Splendor in the Bluegrass

A Cookbook by the Junior League of Louisville

Published by the Junior League of Louisville, Inc.
Copyright © 2000 by the
JUNIOR LEAGUE OF LOUISVILLE, INC.
PO Box 6066
Louisville, Kentucky 40206-0066
(502) 584-7271

All proceeds from the sale of *Splendor in the Bluegrass* will benefit
the community through the charitable activities of the
Junior League of Louisville, Inc.

To obtain additional copies of *Splendor in the Bluegrass* for $29.95
each plus tax and shipping, or for more information about the
Junior League of Louisville, please contact us at:

PO Box 6066
Louisville, Kentucky 40206-0066
(502) 584-7271
Fax (502) 584-3562
E-mail: jll@ntr.net
www.juniorleaguelouisville.org

First printing, 20,000 copies
Edited and Manufactured in the United States of America by
FRP™
an imprint of
Favorite Recipes® Press, 2451 Atrium Way, Nashville, Tennessee 37214

Library of Congress Number: 00-090478
ISBN: 0-9613330-1-4

Contents

Splendor in the Bluegrass

Gathering around the table has been a foundation of Kentucky family life since our state's frontier beginnings. Laughter is heard, memories are made, and problems are solved while sharing a meal. Food and drink provide sustenance to the body and soul of our community as well as to ourselves. In short, cooking is a lifeline to our heritage, as recipes passed down generation to generation become infused with life's lessons and so much more.

By sharing these recipes in *Splendor in the Bluegrass*, the Junior League of Louisville acknowledges the strength and endurance of family tradition. Through this act of sharing, we continue to build our community. Proceeds from this cookbook help provide funding for our numerous projects, including Habitat for Humanity, The Family Place, the Home of the Innocents, Kidspace/Kidzone at the Louisville Science Center, Waterfront Park Playground, Portland Pride, Cabbage Patch Settlement House, and an interactive gallery at the Laramie L. Leatherman Art Learning Center at The Speed Museum.

Striking out eighty years ago, with little more than voracious appetites to make a difference, our founding members sought to improve the lives of Louisville's women and children. This is evidenced by the commitment of hundreds of thousands of volunteer hours and the contributions in excess of $3 million for community projects. During the early decades, we established scholarship funds, well-baby clinics, and occupational therapy departments at area hospitals; we purchased a respirator for the local children's hospital; and we developed the Children's Theatre, now known as Stage One. In the seventies, with the acquisition and renovation of a historic building called Stairways, we played an integral role in the revitalization of Main Street in downtown Louisville. During the next decade, we were instrumental in the establishment of the Ronald McDonald House and the Youth Career Development Program, still used today within Jefferson County Public Schools. Over the past four years, we have renewed our commitment to women's and children's health issues, particularly through our relationship with the Susan G. Komen Breast Cancer Foundation Race for the Cure®. We have raised more than $500,000 for breast cancer research, education, awareness, and screenings. Seventy-five percent of the proceeds have stayed in the greater Louisville community to purchase a new mammography unit for a mobile van and to create *Keep in Touch*, our signature breast cancer awareness project.

As we enter the new millennium, we commemorate the 80th anniversary of the Junior League of Louisville. Throughout our history, we have been dedicated to the needs of women and children and committed to a tradition of volunteerism. We are the beneficiaries and the caretakers of our founders' vision to improve our community through the effective action and leadership of trained volunteers.

Your purchase of this book helps the Junior League of Louisville fulfill its vision. Our recipe for success includes you.

Thank you.

Photo on facing page,
Brookside Farm
Woodford County, Kentucky

Entertainment

The Woodford Reserve Mint Julep
(Photo, pages 6–7)

Of all the libations
identified with the South,
the most celebrated
and romanticized is
surely the mint julep,
a disarmingly simple
(and potent) refreshment
for which claims have
been voiced from Virginia
to Louisiana.

John Egerton
Southern Food: At Home,
on the Road, in History

TEA TIME IN THE GARDEN
MENU

Prosciutto and Parmigiana Puffs

Goat Cheese Tartlets

Hazelnut Scones

Zucchini Bread with Zesty Spread

Praline Cheesecake Bars

Rose Geranium Cake

Tea Suggestions: Earl Grey, Darjeeling Tea, or
Rose Tea (Black China Tea blended with rose petals)

FLORAL FLOURISHES

Baby's Breath, Hibiscus, Marigold
Pansy, Lilac, Fruit Tree Leaves, Herb Leaves

TAMARIND TEA WITH SCENTED GERANIUMS

*One of the most flavorful herbal teas is made from scented geraniums. Scented
geraniums are easy to grow and come in a wide variety of scents.
The following recipe has tamarind pulp, which gives an added flavor dimension.
Tamarind pulp is available both in Hispanic and Southeast Asian markets.*

**2¹/₂ tablespoons tamarind pulp or concentrate
2 tablespoons honey, or to taste
2¹/₂ cups Fetzer Sundial Chardonnay, water or apple juice
3 to 4 large lemon geranium leaves, or zest from 1 small lemon**

Combine the tamarind pulp, honey, wine and geranium leaves in a
saucepan. Bring to a simmer. Partially cover and simmer for 3 minutes.
Remove from heat. Let steep and cool.
Strain and serve hot or cold over ice cubes.

Serves 4

Tea Terms

*High Tea is a term,
originating in Britain, used
to describe a light supper
accompanied by a pot of tea.
The term "high" has nothing
to do with the elegance of
the meal. "High" meant
that the meal was taken at
a high dining table.*

*Afternoon Tea is a leisurely
afternoon uncooked meal that
may be served in fine fashion
and in several courses.
Afternoon teas are generally
more elegant than evening
high teas.*

*Cream Tea is a term for a
pot of tea accompanied by
sumptuous scones with clotted
or whipped cream and jam.
Cream teas may be found
in tearooms across the
British Isles.*

CURTAIN CALL CUISINE
MENU

Marinated Goat Cheese

Shrimp Artichoke Bake

Kentucky Country Ham and Spinach Salad

Herbed and Spiced Beef Tenderloin with Red Wine Sauce

Easy Oven-Baked Mushroom Risotto

Elegant Broccoli with Sautéed Garlic

Wine Suggestions: Jekel Chardonnay or Jekel Johannisberg Riesling
and Bolla Amarone della Valpolicella

Southern Apple Tart

Korbel Brandy

Louisville, Kentucky, boasts a thriving performing arts scene
that few cities its size can match. The city is home to professional theater,
opera and ballet companies, and a symphony orchestra,
as well as many semiprofessional and amateur troupes.
The cultural choices abound, and any one of them would make the
perfect artistic accompaniment to this menu.

Entertaining Is Love

"Social historians might say that the most important thing to happen in Kentucky cooking was the development of a certain fast food chicken. But I would say that we've spent the last 25 years trying to get women out of the kitchen only to realize that preparing food is a way of saying 'welcome'; entertaining is love; leaning across a kitchen table is humbling; and sharing a meal is pure joy because it means exchanging stories and laughing with family and friends. From county to county across this Commonwealth, women share secret bonds of spending days cooking because it takes us back to our roots and gives us a sense of reality in our hybridized worlds."

GENIE K. POTTER, AUTHOR
KENTUCKY WOMEN

FIRST SATURDAY IN MAY DERBY BRUNCH

MENU

Asparagus and Yellow Pepper Frittata

Green Bean and Sun-Dried Tomato Salad

Fresh Seasonal Fruit

Grits Gruyère

Kentucky Country Ham

Buttermilk Cheese Biscuits

Early Times Triple Turf Pie

The Woodford Reserve Mint Julep

Korbel Mimosa or Strawberry Sparkler

This menu is as traditional as the first Saturday in May,
when thousands of visitors flock to Louisville, Kentucky, for
"the most exciting two minutes in sports." For more than 125 years,
the horse race known as the Derby has been the perfect occasion for
Kentuckians to extend their Bluegrass hospitality.

CENTER OF ATTENTION

Consider these arrangements with a "springtime in Kentucky" theme:

Place a floral oasis in the bottom of a glass vase. Cover the oasis with
lemons and limes. Arrange tiger lilies, yellow lilies, red roses,
and purple larkspur in the oasis.

Arrange red roses tightly in mint julep cups with Queen Anne's Lace.
The Charlotte Red Rose, which opens full and is a bright red,
is recommended.

Make the Rose in Gelée recipe on page 240 using a brilliant red rose.

A Hint of Mint

*Nineteenth-century
Louisville business leader
and newspaper editor,
"Marse Henry" Watterson,
suggests the poetic approach
to making a mint julep:*

*"Pluck the mint gently from
its bed, just as the dew of the
evening is about to form upon
it. Select the choicer sprigs
only, but do not rinse them.
Prepare the simple syrup
and measure out a half-
tumbler of whiskey. Pour the
whiskey into a well-frosted
silver cup,* throw the other
ingredients away and drink
the whiskey."

"MARSE HENRY" WATTERSON

*Photo on facing page,
Twin Spires of Churchill Downs®
Louisville, Kentucky*

Menu

Fiesta Corn Salad

Bluegrass Salad

Grilled Bourbon Shrimp Skewers

Kentucky Sweet-and-Sour Ribs

Grilled Vegetables over Rice

Wine Suggestions: Fetzer Home Ranch Zinfandel and Bolla Pinot Grigio

Blueberry Ice Cream

Gone-in-a-Day Cookies

Barbecue Tips

You don't need fancy equipment. You can make great barbecue on a
charcoal grill if that's what you have. The key is simple: tender loving
care. Take your time and take care.

The clue to great 'que: low and slow. Cook your meat on
low heat for a long time.

Cook with heat, not with fire. Don't put your meat directly over the flame.
Put it to the side and open your grill vents to draw the smoke to the meat.

Don't play with your food. Once you get your fire going, you don't
have to check on the meat every five minutes. Remember, every time
you open the lid, you are letting heat escape. Let the barbecue cook.
Checking every half-hour is often enough until the meat is done.

Sauce is a complement, not an end unto itself. The meat is the barbecue.
Serve your sauce on the side and let your guests decide how much they want.

Cook plenty of meat because, if you have followed the steps above,
your guests will want lots and lots of your barbecue.

VINCE STATEN, VINCE STATEN'S OLD TIME BARBECUE

PICNIC FOR FOUR IN
LOUISVILLE'S CHEROKEE PARK

MENU

Pesto and Sun-Dried Tomato Cheesecake

Garden Vegetable Sandwich

Grilled Steak Sandwiches on Baguettes

Derby Pasta Salad

Chocolate Chess Bars

Wine Suggestions: Fetzer Echo Ridge Fumé Blanc and Bolla Merlot

Drink Suggestion: Watermelon Lemonade

Often referred to as an emerald necklace of greenery around Louisville, the city's park system was designed more than a century ago by Frederick Law Olmsted, the designer of New York City's Central Park. Louisville's Cherokee Park is just one such jewel where you can leisurely enjoy this menu.

Picnic Checklist

Picnic basket

Cooler

Ice

Two large cotton blankets

Crackers

Cocktail napkins

Four cotton napkins rolled
    with your choice of flatware

Plates

Cups

Small knife

Bottled water

Wine glasses

Corkscrew

Four small citronella candles
    in clay pots

Matches

Glass canning jar filled with
    seasonal fresh flowers

Insect repellent

Football

Your dog (with leash)

A significant other

A set of friends

Kentucky Cocktail Celebration for Twenty

Menu

Thai Chicken Satay

Salmon Pot Stickers

Spicy Two-Cheese Crostini

Coconut-Fried Shrimp and Citrus Sauce

Sausage and Pepper Jack Cheese Tartlets

Corn and Crab Fritters with Spicy Red Pepper Aïoli

Drink Specials:

Lavender Margarita

Finlandia Cosmopolitan Martini

Stock the Bar

Liquor

One liter of Woodford Reserve Kentucky Straight Bourbon Whiskey
One liter of Jack Daniel's Tennessee Whiskey
One liter of Finlandia Vodka
One 750 ml bottle of Cranberry Finlandia Vodka
One bottle of Gin
One 750 ml bottle of sweet Noilly Prat Vermouth
One 750 ml bottle of Noilly Prat Dry Vermouth
One liter of Glenmorangie 10 year Scotch
Three or four bottles of Bonterra Chardonnay
One or two bottles of Jekel Johannisberg Riesling
Two or three bottles of Jekel Merlot

Mixers

One bottle of
sweet and sour mix
One bottle of
Bloody Mary mix
One liter of club soda
One liter of tonic water
12-pack of cola
12-pack of ginger ale
6-pack of diet cola
Pitcher of orange juice
Pitcher of cranberry juice

Supplies and Garnishes

Drink stirrers
Cut wedges and twists of
lemons and limes
Maraschino cherries
Small jar of green olives
Small jar of cocktail onions

*Photo on facing page,
Labrot & Graham Distillery
Woodford County, Kentucky*

WINTER FIRESIDE REPAST

MENU

Spiced Walnuts and Mixed Greens

Chicken and Kentucky Country Ham Pot Pie

Tender Peas with Parmesan

Cranberry Caramel Squares

Wine Suggestions: Fetzer Reserve Chardonnay and Bolla Colforte

TIPS ON WINE AND FOOD PAIRING

Pair higher acid foods (tomatoes, citrus fruits, goat cheese) with higher acid wines such as Sauvignon Blanc, Sangiovese, and Pinot Noir.

Pair richer and fattier foods (duck, lamb, beef, cheese) with either slightly oaky white wines, such as Chardonnay, or with young red wines, such as Cabernet Sauvignon, Merlot, Zinfandel, and Nebbiolo.

Spicy, salty or smoked, and more heavily seasoned dishes are paired with lighter, fruity wines, such as Gewürztraminer, Bardolino, and Pinot Grigio.

Wines should follow each other at the table in a natural progression from driest to sweetest.

PRINTED WITH PERMISSION FROM FETZER VINEYARDS.

See pages 257–259 for more wine and food pairing tips.

The Uncommon Wealth of Dinner in Kentucky

"Eating dinner in Kentucky is more than a physiological refueling of the human body, it is a joyous social ritual. The table is the great yarning place for the state. There is something about a Kentucky dinner that stretches a yarn or puts spirit into a bit of gossip."

THOMAS D. CLARK
THE KENTUCKY

NEW YEAR'S EVE GOURMET GATHERING

MENU

Savory Feta Cheese Log

Red Pepper Crab Bisque

Endive with Apples and Stilton

Wine Suggestion: Sonoma-Cutrer Russian River Ranches Chardonnay

Grilled Veal Chops with Cabernet Sauce

Rosemary and Garlic Red Potatoes

Spinach Timbales

Wine Suggestion: Fetzer Reserve Cabernet Sauvignon

Amaretto Buttercream Chocolate Cake

Toast at 11:59 p.m. — Korbel Natural Champagne

HOW TO OPEN A CHAMPAGNE BOTTLE

Avoid shaking the bottle as much as possible since it creates unnecessary pressure inside and increases the chances of the cork popping itself off. The "popping" of a cork may sound festive and exciting, but it wastes Champagne.

Remove the foil and loosen and remove the wire muzzle, keeping the thumb of your other hand on the cork to prevent it from accidentally shooting out of the bottle.

Tilt the bottle at 45-degree angle while holding the cork firmly with one hand and the base of the bottle with the other. Be sure to point the bottle away from people.

Do not twist the cork! Rather, twist the bottle slowly while holding the cork tight and letting it glide out, emitting a gentle "sigh."

Never use a corkscrew. A Champagne cork is highly compressed; if a corkscrew is inserted at an angle, you may literally have an exploding bottle in your hand.

The Quick Chill

Give your Champagne bottle the quick chill by submerging the bottle in a solution of $1/2$ ice and $1/2$ water. This will cause the Champagne to chill faster than if placed in ice alone.

HOW TO OPEN A CHAMPAGNE BOTTLE PRINTED WITH PERMISSION FROM FETZER VINEYARDS.

HOLIDAY DESSERT SOIRÉE

MENU

Elegant Pumpkin Roll with Caramel Sauce

Miss Pepper's Christmas Cake

Woodford Reserve Chocolate Torte

Currant Jelly Cookies

Sugar and Spice Ginger Cookies

Praline Cookies

Cranberry Kir Noël

Wine Suggestions: Jekel Late Harvest Riesling or
Korbel Brut Rosé Champagne

COFFEE STATION ESSENTIALS

French Roast coffee—decaffeinated and regular
Hazelnut coffee—decaffeinated and regular
Hot chocolate
Homemade whipped cream
Chocolate shavings
Cinnamon sticks
Ground nutmeg and cinnamon
Cream
Half-and-Half
Sugar cubes
Tray of Old Forester Bourbon Balls

ROMANTIC RENDEZVOUS BY CANDLELIGHT

MENU

Gremolata-Topped Yellow Pepper Soup

Sesame Soy Vinaigrette over Greens

Wok-Seared Asian Salmon with Spicy Shrimp Fried Rice

Green Bean Bundles

Wine Suggestions: Jekel Pinot Noir and Fetzer Gewürztraminer

Fall Dessert—Pears in White Zinfandel

Spring & Summer Dessert—Frozen Lemon and Fresh Berry Parfaits

Korbel Chardonnay Champagne

CANDLE CREATIONS

Use one large clear glass vase, approximately $8^1/2$ inches in diameter. Place a piece of floral foam, approximately one-half the height of the glass vase, in the bottom of the vase. Disguise the floral foam by tucking unique looking commercial moss around all exposed sides of the foam. Place a 4-inch square pillar candle on top of the moss-covered foam. Arrange circular slices of oranges, lemons, and limes on top of the moss around the base of the candle. If desired, place additional oranges, lemons, limes, and greenery around the outside base of the vase.

Group together three glass vases, 3 inches in diameter, in varying heights (6-inch, 9-inch, and 11-inch). Fill each vase three-quarters full with water. Submerge your favorite flower, fruit, or greenery in the water. For example, use Gerber daisies, snapdragons, and fruits such as lemons, limes, or pomegranates. For the holiday season, submerge pinecones or holly. Place a $2^1/2$-inch by $2^3/4$-inch-diameter floating candle on top of the submerged arrangement.

Marinated Goat Cheese
(Photo, pages 22–23)

If, beyond the pearly gates,
I am permitted to select
my place at the table, it will
be among Kentuckians.

Thomas D. Clark
The Kentucky

BLACK BEAN SALSA DIP

Serves 20 to 25

2 (16-ounce) cans black beans, drained, rinsed
2 (11-ounce) cans white Shoe Peg corn, drained
2 (4-ounce) cans chopped green chiles, drained
1 red bell pepper, chopped
1 small can chopped jalapeño chiles
1 small bunch cilantro, minced
2/3 cup apple cider vinegar
1/3 cup vegetable oil
Pepper to taste

Combine the beans, corn, green chiles, bell pepper, jalapeños and cilantro in a bowl and mix well. Whisk the vinegar, oil and pepper in a bowl until blended. Add to the bean mixture gradually and mix well.

Chill, covered, for 2 hours or longer. Serve with tortilla chips.

MI CASA MEXICAN DIP

Serves 10

1 (10-ounce) package frozen chopped spinach, thawed, drained
8 ounces cream cheese, softened
2 cups shredded sharp Cheddar cheese
1 (16-ounce) jar mild, medium or hot salsa
1 (4-ounce) can chopped black olives, drained
1 tablespoon red wine vinegar

Press the excess moisture from the spinach. Beat the cream cheese and Cheddar cheese in a mixing bowl until blended. Stir in the spinach, salsa, black olives and wine vinegar.

Spoon the cheese mixture into a 3 × 6-inch or 8 × 8-inch baking dish sprayed with nonstick cooking spray. Bake at 350 degrees for 30 minutes. Serve warm with tortilla chips.

SHRIMP SALSA

Serves 10 to 12

2 large tomatoes, peeled, seeded, chopped
1/2 medium yellow bell pepper, chopped
1/2 medium red bell pepper, chopped
1/2 cucumber, chopped
1/2 cup fresh whole corn kernels
2 tablespoons finely chopped cilantro
2 tablespoons finely chopped parsley
1 jalapeño chile, seeded, finely chopped
2 1/2 tablespoons fresh lime juice
1 1/2 teaspoons salt
1/4 teaspoon pepper
8 ounces peeled steamed small shrimp
1 ripe avocado, cut into 1/2-inch pieces

Combine the tomatoes, bell peppers, cucumber, corn, cilantro, parsley, chile, lime juice, salt and pepper in a serving bowl and mix gently. Chill, covered, for 1 hour.

Stir the shrimp and avocado into the tomato mixture just before serving. Serve with tortilla chips.

BLOOMER DROPPERS

Bloomer Droppers are wonderful served at summer picnics or at the beach. For a special treat for children, simply omit the liquor.

Serves 6

6 ounces frozen lemonade
    concentrate
2 unpeeled peaches, chopped
6 ounces Finlandia Vodka
6 ounces lemon-lime soda
1 tablespoon confectioners'
    sugar

Combine the lemonade concentrate, peaches, vodka, soda and confectioners' sugar in a blender container. Process adding ice cubes as needed until of a slushy consistency. Serve immediately or store, covered, in the freezer until serving time.

HOT OLIVE CHEESE SPREAD

Serves 12 to 15

1¹/₂ cups pimento-stuffed green olives, finely chopped
³/₄ cup black olives, finely chopped
1 cup shredded mozzarella cheese
1 cup shredded Cheddar cheese
2 small green onions, finely chopped
1 cup mayonnaise

Combine the green olives, black olives, mozzarella cheese, Cheddar cheese and green onions in a bowl and mix well. Stir in the mayonnaise. Spoon into an ungreased 1-quart baking dish.

Bake at 350 degrees for 25 minutes. Serve warm with tortilla chips, large corn chips and/or assorted party crackers.

HOT BRANDIED CHEESE SPREAD

The perfect way to warm up a crisp autumn day.

Serves 10 to 12

8 ounces cream cheese, softened
1 cup sour cream
3 tablespoons Korbel Brandy
1¹/₂ cups shredded Gouda cheese
¹/₄ cup chopped walnuts
2 medium apples, sliced

Combine the cream cheese, sour cream and brandy in a bowl and stir until blended. Add the Gouda cheese and mix well. Spoon into an 8-inch quiche dish.

Bake at 350 degrees for 30 minutes or until light brown. Arrange the walnuts in a decorative pattern in the center. Serve warm with the apples.

Create an attractive olive flower garnish with one large black olive and a sprig of parsley. Cut the olive lengthwise into five strips and arrange like flower petals on top of the spread. Place a small sprig of parsley in the center of the petals.

SAVORY FETA CHEESE LOG

Serves 12 to 15

8 ounces feta cheese, crumbled
4 ounces cream cheese, softened
2 tablespoons extra-virgin olive oil
1 small garlic clove, minced
1/2 cup chopped black olives
2 tablespoons sliced green onions
1/2 cup chopped walnuts
1/3 cup chopped fresh parsley

Combine the feta cheese, cream cheese, olive oil and garlic in a mixing bowl. Beat at medium speed until blended. Stir in the black olives and green onions. Shape the cheese mixture into a 10-inch log. Chill, covered in plastic wrap, in the refrigerator.

Toast the walnuts in a nonstick skillet over medium-high heat for 5 minutes or until light brown, stirring constantly. Let stand until cool.

Roll the cheese log in the walnuts and parsley. Chill, covered in plastic wrap, until serving time. Serve with assorted party crackers.

For a festive look, add 1/4 cup chopped, well-drained, oil-pack sun-dried tomatoes to the cheese mixture.

THE OLD-FASHIONED

1 teaspoon, 1 envelope or
   1 cube sugar
2 dashes of Angostura Bitters
1 ounce soda water
2 ounces Old Forester

Muddle the sugar and bitters or mix together with the back of a spoon in an old-fashioned glass. Add the soda water. Pack the glass with ice. Add the bourbon and stir. Garnish with a lemon twist, orange slice and maraschino cherry.

PESTO AND SUN-DRIED TOMATO CHEESECAKE

Serves 20

Crust
3 slices bread, toasted, crumbled (about 1 cup)
1/2 cup grated Parmesan cheese
1/2 cup (1 stick) butter, melted

Pesto Filling
32 ounces cream cheese, softened
2 cups pesto
4 eggs
1/4 cup heavy cream
1 (7-ounce) jar oil-pack sun-dried tomatoes, drained, chopped

For the crust, combine the bread crumbs, Parmesan cheese and butter in a bowl and mix well. Press over the bottom of a 9-inch springform pan. Bake at 325 degrees for 5 to 10 minutes or until light brown.

For the filling, beat the cream cheese in a mixing bowl until smooth. Add the pesto, eggs and heavy cream. Beat until blended, scraping the bowl occasionally. Spread over the crust. Place the springform pan on a baking sheet with sides. Bake for 1 to 1 1/2 hours or until set.

Chill, covered, for several hours or for up to several days. Run a sharp knife around the edge of the pan to loosen the cheesecake. Remove the side of the pan. Transfer the cheesecake to a platter. Top with the sun-dried tomatoes. Serve with assorted party crackers and/or party bread.

Halve the recipe and bake in a 6-inch springform pan for approximately 1 hour if your crowd is smaller. You may freeze for future use.

APPLEJACK

1 ounce Jack Daniel's
2 ounces Sour Apple Schnapps
1 ounce sweet-and-sour mix
1 ounce club soda
Bitters to taste

Combine the whiskey, schnapps, sweet-and-sour mix and club soda in a shaker and mix well. Stir in bitters to taste and for desired color. Pour over ice in a highball or 8-ounce glass.

TEMPTING CRAB AND MUSHROOM CHEESECAKE

Serves 16 to 20

Crust
1 cup freshly grated
   Parmesan cheese

1³/4 cups bread crumbs
6 tablespoons butter, melted

Crab and Mushroom Filling
1 cup chopped onion
1/2 cup chopped green bell pepper
1/2 cup chopped red bell pepper
1 tablespoon olive oil
4 cups coarsely chopped assorted
   wild mushrooms
   (cremini, oyster and shiitake)
28 ounces cream cheese, softened

2 teaspoons salt
1 teaspoon pepper
4 eggs
1/2 cup whipping cream
10 ounces crab meat, drained
1 cup shredded smoked
   Gouda cheese
1/2 cup chopped fresh parsley

THE MANHATTAN

1 dash of Angostura Bitters
1 dash of Peychaud Bitters
1 splash grenadine
1/2 ounce sweet vermouth
2¹/2 ounces Woodford
   Reserve Bourbon
1 maraschino cherry

Fill a mixing glass with ice.
Add the bitters, grenadine,
vermouth and bourbon and
stir. Strain into a chilled
cocktail glass. Top with
a cherry.

For the crust, combine the cheese, bread crumbs and butter in a bowl and
mix well. Press the crumb mixture over the bottom of a 9-inch springform
pan. Bake at 350 degrees for 15 minutes or until golden brown. Let stand
until cool.

For the filling, sauté the onion and bell peppers in the heated olive oil in a
skillet over medium-high heat for 2 minutes. Stir in the mushrooms. Sauté
for 10 minutes or until the liquid evaporates and the mushrooms begin to
brown. Let stand until cool.

Beat the cream cheese, salt and pepper in a mixing bowl until fluffy,
scraping the bowl occasionally. Add the eggs 1 at a time, beating well after
each addition. Beat in the whipping cream. Stir in the mushroom mixture,
crab meat, Gouda cheese and parsley. Spoon into the prepared pan.

Place the springform pan on a baking sheet. Bake for 1¹/2 hours or until
the cheesecake puffs and browns and the center moves just slightly when
the pan is shaken. Cool in the pan on a wire rack. Run a sharp knife
around the edge of the pan to loosen the cheesecake. Remove the side of
the pan. Transfer the cheesecake to a platter. Serve with baguette slices at
room temperature or chilled.

GARDEN VEGETABLE PÂTÉ

Serves 16

16 ounces reduced-fat cream cheese, softened
3/4 cup nonfat sour cream
2 tablespoons flour
4 eggs
2 garlic cloves, minced
2 tablespoons lemon juice
1 teaspoon salt
1 teaspoon chili powder
1/2 teaspoon pepper
1/4 teaspoon paprika
1/4 teaspoon hot sauce
1 cup shredded Cheddar cheese
1/2 cup finely chopped carrot
1/4 cup finely chopped broccoli
1/4 cup finely chopped green onions
1 cup chopped tomato
2 tablespoons chopped fresh parsley
2 tablespoons chopped fresh chives

Combine the cream cheese, sour cream and flour in a mixing bowl and beat until blended, scraping the bowl occasionally. Add the eggs 1 at a time, beating well after each addition. Add the garlic, lemon juice, salt, chili powder, pepper, paprika and hot sauce and mix well. Fold in the Cheddar cheese, carrot, broccoli and green onions.

Spoon the vegetable mixture into a greased 9-inch springform pan. Bake at 375 degrees for 35 to 45 minutes or until set. Cool in the pan on a wire rack. Remove the side of the pan. Chill, covered, in the refrigerator until serving time.

Sprinkle the tomato, parsley and chives over the top just before serving. Serve with assorted party crackers.

CURRIED SHERRY PÂTÉ

Serves 8 to 10

8 ounces cream cheese, softened
1 cup shredded Cheddar cheese
4 teaspoons sherry
1/2 to 1 teaspoon curry powder, or
   to taste
1/2 teaspoon garlic powder

1/4 teaspoon salt
1 (9-ounce) jar chutney,
   finely chopped
1 bunch green onions with tops,
   finely chopped

Beat the cream cheese, Cheddar cheese, sherry, curry powder, garlic powder and salt in a mixing bowl until blended. Pat into the desired shape on a serving platter. Spread with the chutney and sprinkle with the green onions. Serve with rice crackers.

EGG PÂTÉ WITH CAVIAR

Serves 20 to 25

1 envelope unflavored gelatin
1/3 cup cold water
16 hard-cooked eggs, chopped
1 cup mayonnaise
1/2 cup Durkee sauce
6 tablespoons finely chopped onion

1 tablespoon chopped
   fresh dillweed
1 teaspoon minced garlic
1/2 teaspoon cayenne pepper
Sour cream
Caviar

Combine the gelatin and cold water in a microwave-safe bowl and mix well. Microwave for 30 to 60 seconds or until the gelatin dissolves. Let stand until cool.

Combine the eggs, mayonnaise, Durkee sauce, onion, dillweed, garlic and cayenne pepper in a bowl and mix well. Stir in the gelatin mixture. Spoon into an oiled 6-cup ring mold. Chill for several hours or until set.

Invert the pâté onto a serving platter. Spread the top and side with sour cream. Spoon the caviar into a small bowl and place in the center. Garnish with sprigs of dillweed. Serve with assorted party crackers.

FINLANDIA COSMOPOLITAN MARTINI

3 ounces Finlandia
   Cranberry Vodka
Splash Triple Sec

Fill a martini shaker with ice. Pour the vodka and liqueur over the ice. Cover and shake vigorously. Pour into a martini glass. Garnish with a lime twist.

KATHERINE DOLL'S CHEESE TORTE

Serves 8 to 10

8 ounces cream cheese, softened
1/4 cup minced baby spinach
1 1/2 tablespoons chutney
2 cups shredded Cheddar cheese
2/3 cup mayonnaise
1/2 cup pecan pieces
1/4 cup finely chopped white onion
Dash of Tabasco sauce

Combine 4 ounces of the cream cheese with the minced spinach in a bowl and mix well. Stir the chutney into the remaining cream cheese in a separate bowl. Combine the Cheddar cheese, mayonnaise, pecans, onion and Tabasco sauce in a third bowl and mix well.

Layer half the Cheddar cheese mixture, the spinach mixture, the chutney mixture and the remaining Cheddar cheese mixture in the order listed in a 2-cup mold or container. Chill, covered, for 8 to 10 hours.

Invert the mold onto a platter lined with additional baby spinach. Garnish with grapes and strawberries. Serve with assorted party crackers.

For a spicier torte, add 1 minced garlic clove to the Cheddar cheese mixture. You may substitute 1/4 cup drained thawed frozen spinach for the spinach cream cheese layer, omitting the 4 ounces of cream cheese.

A Kentucky Tradition

"If there was ever a way to sip the essence of the South, it would be through a mint julep. The taste conjures up images of a comfortably warm evening stirred by a cool breeze with the aromas of summer in the air. The julep is a simple and time-honored Kentucky tradition encompassing all that is good about the Commonwealth."

LINCOLN HENDERSON
MASTER DISTILLER
BROWN-FORMAN CORPORATION

CHEESY CRAB TARTS

Makes 40 tarts

8 ounces crab meat, flaked
1/4 cup chopped onion
1 tablespoon butter
8 ounces cream cheese
2 cups shredded Cheddar cheese
1/4 cup chopped fresh parsley
Dash of liquid red pepper
40 phyllo shells

Remove any shell fragments from the crab meat. Combine the onion and butter in a microwave-safe dish. Microwave, covered, for 30 to 45 seconds or until the onion is tender.

Microwave the cream cheese in a microwave-safe dish until soft. Stir in the onion mixture. Add the Cheddar cheese, crab meat, parsley and liquid red pepper.

Spoon the crab meat mixture into the phyllo shells. Arrange the shells on a baking sheet. Bake at 350 degrees for 15 to 20 minutes or until heated through.

THE WOODFORD RESERVE MINT JULEP

1 cup sugar
1 cup water
1 bunch fresh mint
1 tablespoon water
2 ounces Woodford Reserve Bourbon

Bring the sugar and 1 cup water to a boil in a saucepan. Boil for 5 minutes; do not stir. Pour over the mint in a heatproof bowl, gently crushing the mint with the back of a spoon. Pour the syrup into a jar with a tight-fitting lid. Chill for 8 to 10 hours. Strain, discarding the mint. You may store the syrup in the refrigerator for several weeks, preparing individual juleps as desired. For each serving, crush a few mint leaves in the bottom of an 8-ounce glass. Fill with crushed ice. Add 1 tablespoon of the syrup and 1 tablespoon water. Add the bourbon, stirring gently until the glass is frosted. Garnish with a sprig of fresh mint.

CORN AND CRAB FRITTERS

Created by Chef Jim McKinney, Club Grotto

Makes 24 fritters

Fritters
1 pound crab meat, drained
2¹/₂ cups flour
1 tablespoon baking powder
1 tablespoon kosher salt
4 cups frozen whole kernel corn
1 bunch green onions, chopped
2 eggs, beaten
1 cup chicken stock
Vegetable oil

Spicy Red Pepper Aïoli
1 red bell pepper, roasted, seeded, finely chopped
1¹/₂ teaspoons sambal
1¹/₂ teaspoons minced fresh parsley
1 cup mayonnaise
Juice of 1 lemon

For the fritters, remove any shell fragments from the crab meat. Combine the flour, baking powder, salt, 2 cups of the corn and green onions in a bowl and mix well. Stir in the eggs and stock.

Process the remaining 2 cups frozen corn in a food processor until finely ground. Add to the flour mixture, stirring until mixed. Fold in the crab meat. Shape the mixture into 24 patties. Sauté the patties in oil until light golden brown and firm to the touch. Drain on paper towels.

For the sauce, combine the roasted bell pepper, sambal and parsley in a bowl and mix well. Stir in the mayonnaise and lemon juice. Serve on the side with the fritters.

Sambal can be found in most Asian markets.

"Don't be AFRAID to experiment with your recipes! How do you think we (chefs) created the food that is served in our restaurants? Have fun with it!"

JIM MCKINNEY
CLUB GROTTO

MUSSELS DIJONNAISE

Serves 6

 24 mussels
1 tablespoon vegetable oil
1 cup Bolla Pinot Grigio
1 medium shallot, crushed
1/2 garlic clove, crushed
1 tablespoon Dijon mustard
1 tablespoon lemon juice
1 1/2 teaspoons soy sauce
1/8 teaspoon salt
1/8 teaspoon ground pepper
1/4 cup olive oil

Never eat a cooked mussel if the shell does not part upon cooking. When a healthy clam, mussel, or oyster expires, so does the holding power of the muscle that keeps the shell tightly closed. If the shell does not open after the bivalve is cooked, it was not alive in the first place and is not safe to eat.

Scrub the mussels. Heat the vegetable oil in a stockpot until the oil begins to smoke. Add the mussels and wine. Cook, covered, over medium heat for 7 minutes or until the mussels open, shaking the stockpot frequently. Remove the mussels with a slotted spoon to a platter. Let stand until cool.

Combine the shallot, garlic, Dijon mustard, lemon juice, soy sauce, salt and pepper in a bowl and mix well. Whisk in the olive oil gradually.

Remove the mussels from the shells. Disconnect the shells, reserving the clean shell. Place one mussel in each clean shell so as to cradle the mussel. Arrange on a serving platter. Spoon some the sauce over each mussel. Garnish with lemon slices and sprigs of fresh parsley.

SALMON POT STICKERS

Created by Chef Jim McKinney, Club Grotto

Serves 4 to 6

Salmon Filling
1 3/4 pounds fresh salmon, skinned, boned
1/4 cup thinly sliced scallion tops
1/4 cup sesame oil

2 tablespoons soy sauce
2 tablespoons minced gingerroot
1/8 teaspoon salt

Pot Stickers
1 package gyoza wrappers
1 egg
1/4 cup water

Cornmeal
6 tablespoons sesame oil
Ponzu Sauce (at right)

For the filling, place the salmon in a food processor. Pulse until coarsely puréed. Combine the salmon, scallions, sesame oil, soy sauce, gingerroot and salt in a bowl and mix well.

For the pot stickers, place 5 wrappers on a work surface. Brush the edges lightly with a mixture of the egg and water. Place 1 rounded teaspoon of the filling in the center of each wrapper. Place the wrappers in a pot sticker press, making sure they are centered, and close the press to crimp the edges to seal. If the pot stickers burst, try again with less filling. If the finished pot stickers do not seem nice and plump, add additional filling. Place the pot stickers on a plate sprinkled with cornmeal. Repeat the process with the remaining wrappers, filling and egg wash.

Heat the sesame oil in a heavy sauté pan until hot and almost smoking. Add the pot stickers 1 at a time, making sure the edges do not touch. Cook until golden brown on both sides; drain. If the pot stickers stick to the pan initially, do not panic. Once the wrapper has cooked, you will be able to slide a thin spatula under the pot sticker and turn it. Serve with the warm Ponzu Sauce. Any leftover filling may be frozen for future use.

You may purchase an inexpensive pot sticker press at most Asian markets.

PONZU SAUCE

1 cup aji mirin (rice wine)
1/2 cup pineapple juice
1/2 cup soy sauce
2 tablespoons lemon juice
2 teaspoons crushed red pepper
2 tablespoons water
1 tablespoon cornstarch

Combine the aji mirin, pineapple juice, soy sauce, lemon juice and red pepper in a saucepan and mix well. Bring to a simmer. Simmer for 5 minutes, stirring occasionally. Strain, discarding the solids. Return the liquid to the saucepan. Stir in a mixture of the water and cornstarch. Bring to a simmer. Simmer for 1 minute, stirring constantly. Remove from the heat. Cover to keep warm.

SHRIMP ARTICHOKE BAKE

Serves 16

1 (14-ounce) can artichoke hearts, drained, finely chopped
8 ounces peeled steamed shrimp, finely chopped
1 cup mayonnaise
3/4 cup grated Parmesan cheese
1/2 cup grated Romano cheese
1/4 teaspoon freshly ground pepper
Dash of Tabasco sauce, or to taste
1/8 teaspoon grated lemon zest
Salt to taste

Combine the artichokes, shrimp and mayonnaise in a bowl and mix well. Stir in the Parmesan cheese, Romano cheese, pepper, Tabasco sauce and lemon zest. Season with salt. Spoon into a shallow 1-quart baking dish.

Bake the shrimp-artichoke mixture at 400 degrees for 10 minutes or until hot and bubbly. Serve hot with crusty French bread, melba toast and/or whole wheat crackers.

RASPBERRY LEMONADE

Makes 2 quarts

1 cup fresh raspberries
1 3/4 cups water
1 1/2 cups sugar, or to taste
1 1/4 cups fresh lemon juice
3 cups carbonated water, chilled

Place 1 raspberry in each cube of an ice tray and fill with water. Freeze until firm. Bring 1 3/4 cups water and sugar to a boil in a saucepan. Boil for 2 minutes or until the sugar dissolves, stirring occasionally. Let stand until cool. Combine the syrup and lemon juice in a covered container and mix well. Chill for 2 hours or longer. Stir in the carbonated water just before serving. To serve, drop several raspberry ice cubes into each serving glass. Fill with the lemonade.

COCONUT-FRIED SHRIMP AND CITRUS SAUCE

Serves 8 to 10

Spicy Citrus Sauce
1 (10-ounce) jar orange marmalade
3 tablespoons spicy brown mustard
1 tablespoon fresh lime juice

Shrimp
³/4 cup baking mix
1 tablespoon sugar
³/4 cup beer
1 pound shrimp, peeled
³/4 cup flour
2 cups flaked coconut
2¹/2 cups (about) vegetable oil

For the sauce, combine the marmalade, brown mustard and lime juice
in a saucepan and mix well. Cook over medium heat until the marmalade
melts, stirring constantly. Remove from the heat.

For the shrimp, combine the baking mix and sugar in a bowl and mix
well. Add the beer, stirring until smooth. Coat the shrimp with the flour.
Dip in the beer mixture; shake to remove excess batter. Roll the shrimp
in the coconut.

Pour the oil into a saucepan to a depth of 3 inches. Heat to 350 degrees.
Fry the shrimp in batches in the hot oil for 1 to 2 minutes or until golden
brown; drain. Serve immediately with the sauce.

Creative Containers

*Edible containers are a
conversation piece and
provide a touch of surprise
to a party. Anything that
can be hollowed out makes
a unique container for dips,
sauces, spreads, or fillings.
Here are a few suggestions:
cabbages, bell peppers, acorn
squash, pumpkins, coconuts,
pineapple, and melons.*

*Photo on facing page,
Cumberland Gap in
Eastern Kentucky*

SHRIMP WITH GREEN CHILE PESTO

Serves 26 to 30

 Green Chile Pesto
4 ounces Parmesan cheese, grated
2 garlic cloves
6 whole mild green chiles, stems and seeds removed
1/2 cup pine nuts, toasted
1/2 cup fresh parsley leaves
1/4 cup fresh cilantro leaves
2 to 3 tablespoons safflower oil

Shrimp
11/2 pounds shrimp (26- to 30-count), peeled, deveined

For the pesto, combine the cheese and garlic in a food processor container fitted with a steel blade. Process until blended. Add the green chiles, pine nuts, parsley, cilantro and safflower oil. Process until of the consistency of a smooth paste. The pesto may be stored, covered, at this point in the refrigerator for up to 1 month.

For the shrimp, toss the shrimp with the pesto in a bowl. Chill, covered, for 1 hour or longer. Arrange the shrimp in a single layer on a baking sheet. Bake at 350 degrees for 15 to 20 minutes or until the shrimp are cooked through.

Arrange the shrimp on a large serving platter. Garnish with whole green chiles and/or sprigs of fresh parsley or cilantro. Serve warm or at room temperature.

For a quick and easy entrée, spoon the shrimp over hot cooked angel hair pasta. You may substitute two 4-ounce cans mild green chiles for the fresh chiles.

DOWN HOME PUNCH

1 ounce Jack Daniel's
1 ounce Peach Schnapps
2 ounces sweet-and-sour mix
2 ounces orange juice
1/2 ounce Sloe Gin

Combine the whiskey, schnapps, sweet-and-sour mix, orange juice and gin in a shaker and mix well. Pour over ice in a highball or 8-ounce glass.

Lynn's Black Bean Quesadillas

Lynn Winter, Lynn's Paradise Cafe

Serves 2

Salsa Fresca
1 medium ripe tomato, chopped
1 tablespoon chopped fresh cilantro
1 fresh jalapeño chile, finely chopped
1 teaspoon olive oil
1 teaspoon lime juice
1/4 teaspoon minced garlic
1/8 teaspoon sugar
Salt and pepper to taste

Quesadillas
1 (16-ounce) can black beans or black bean chili
1 medium onion, chopped
5 to 6 ounces Bass Ale or other beer with high sugar content
2 tablespoons chopped fresh cilantro
1 tablespoon cumin
1 tablespoon chili powder
4 (6- to 8-inch) flour tortillas
1 cup shredded Monterey Jack cheese
1 to 2 tablespoons lime juice
1 cup sour cream

For the salsa, combine the tomato, cilantro, chile, olive oil, lime juice, garlic, sugar, salt and pepper in a bowl and mix gently. Adjust the seasonings. Chill, covered, in the refrigerator.

For the quesadillas, combine the black beans, onion, beer, cilantro, cumin and chili powder in a saucepan and mix well. Cook until thickened, stirring frequently. Arrange the tortillas on a hot lightly greased griddle. Spread the bean mixture over the surface of 2 of the tortillas. Sprinkle the cheese on the remaining 2 tortillas. Bake until the bean mixture and cheese is hot and bubbly. Flip the cheese sides over onto the bean sides. Remove the quesadillas to a cutting board.

Stir the lime juice into the sour cream in a bowl. Top each quesadilla with 1/2 cup of the sour cream mixture and 1/4 cup of the salsa. Cut each quesadilla into wedges. Serve immediately.

Lavender Margaritas

Serves 10

1 cup Pepe Lopez Tequila
1 cup canned coconut milk
1/2 cup blue curaçao or other orange liqueur
1/3 cup lime juice
2 cups frozen unsweetened raspberries
2 cups frozen unsweetened blueberries
4 cups ice cubes
Lime wedge
1 tablespoon sugar
Sprigs of fresh lavender (optional)

Process the tequila, coconut milk, curaçao and lime juice in a blender at high speed. Add the raspberries, blueberries and ice cubes gradually, processing constantly until smooth and slushy. Rub the rim of each glass with the lime wedge to moisten. Dip the rims in the sugar. Pour the margaritas into the glasses. Top with sprigs of fresh lavender.

THAI CHICKEN SATAY

Serves 10 to 12

1 pound boneless skinless chicken
   breasts, cubed
$1/4$ cup vegetable oil
$1^1/2$ to 3 tablespoons minced Thai
   bird chiles

Freshly ground pepper
$1/4$ cup fish sauce
1 teaspoon brown sugar
1 cup fresh basil leaves, or
   1 tablespoon dried basil

Sauté the chicken in the oil in a skillet for 1 minute or until cooked through. Remove the chicken with a slotted spoon to a platter, reserving the pan drippings. Add the chiles and pepper to the reserved drippings. Sauté for $1^1/2$ minutes. Remove the chile mixture with a slotted spoon and discard, reserving 2 teaspoons of the pan drippings. Heat the reserved drippings until hot. Return the chicken to the skillet. Stir in the fish sauce and brown sugar. Sauté for 30 seconds. Stir in the basil just before serving.

PEPPERONI ARTICHOKE PIE

Serves 16 to 20

2 refrigerator pie pastries
2 (14-ounce) cans artichoke hearts, drained, coarsely chopped
8 ounces mozzarella cheese, shredded
8 ounces Swiss cheese, shredded
1 (8-ounce) jar oil-pack roasted red bell peppers, drained, chopped
6 ounces pepperoni, chopped
2 eggs, beaten

Pat the pastries over the bottom and up the sides of a 9 × 13-inch baking dish, pressing the edges to seal. Combine the artichokes, mozzarella cheese, Swiss cheese, bell pepper and pepperoni in a bowl and mix well. Stir in the eggs.

Spoon the pepperoni mixture into the prepared baking dish. Bake at 350 degrees for 1 hour or until set. Cut into squares.

MARINATED GOAT CHEESE

Serves 12 to 18

1½ pounds Capriole goat cheese
1½ cups extra-virgin olive oil
1½ tablespoons dried thyme
1 tablespoon green or mixed
    peppercorns

4 bay leaves
3 large garlic cloves, minced
3 tablespoons sliced fresh basil
1 tablespoon pink peppercorns

Freeze the goat cheese for 10 minutes before slicing. Cut into ½-inch slices. Arrange the slices in a single layer in a 9 × 12-inch dish.

Combine the olive oil, thyme, green peppercorns and bay leaves in a saucepan. Heat until hot. Pour over the cheese. Sprinkle with the garlic, basil and pink peppercorns. Marinate, covered, in the refrigerator for 8 to 10 hours. Let stand until room temperature. Discard the bay leaves. Serve with baguette slices and/or assorted party crackers.

Use a thin-bladed knife heated in a glass of hot water to cut smooth slices from a fresh goat cheese log.

Chèvre

Chèvre, which is the French word for goat, is a fresh, tangy, zesty white cheese that is available in an assortment of shapes—rolls, pyramids, and rounds. Its consistency can vary from moist to moderately firm. Chèvre can be stored, tightly wrapped, in the refrigerator for up to two weeks and can be found in most supermarkets.

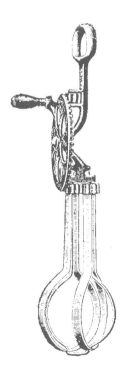

GOAT CHEESE TARTLETS

Makes 24 tartlets

 2 cups crumbled Capriole goat cheese
1 egg, beaten
1 tablespoon half-and-half
1/2 teaspoon salt
1/4 cup chopped sun-dried tomatoes
1 tablespoon finely chopped fresh chives
24 miniature tart shells

Combine the goat cheese, egg, half-and-half and salt in a bowl and mix gently; do not overmix and cause the cheese to become too soft. Fold in the sun-dried tomatoes and chives; overmixing will make the filling pink.

Spoon or pipe the goat cheese mixture just over the top edge of each of the tart shells. Arrange the filled shells on a baking sheet. Bake at 400 degrees for 10 to 12 minutes or until heated through. Garnish with sprigs of fresh chives, minced bell peppers, tiny rolls of prosciutto and/or olive fans.

The Best of Times

"The year is 1917. 'Omar Khayyam' wins the 43rd Derby. It is the best of times. The Seelbach Cocktail becomes the hotel drink for elegant ladies and well-groomed gentlemen. Whenever there is celebration involving wining and dining, there are guests sipping The Seelbach Cocktail. Its elegant Champagne flute holds a golden blend of zest of orange, Korbel Champagne (California's oldest continuously operating winery), a touch of Louisville's Old Forester Bourbon (America's first bottled bourbon), and the bartender's then secret ingredients."

MAX ALLEN, JR.
THE SEELBACH HILTON
BARTENDER EMERITUS

Sausage and Pepper Jack Cheese Tartlets

Makes 24 tartlets

12 ounces Purnell's "Old Folks" Italian Sausage
$1/2$ cup medium-hot salsa
$1/2$ cup shredded Pepper Jack cheese
$1/2$ cup shredded sharp Cheddar cheese
$1/2$ (4-ounce) can diced green chiles
Olive oil
24 won ton wrappers
Sour cream
Finely chopped green onions

Brown the sausage in a heavy skillet over medium-high heat, stirring until crumbly; drain. Stir in the salsa, Pepper Jack cheese, Cheddar cheese and green chiles. Simmer for 5 minutes or until thickened, stirring frequently. Let stand until cool.

Brush 24 miniature muffin cups with olive oil. Press 1 won ton wrapper into each oiled muffin cup; the wrappers will extend beyond the top of the cups. Fill each cup with 1 rounded tablespoon of the sausage mixture. May be prepared up to 3 hours in advance at this point and stored, covered, in the refrigerator.

Bake at 350 degrees for 10 minutes or until the edges of the won ton wrappers begin to brown. Transfer the tartlets to a baking sheet. Bake for 10 minutes longer or until the bottoms are crisp. Arrange the tartlets on a serving platter. Top each with sour cream and sprinkle with green onions.

The Seelbach Cocktail

$1/2$ ounce Triple Sec, chilled
7 dashes of Angostura Bitters
7 dashes of Peychaud Bitters
1 ounce Old Forester, chilled
5 ounces Korbel Brut
**   Champagne, chilled**

Combine the liqueur, bitters and bourbon in a shaker and mix. Pour into a Champagne flute. Add the Champagne. Garnish with orange zest. Serve immediately.

Sausage Puffs and Chili Sauce

Makes 24 to 30 puffs

Puffs
1 pound Purnell's "Old Folks" Italian Sausage, crumbled
1 medium tomato, peeled, seeded, chopped
1 cup shredded fontina cheese
2 or 3 green onions, minced, or equal amount of fresh chives
1 tablespoon oregano
1/2 teaspoon Tabasco sauce
2 sheets frozen puff pastry, thawed

Sour Cream Chili Sauce
1 1/2 cups sour cream
1/2 cup chili sauce

For the puffs, combine the sausage, tomato, cheese, green onions, oregano and Tabasco sauce in a bowl and mix well. Cut each pastry sheet lengthwise into halves; reserve one half for another use.

Shape the sausage mixture into 3 logs the length of the pastry. Wrap the pastry around the logs to enclose completely, pressing the edges to seal. Brush the edges with water. Slice the logs and arrange the slices on a baking sheet. Bake at 375 degrees for 20 minutes or until the sausage is cooked through.

For the sauce, combine the sour cream and chili sauce in a bowl and mix well. Serve with the puffs.

You may prepare in advance and store the unbaked logs in the freezer for future use. May be prepared 1 day in advance and stored, covered, in the refrigerator. Slice and bake just before serving.

PROSCIUTTO AND PARMIGIANA PUFFS

Makes 18 to 24 puffs

8 ounces puff pastry, thawed
3 ounces freshly grated Parmigiano-Reggiano
Freshly ground pepper
10 ounces thinly sliced imported prosciutto
1 egg, beaten
3 tablespoons freshly grated Grana Padano, or other hard cheese

Roll the puff pastry into a very thin rectangle on a lightly floured surface. Sprinkle with the Parmigiano-Reggiano and pepper. Arrange the prosciutto over the cheese to cover the entire surface. Cut into 3-inch triangles with a pastry wheel.

Roll the triangles up from the wide end, enclosing the cheese and prosciutto.

Arrange on a baking sheet and shape into crescents. Brush with the egg and sprinkle with the Grana Padano. Bake at 375 degrees for 20 minutes or until golden brown and crisp.

A Passion for Prosciutto

Prosciutto means ham in Italian. This ham is seasoned, salt-cured, air-dried, and pressed, resulting in a firm, dense texture with a delicate taste. Italians identify prosciutto as Parma ham because the residents of Parma, Italy, have developed a special breed of pigs, which are fed the leftover whey from the processing of Parmesan cheese. Prosciutto is available in specialty markets or in the deli section of the supermarket. As an appetizer, drape thinly sliced prosciutto over a platter covered with chunks or wedges of seasoned fresh fruits sprinkled with freshly squeezed lemon juice. Thicker slices of prosciutto can be added to cooked pasta or vegetables. However, do not overcook prosciutto because it will toughen.

SPICY TWO-CHEESE CROSTINI

Makes 30 to 36 crostini

1 French bread baguette, cut into $^1/_2$-inch slices
$^1/_2$ cup olive oil
8 ounces cream cheese, softened
$^3/_4$ cup freshly grated Parmesan cheese
2 teaspoons Italian seasoning
2 teaspoons garlic powder
1 teaspoon cayenne pepper
2 tablespoons parsley flakes

Arrange the bread slices in a single layer on a baking sheet. Brush 1 side with the olive oil. Bake at 400 degrees for 5 to 6 minutes or until light brown. Cool for 10 minutes.

Beat the cream cheese, Parmesan cheese, Italian seasoning, garlic powder and cayenne pepper in a mixing bowl until blended, scraping the bowl occasionally. Spread 1 to 2 teaspoons of the cream cheese mixture over the toasted side of each bread slice. Sprinkle with the parsley. Bake at 400 degrees for 5 minutes or until slightly puffy. Serve warm.

To freeze for up to thirty days, arrange the unbaked crostini in a single layer on a baking sheet lined with parchment paper. Freeze until firm. Transfer the crostini to a sealable freezer plastic bag. Store in the freezer. Bake at 375 degrees for 10 to 12 minutes or until slightly puffy.

LYNCHBURG LEMONADE

1 ounce Jack Daniel's
1 ounce Triple Sec
1 ounce sweet-and-sour mix
2 ounces lemon-lime soda

Combine the whiskey, liqueur, sweet-and-sour mix and soda in a shaker and mix well. Pour over ice in a highball or 8-ounce glass. Garnish with a lemon slice and maraschino cherry.

SPRING STRUDEL

This versatile dish, from Randolph House Bed & Breakfast in Danville, Kentucky, may be served as a vegetable side dish, a vegetarian entrée or in a brunch buffet.

Serves 6

1/2 teaspoon salt
1 pound asparagus, trimmed, cut into 2-inch slices
6 tablespoons butter, melted
1/3 cup finely chopped onion
3 Roma tomatoes, chopped
1 garlic clove, minced
1/4 teaspoon salt
1 pound mushrooms, thinly sliced

2 tablespoons chopped fresh parsley
1/2 teaspoon salt
1/2 cup finely chopped walnuts, toasted
2 tablespoons bread crumbs
1 package frozen puff pastry, thawed
1 cup shredded provolone cheese

Add enough water to a 12-inch skillet to measure 1/2 inch. Stir in 1/2 teaspoon salt. Bring to a boil; reduce heat. Add the asparagus. Cook for 4 to 6 minutes or until the asparagus is tender; drain. Transfer the asparagus to a platter.

Wipe the skillet dry with a paper towel. Add 1 tablespoon of the butter. Heat until hot. Sauté the onion, tomatoes, garlic and 1/4 teaspoon salt in the butter until the vegetables are tender. Remove the tomato mixture with a slotted spoon to a bowl. Add 1 tablespoon of the remaining butter. Add the mushrooms, parsley and 1/2 teaspoon salt. Cook until the mushrooms are brown and liquid evaporates, stirring frequently. Let stand until cool.

Combine the walnuts and bread crumbs in a bowl and mix well. Roll 1 sheet of the pastry into a 12-inch square on a lightly floured surface. Cut into 6 equal squares. Sprinkle each square with some of the walnut mixture. Top with some of the asparagus mixture and some of the tomato mixture. Sprinkle with some of the cheese.

Roll each filled square into a packet and tuck the edges under; seal edges with water. Arrange the packets seam side down on a generously greased baking sheet. Brush with some of the remaining butter. Repeat the process with the remaining ingredients. Bake at 375 degrees for 15 to 20 minutes or until light brown.

WATERMELON LEMONADE

Makes 2 quarts

1 cup sugar, or to taste
1 cup water
2 cups chopped seeded watermelon
1 cup fresh lemon juice
3 cups carbonated water

Bring the sugar and water to a boil in a saucepan. Boil for 2 minutes or until the sugar dissolves, stirring occasionally. Pour into a container with a cover. Chill in the refrigerator. Press the watermelon with the back of a spoon through a fine mesh strainer into a bowl, discarding the pulp. Combine the watermelon juice, syrup and lemon juice in a container with a cover and mix well. Chill in the refrigerator. Pour into a 2-quart pitcher. Stir in the carbonated water just before serving. Pour over ice in glasses.

Soups & Salads

Kentucky Country Ham and
Spinach Salad
(Photo, pages 52–53)

Kentucky is not only a
state of the union but a
state of mind. What you
need to do is relax. Good
Kentucky food, like good
food anywhere, depends on
using natural ingredients
and knowing that Mother
Nature doesn't operate
with scientific exactness.

Charles Patteson
Charles Patteson's Kentucky Cooking

Mediterranean Meatball Soup

Serves 8 to 10

1 pound ground chuck
1 egg, beaten
1 ounce Parmesan cheese, grated
1 teaspoon garlic salt
1/2 teaspoon ground black pepper
6 ounces onion, coarsely chopped
4 ounces carrots, coarsely chopped
4 ounces celery, coarsely chopped
1 tablespoon olive oil
2 garlic cloves, minced
2 1/2 quarts chicken stock,
   defatted homemade or canned
   reduced-sodium
1/2 cup Bolla Merlot
1 teaspoon dried thyme, or
   1 tablespoon chopped fresh
   thyme

1 (28-ounce) can crushed tomatoes
8 ounces eggplant, coarsely
   chopped
1 pint chicken stock
8 ounces zucchini, coarsely chopped
3 ounces spinach, cut into
   1/2-inch strips
2 teaspoons sugar
1 teaspoon dried basil, or
   1 tablespoon minced fresh basil
1 teaspoon dried oregano, or
   1 tablespoon minced
   fresh oregano
1/2 teaspoon cayenne pepper
Ground black pepper to taste
2 tablespoons chopped
   fresh parsley

Combine the ground chuck, egg, cheese, garlic salt and 1/2 teaspoon black pepper in a bowl and mix well. Shape the ground chuck mixture into marble-size meatballs and set aside. Sauté the onion, carrots and celery in the olive oil in a stockpot just until the vegetables begin to soften. Add the garlic. Sauté for 30 seconds. Add 2 1/2 quarts chicken stock, red wine and thyme and mix well. Simmer for 30 minutes or until the vegetables are tender-crisp, stirring occasionally. Stir in the undrained tomatoes and eggplant. Cook for 15 minutes longer, stirring occasionally.

Bring 1 pint chicken stock to a simmer in a saucepan. Add half the meatballs. Poach for 10 minutes or until the meatballs float to the top. Remove the meatballs with a slotted spoon to the soup mixture. Repeat the process with the remaining meatballs and add to the soup, discarding the poaching liquid. Simmer the soup for 10 minutes, stirring occasionally.

Add the zucchini, spinach, sugar, basil, oregano, cayenne pepper and black pepper to taste 5 minutes before serving and mix well. Stir in the parsley just before serving. Ladle into soup bowls. Garnish with additional Parmesan cheese and/or pasta such as ditalini cooked al dente.

Hearty Tortellini and Sausage Soup

Serves 6

1 pound Purnell's "Old Folks" Italian Sausage
1 cup chopped onion
2 large garlic cloves, sliced
5 cups beef stock or canned broth
2 cups chopped fresh tomatoes
1 (8-ounce) can tomato sauce
1 large zucchini, sliced
1 large carrot, thinly sliced
1 medium green bell pepper, chopped
1/4 cup chopped banana peppers
1/2 cup Bolla Valpolicella
2 tablespoons basil
2 tablespoons oregano
8 to 10 ounces fresh cheese tortellini
Salt and pepper to taste
Freshly grated Parmesan cheese

Brown the sausage in a heavy saucepan over medium-high heat for 10 minutes or until crumbly and cooked through, stirring constantly. Transfer the sausage with a slotted spoon to a large bowl. Drain the pan drippings, reserving 1 tablespoon. Sauté the onion and garlic in the reserved drippings for 5 minutes or until the onion is tender. Return the sausage to the saucepan. Stir in the stock, tomatoes, tomato sauce, zucchini, carrot, bell pepper, banana peppers, wine, basil and oregano.

Simmer for 40 minutes or until the vegetables are tender, stirring occasionally. May be prepared to this point up to 2 days in advance and stored, covered, in the refrigerator. Bring to a simmer before continuing. Add the pasta and mix gently. Cook for 8 minutes or until the pasta is tender, stirring occasionally. Season with salt and pepper. Ladle into soup bowls. Sprinkle with cheese.

The Blessing of Food

"Good food blesses all, the one who cooks it and the one who eats it."

CAMILLE GLENN
THE HERITAGE OF SOUTHERN COOKING

TEX-MEX SOUP

Serves 6 to 8

1 small onion, coarsely chopped
3 tablespoons shortening
1 (16-ounce) can chicken broth
1 (14-ounce) can beef broth
1 (16-ounce) can stewed tomatoes
1 (4-ounce) can chopped green chiles
2 tablespoons Worcestershire sauce
1 teaspoon Tabasco sauce
1 teaspoon cumin seeds
1 teaspoon chili powder
3 or 4 fresh or frozen flour tortillas, cut into ¼- to ½-inch strips
3 boneless skinless chicken breasts, cooked, coarsely chopped

Sauté the onion in the shortening in a heavy saucepan until tender. Stir in the chicken broth, beef broth, undrained tomatoes, chiles, Worcestershire sauce, Tabasco sauce, cumin seeds and chili powder.

Simmer for 1 hour, stirring occasionally. Add the tortillas and mix gently. Cook until the tortillas are tender. Stir in the chicken. Cook just until heated through. Ladle into soup bowls. Garnish with tortilla chips, sour cream and chopped fresh cilantro.

Triple the recipe for a crowd, substituting 1 shredded cooked whole chicken for the chicken breasts.

ROASTED TOMATO CLAM CHOWDER

Serves 6 to 8

9 Roma tomatoes
2 teaspoons olive oil
1 teaspoon minced fresh thyme
Salt and black pepper to taste
1 tablespoon olive oil
2 cups finely chopped onions
2 cups finely chopped celery
1 tablespoon minced fresh thyme
2 teaspoons minced garlic
$1/8$ teaspoon red pepper flakes
$1/2$ cup water
1 (16-ounce) package frozen white
   Shoe Peg corn, thawed

2 (8-ounce) bottles clam juice
1 (14-ounce) can chicken broth
1 (14-ounce) can diced tomatoes
8 ounces Polish sausage, cut into
   $1/4$-inch slices
2 cups coarsely chopped Yukon
   Gold potatoes
1 cup Bolla Merlot
1 (10-ounce) bottle vegetable
   juice cocktail
1 bay leaf
2 (6-ounce) cans chopped clams
1 tablespoon minced fresh basil

Cut off the stem ends of the tomatoes. Cut the tomatoes lengthwise into halves. Mix 2 teaspoons olive oil, 1 teaspoon thyme, salt and black pepper in a bowl. Add the tomatoes and toss to coat. Arrange the tomatoes cut side down on a baking sheet sprayed with nonstick cooking spray.

Roast at 400 degrees for 20 minutes or until the tomatoes begin to brown. Transfer the tomatoes and any accumulated juices to a food processor container. Process until puréed.

Heat 1 tablespoon olive oil in a 5-quart Dutch oven over medium-high heat until hot. Add the onions, celery, 1 tablespoon thyme, garlic and red pepper flakes. Sauté for 3 minutes. Reduce the heat to medium-low. Stir in the water.

Cook for 5 minutes or until the vegetables begin to soften, stirring occasionally. Stir in the roasted tomato purée, corn, clam juice, broth, undrained canned tomatoes, sausage, potatoes, wine, vegetable juice cocktail and bay leaf. Bring to a boil; reduce heat. Simmer for 45 minutes or until the vegetables are tender, stirring occasionally. Stir in the undrained clams and basil. Cook for 5 minutes, stirring occasionally. Discard the bay leaf. Ladle into soup bowls.

Clams can become tough when cooked. If you object to this texture in chowder, place the undrained clams in a food processor container. Pulse until finely minced and add to the chowder.

THE OAKROOM'S ROASTED CORN CHOWDER

Created by Chef Jim Gerhardt, The Oakroom at The Seelbach Hilton

Serves 10 to 12

3 ears unhusked Kentucky
    white corn
2 medium baking potatoes
1 small onion, finely chopped
2 ribs celery, finely chopped
1 small red bell pepper,
    finely chopped
1 small green bell pepper,
    finely chopped
1 tablespoon olive oil
3 garlic cloves, finely chopped
4 ounces Kentucky country ham,
    finely chopped or ground

2 quarts chicken stock
2 cups shrimp stock
2 cups heavy cream
1 tablespoon minced fresh thyme,
    or 1 teaspoon dried thyme
2 tablespoons cornstarch
1 tablespoon water
Salt and freshly ground pepper
    to taste
Crawfish tails, cooked

"What influenced me to become a chef was that I always enjoyed going to restaurants with the family as a kid as well as eating. This made me want to run a great restaurant.

"I also enjoyed watching Graham Kerr as a kid. I could not believe how much fun he made this profession look."

CHEF JIM GERHARDT
THE OAKROOM AT
THE SEELBACH HILTON

Arrange the corn and potatoes on a nonstick baking sheet. Roast at 400 degrees for 30 minutes. Cool slightly. Remove the husks and silk from the corn. Cut the corn kernels with a sharp knife into a bowl; scrape the corncob with a knife to remove the juices. Peel the potatoes and cut into 1/2-inch pieces.

Sauté the onion, celery and bell peppers in the olive oil in a 4-quart stockpot for 2 minutes. Add the garlic. Sauté for 1 minute. Stir in the corn, ham, chicken stock, shrimp stock, heavy cream and thyme. Bring just to a boil, stirring constantly. Stir in a mixture of the cornstarch and water; reduce heat.

Simmer until of the desired consistency, stirring frequently. Add the potatoes and mix gently. Season with salt and pepper to taste. Simmer just until heated through. Ladle into soup bowls. Top each serving with 3 crawfish tails.

You may substitute shrimp base or bouillon for the shrimp stock.

RED PEPPER CRAB BISQUE

Serves 6

3 cups coarsely chopped red bell peppers
1 cup coarsely chopped celery
3/4 cup chopped shallots
2/3 cup coarsely chopped carrot
1/2 cup coarsely chopped red onion
2 tablespoons extra-virgin olive oil
2 teaspoons tarragon
1/4 teaspoon chipotle chile
2 (14-ounce) cans diced peeled tomatoes in juice
3 (8-ounce) bottles clam juice
1 cup Fetzer Echo Ridge Fumé Blanc
1 cup whipping cream
12 ounces crab meat
Salt and pepper to taste
1/4 cup chopped shallots

Sauté the bell peppers, celery, 3/4 cup shallots, carrot and red onion in the olive oil in a heavy saucepan for 12 minutes or until the vegetables are tender. Stir in the tarragon and chile. Add the undrained tomatoes, clam juice and wine and mix well. Bring to a boil; reduce heat.

Simmer over low heat for 30 minutes, stirring occasionally. Stir in the whipping cream. Simmer for 20 minutes longer, stirring occasionally. Add the crab meat and mix well. Cook for 5 minutes or until heated through, stirring occasionally. Season with salt and pepper. Ladle into soup bowls. Sprinkle with 1/4 cup shallots.

Creative Serving Idea

Serve this soup in bell pepper bowls created by cutting the tops off red, yellow, or green bell peppers. Reserve the tops. Hollow out the inside of the peppers by removing the seeds and membranes. It may be necessary to shave some peel off the bottoms of the peppers to make them sit upright (be careful not to cut a hole). Spoon the soup into the pepper bowls and place the tops on them to keep the soup warm until it is ready to serve.

GREMOLATA-TOPPED YELLOW PEPPER SOUP

Serves 10 to 12

Parmesan Gremolata
5 ounces Parmesan cheese, grated
Leaves of 1 bunch parsley, minced
5 tablespoons chopped fresh basil
4 garlic cloves, minced
Finely chopped zest of 2 lemons

Yellow Pepper Soup
6 tablespoons extra-virgin olive oil
2 carrots, peeled, minced
2 ribs celery, minced
2 small shallots, chopped
2 garlic cloves, minced
4 oil-pack sun-dried tomatoes, drained, minced
8 yellow bell peppers, roasted, peeled, chopped
2 quarts chicken stock (preferably homemade)
1 cup Bel Arbor Chardonnay
5 tablespoons chopped fresh basil
1/2 cup light cream
Salt and freshly ground pepper to taste

For the gremolata, toss the cheese, parsley, basil, garlic and lemon zest in a bowl.

For the soup, heat the olive oil in a stockpot over medium-high heat. Stir in the carrots, celery, shallots, garlic and sun-dried tomatoes. Cook for 5 minutes, stirring frequently. Reduce the heat to medium. Cook for 15 minutes longer, stirring occasionally. Stir in the bell peppers, chicken stock and wine.

Simmer for 15 minutes, stirring occasionally. Add the basil and mix well. Simmer for 2 minutes. Remove from the heat. Stir in the cream. Process the soup in batches in a blender until puréed. Return the soup to the stockpot. Season with salt and pepper.

Bring the soup to a simmer, stirring occasionally. Ladle into heated soup bowls. Top each serving with a heaping spoonful of the gremolata.

AUTUMN PUMPKIN SOUP

Enjoy autumn's harvest with this delightful soup.

Serves 14

¹/₄ cup whipping cream
¹/₄ cup sour cream
¹/₂ teaspoon fresh lime juice
3 tablespoons butter
3 cups finely chopped Vidalia onions
3 (15-ounce) cans solid-pack pumpkin
1 cup milk
1 teaspoon minced chipotle chile
4¹/₂ cups canned chicken broth
Salt and pepper to taste
¹/₂ cup pumpkin seeds, toasted

Whisk the whipping cream, sour cream and lime juice in a bowl until blended. Chill, covered, for 2 hours. May be prepared up to 1 week in advance and stored, covered, in the refrigerator.

Heat the butter in a heavy saucepan over medium heat. Add the onions. Sauté for 10 minutes or until tender. Stir in the pumpkin, milk and chile. Process the pumpkin mixture in batches in a blender until puréed. Return the mixture to the saucepan. Stir in the broth.

Simmer for 10 minutes, stirring occasionally. Season with salt and pepper. Ladle into soup bowls. Top each serving with some of the sour cream mixture and sprinkle with some of the pumpkin seeds.

The soup may be prepared up to 1 day in advance and stored, covered, in the refrigerator. Reheat just before serving.

The Pumpkin Patch

It would not be fall without pumpkins. Not only are they wonderful in recipes, but they have many festive uses.

Hollow out a large pumpkin and use it as a soup tureen. Cut off the top of the pumpkin and scoop out the insides. Fill with hot or cold soup and garnish the base with fresh greens or flowers and you have an inexpensive serving piece.

Smaller pumpkins make great containers for fresh flowers. Cut off the top and remove the pumpkin's insides. Insert a suitable size plastic or glass container filled with water and arrange flowers.

Miniature pumpkins can be used as table place cards. Tie a name card on the stem with raffia or ribbon or write names directly on the pumpkin. For a more elegant look, spray paint the pumpkins gold or silver.

TOMATO BASIL SOUP

Serves 10 to 12

1/3 **cup fruity olive oil**
4 leeks, minced
3 carrots, peeled, minced
1 medium red onion, chopped
3 garlic cloves, minced
Grated zest of 1 lemon
1 tablespoon thyme
1 teaspoon fennel seeds
1 teaspoon saffron threads
Tabasco sauce to taste
12 large ripe tomatoes, seeded, chopped
3 (35-ounce) cans Italian plum tomatoes
2 quarts chicken stock (preferably homemade)
1 cup orange juice
Salt and freshly ground pepper to taste
1 cup chopped fresh basil

Heat the olive oil in a stockpot over high heat. Add the leeks, carrots,
onion and garlic and mix well. Cook for 15 minutes, stirring frequently.
Stir in the lemon zest, thyme, fennel seeds, saffron threads and Tabasco
sauce. Cook for 3 minutes, stirring frequently. Add the fresh tomatoes,
undrained canned tomatoes, chicken stock and orange juice and mix well.

Simmer over medium heat for 30 minutes, stirring occasionally. Remove
from heat. Process the soup in batches in a blender or food processor
fitted with a steel blade until puréed. Season with salt and pepper.

Return the soup to the stockpot. Bring just to a simmer, stirring
occasionally. Stir in the basil just before serving. Ladle into soup
bowls. Garnish each serving with a dollop of sour cream and chopped
fresh chives.

Photo on facing page,
Farmland in
Western Kentucky

CURRIED CHICKEN MANGO SALAD

Savor the light, fresh, and cool flavors of summer in this salad.

Serves 6

**3 pounds boneless skinless chicken breasts, poached,
  cut into bite-size pieces**
2 mangoes, cut into 3/4-inch pieces
2 tablespoons fresh lemon juice
1 cup chopped celery
4 scallions with tops, sliced
1/4 cup plain yogurt
1/4 cup mayonnaise
2 1/2 teaspoons curry powder
1/2 teaspoon cumin
Salt and pepper to taste
1 cup cashews, roasted, chopped
2 tablespoons chopped fresh coriander (optional)

Toss the chicken, mangoes and lemon juice in a bowl until mixed. Stir in
the celery and scallions.

Whisk the yogurt, mayonnaise, curry powder and cumin in a bowl.
Add to the chicken mixture and mix well. Season with salt and pepper.
Chill, covered, until serving time. Stir in the cashews and coriander.

Spoon the chicken salad onto a lettuce-lined serving platter. Serve
immediately. May be prepared 1 day in advance and stored, covered, in
the refrigerator until serving time.

MEDITERRANEAN ORZO AND SHRIMP SALAD

Serve this salad with crusty baguettes as an entrée for a light summer dinner.

Serves 4

Dill Salad Dressing
1/4 cup plus 2 tablespoons packed fresh dillweed
1 1/2 garlic cloves
3 tablespoons olive oil
3 tablespoons fresh lemon juice
1 1/2 tablespoons red wine vinegar or balsamic vinegar
1/2 teaspoon salt
Freshly ground pepper to taste

Salad
3/4 cup orzo, cooked, rinsed, drained
1 teaspoon vegetable oil
1 pound large peeled cooked shrimp
3 1/2 ounces feta cheese, crumbled
2 small Roma tomatoes, seeded, chopped
1 (2-ounce) can sliced black olives, drained
2 shallots, chopped

For the dressing, place the dillweed in a food processor container fitted with a steel blade. Add the garlic through the feed tube, processing constantly until minced. Scrape down the side of the bowl. Add the olive oil, lemon juice, wine vinegar, salt and pepper. Process for 5 seconds or until blended.

For the salad, combine the orzo and oil in a bowl and mix well. Chill, covered, in the refrigerator. Combine the chilled orzo mixture, shrimp, feta cheese, tomatoes, black olives and shallots in a bowl and mix gently. Add the dressing and toss to coat.

Mound the salad evenly onto 4 lettuce-lined salad plates. Garnish with sprigs of fresh dillweed.

PAN-ROASTED PRAWN SALAD

Created by Chef John Castro, Winston's at Sullivan College

Serves 1

Thai Basil Oil

4 cups water

2 teaspoons salt

1 cup Thai basil

1/2 cup peanut oil

Salad

1 unshelled prawn or 3 shrimp, butterflied

Szechuan peppercorn salt to taste

1 tablespoon peanut oil

1/4 cup chopped beefsteak or ultra boy tomato

1 tablespoon chopped green tomato

2 tablespoons diagonally sliced garlic chives

2 tablespoons tamari sauce

1 scallion, diagonally sliced

1/4 teaspoon sugar

3 yellow pear tomatoes, cut into halves

5 red currant tomatoes or sweet one hundreds, cut into halves if desired

Sea salt to taste

For the oil, bring the water and salt to a boil in a saucepan. Add the basil. Blanch for 1 minute; drain. Purée the basil and peanut oil in a blender.

For the salad, sprinkle the prawn with Szechuan peppercorn salt. Let stand for 15 minutes. Heat 1 teaspoon of the peanut oil in a sauté pan over high heat. Arrange the prawn shell side down in the pan. Cook for 1 1/2 minutes. Reduce the heat to low and turn the prawn over. Cook for 2 to 3 minutes longer, allowing to caramelize slightly.

Heat the remaining 2 teaspoons peanut oil in a sauté pan. Add the beefsteak tomato and green tomato. Cook for 3 minutes, stirring occasionally. Stir in the garlic chives, tamari sauce, scallion and sugar. Add the pear tomatoes and currant tomatoes and mix gently. Cook for 2 minutes longer or until the tomatoes are heated through and slightly softened but not mushy. Season with salt.

Arrange the tomatoes and prawn on a plate. Garnish with a chiffonade of Thai basil and drizzle with Thai Basil Oil. You may serve over hot cooked rice as a main dish.

"Imagine the warmth of a late August or September day, combined with the dust of a limestone gravel road and a shriveled tomato vine. That vine is almost ready to perish, but it still produces beautiful fruit and seeds to ensure its legacy. Pick one of the tomatoes from the vine. Bite into it and enjoy the rush of its sugary insides. This example shows cooking is both a passion and an art.

"The hours are long, and the kitchens are hot. However, the rewards of family, friends and patrons are many."

CHEF JOHN CASTRO
WINSTON'S AT
SULLIVAN COLLEGE

DERBY PASTA SALAD

You might come to Kentucky for the Derby, but you will want to stick around after the race when this salad is served.

Serves 10 to 12

12 ounces bow tie pasta
1 bunch asparagus, trimmed
1 pound French or Greek feta
   cheese, crumbled
1 red bell pepper, thinly sliced
1 yellow bell pepper, thinly sliced

1/4 cup thinly sliced oil-pack
   sun-dried tomatoes
1/4 cup olive oil
2 tablespoons Red Wine Marinade
   (at right)

Cook the pasta using package directions until al dente; drain. Let stand until cool. Cook the asparagus in boiling water in a saucepan for 2 to 3 minutes or until tender-crisp; drain.

Toss the pasta, asparagus, cheese, bell peppers and sun-dried tomatoes in a bowl. Add the olive oil and Red Wine Marinade and mix well. Serve at room temperature.

RED WINE MARINADE

2 cups sugar
1 cup red wine vinegar

Combine the sugar and red wine vinegar in a saucepan and mix well. Bring to a boil. Cook until the sugar dissolves, stirring constantly. Remove from the heat. Let stand until cool. Store at room temperature in a covered plastic container.

BLUEGRASS SALAD

Serves 8

1/2 cup salad oil
1/4 cup rice vinegar
1 tablespoon balsamic vinegar
2 tablespoons sugar
3/4 cup walnuts
Butter
2 heads green leaf lettuce, romaine
   or 1 package spring salad mix

1 cup asparagus tips, broccoli
   florets or snow peas
2 fresh pears, chopped
1/2 cup crumbled bleu cheese
   or feta cheese or grated
   Parmesan cheese
1/2 cup dried cranberries or cherries
   (optional)

Combine the salad oil, rice vinegar, balsamic vinegar and sugar in a jar with a tight-fitting lid. Shake to mix. Chill for 2 hours or longer before serving. Sauté the walnuts in butter in a skillet until light brown. Remove the walnuts with a slotted spoon to a bowl. Tear the lettuce. Toss the lettuce, asparagus, pears, cheese and walnuts in a bowl. Sprinkle with the cranberries. Add the vinaigrette just before serving and mix well.

FIESTA CORN SALAD

This easy and colorful salad pairs well with anything you toss on the grill.

Serves 4 to 6

2 cups fresh corn kernels
$3/4$ cup water
1 (14-ounce) can black beans, drained, rinsed
$1/2$ cup chopped shallots
$1/2$ cup chopped red bell pepper
$1/4$ cup chopped fresh cilantro
1 small cucumber, seeded, chopped
2 garlic cloves, minced
2 tablespoons corn oil
2 tablespoons rice vinegar
1 tablespoon sunflower oil
1 tablespoon lime juice
1 teaspoon sweet red pepper flakes
$1/4$ teaspoon ginger
$1/4$ teaspoon salt

Combine the corn kernels and water in a saucepan. Bring to a boil; reduce heat. Simmer, covered, for 7 to 8 minutes or until tender; drain. Combine the corn, beans, shallots, bell pepper, cilantro, cucumber and garlic in a bowl and mix well.

Whisk the corn oil, rice vinegar, sunflower oil, lime juice, red pepper flakes, ginger and salt in a bowl. Add to the corn mixture and mix well. Chill, covered, for 2 hours or longer.

ENDIVE WITH APPLES AND STILTON

Serves 6 to 8

Dijon Vinaigrette
3 tablespoons apple cider vinegar
1¹/₂ tablespoons red wine vinegar
³/₄ teaspoon Dijon mustard
¹/₂ teaspoon sugar
3 tablespoons extra-virgin olive oil
2 small green onions, sliced
Salt and freshly ground pepper to taste

Salad
3 tablespoons unsalted butter
1¹/₂ cups walnuts, coarsely chopped
³/₄ teaspoon sugar
3 large heads Belgian endive
3 Granny Smith apples, julienned
³/₄ cup crumbled Stilton cheese
Salt and freshly ground pepper to taste
Romaine lettuce

For the vinaigrette, whisk the apple cider vinegar, red wine vinegar, Dijon mustard and sugar in a bowl. Add the olive oil gradually, whisking constantly until blended. Stir in the green onions, salt and pepper.

For the salad, heat the butter in a saucepan over medium heat until melted. Stir in the walnuts and sugar. Cook for 2 minutes or until the walnuts are golden brown, stirring constantly. Transfer the walnuts to a bowl. Cut the endive lengthwise into julienne strips.

Combine the endive, apples, walnuts and cheese in a bowl and mix well. Add the vinaigrette and toss gently to coat. Season with salt and pepper. Spoon the salad onto salad plates lined with romaine lettuce.

Add a Little Flavor

"Rely on flavorful ingredients. Remember feta cheese, imported black olives, capers, soy sauce, green chilies, garlic, raisins or currants, toasted nuts and fresh ginger give lots of flavor with little extra effort."

SARAH FRITSCHNER
VEGETARIAN EXPRESS
LANE COOKBOOK

Green Bean and Sun-Dried Tomato Salad

Serves 8 to 10

1 cup pine nuts
3/4 cup olive oil
1/4 cup white wine vinegar
2 tablespoons chopped fresh basil
1 teaspoon minced garlic
1/4 teaspoon salt
1/4 teaspoon pepper
1 1/2 pounds fresh green beans
1 small purple onion, thinly sliced
4 ounces oil-pack sun-dried tomatoes, drained
Freshly grated Romano cheese

Spread the pine nuts in a single layer on a baking sheet. Toast at
350 degrees for 3 to 5 minutes or until light brown, stirring occasionally.
Whisk the olive oil, wine vinegar, basil, garlic, salt and pepper in a bowl.
Chill, covered, in the refrigerator.

Cut the beans into thirds. Place the beans in a steamer basket over boiling
water in a saucepan. Steam, covered, for 15 minutes or until tender-crisp.
Plunge the beans into cold water immediately. Drain and pat dry.

Combine the pine nuts, beans, onion and sun-dried tomatoes in a bowl and
toss to mix. Chill, covered, in the refrigerator. Pour the olive oil mixture
over the bean mixture 1 hour before serving. Toss the salad just before
serving and sprinkle with Romano cheese.

ROMAINE BUNDLES WITH MACADAMIA DRESSING

This salad's unique presentation will impress your guests.

Serves 4

Macadamia Dressing
1/2 cup mayonnaise
2 tablespoons fresh lemon juice
2 tablespoons orange juice
2 tablespoons finely chopped macadamias, toasted
1 teaspoon sugar
1 small garlic clove, crushed

Salad
1 medium red onion
1 to 2 heads romaine lettuce (preferably the hearts), separated
Sliced mandarin oranges or cherry tomatoes
2 tablespoons coarsely chopped macadamias, toasted

For the dressing, combine the mayonnaise, lemon juice, orange juice, macadamias, sugar and garlic in a bowl and mix well.

For the salad, slice the onion into four $1/4$-inch slices, discarding all the rings except the larger outer rings of each onion slice. Pull several lettuce leaves through each onion slice and arrange on a salad plate. Top with sliced mandarin oranges or cherry tomatoes. Drizzle the dressing over the bundles. Sprinkle with the macadamias.

This dressing would be delicious served over a variety of fresh fruit.

Dried Herbs vs. Fresh Herbs

Use fewer dried herbs than you would fresh herbs. The loss of moisture strengthens and concentrates the flavor in dried herbs. As a general rule, use only one-half to one-third as many dried herbs as fresh in a given recipe. For example, if a recipe calls for one tablespoon of fresh thyme, you should substitute only one teaspoon of dried thyme. You can usually add more later if necessary.

Tuscan Potato Salad

Serves 12 to 15

3 pounds cubed red or white new potatoes
Salt to taste
1 cup ricotta cheese
2/3 cup grated Parmesan cheese

1/2 cup olive oil
6 tablespoons cider vinegar
1/2 red onion, thinly sliced
4 garlic cloves, crushed
Pepper to taste

Combine the potatoes and salt with enough water to cover in a saucepan. Bring to a boil; reduce heat. Cook until the potatoes are tender; drain. Cover to keep warm.

Combine the ricotta cheese, Parmesan cheese, olive oil, vinegar, onion, garlic, salt and pepper in a bowl and mix well. Add the warm potatoes and mix gently. Serve immediately or chill, covered, in the refrigerator. The flavor of the salad is enhanced if chilled before serving. Garnish with fresh parsley.

Salad Spuds

New potatoes have a low starch content, which means they will absorb less of the cooking water, as well as less of the mayonnaise or vinaigrette dressing when used in a salad. They are also less likely to crumble when the salad is mixed and served.

Sesame Soy Vinaigrette over Greens

Serves 8 to 10

Sesame Soy Vinaigrette
1/2 cup seasoned rice wine vinegar
1/4 cup soy sauce
2 tablespoons sesame oil

1 teaspoon minced fresh gingerroot
1/2 teaspoon minced garlic
1 cup peanut oil

Salad
Baby leaf lettuce
Mustard greens and endive

Shredded red cabbage
Sautéed shiitake mushrooms

For the vinaigrette, combine the wine vinegar, soy sauce, sesame oil, gingerroot and garlic in a food processor or blender container. Add the peanut oil gradually, processing constantly until blended. The vinaigrette will thicken.

For the salad, toss baby leaf lettuce, mustard greens, endive, cabbage and shiitake mushrooms in a bowl. Drizzle with the vinaigrette and mix well.

Kentucky Country Ham and Spinach Salad

Created by Chef John Castro, Winston's at Sullivan College

Serves 4 to 6

Orange and Kentucky Ham Dressing
¹/₄ cup Kentucky country ham or bacon drippings
¹/₄ cup sherry vinegar
¹/₄ cup fresh orange juice
1 tablespoon sugar
1 tablespoon orange oil
Salt and pepper to taste
¹/₂ cup olive oil

Salad
Kentucky country ham, thinly sliced
Baby spinach
Sliced fresh oranges or orange sections

For the dressing, whisk the country ham drippings, sherry vinegar, orange juice, sugar, orange oil, salt and pepper in a bowl until mixed. Add the olive oil gradually, whisking constantly until blended. Let stand at room temperature.

For the salad, sauté the ham in a skillet until crisp; drain. Toss the spinach and ham in a bowl. Drizzle with the dressing. Top with fresh orange slices or sections.

"I treasure the warmth and support of the local farming community, as well as the history and folklore of some of the regional products. I also find Kentucky cooking to be very welcoming. It is decidedly 'Southern' yet with a 'Northern' edge."

Chef John Castro
Winston's at
Sullivan College

SPICED WALNUTS AND MIXED GREENS

Serves 8

Walnut Vinaigrette
6 tablespoons walnut oil
3 tablespoons vegetable oil
3 tablespoons white wine vinegar
Salt to taste
Fresh lemon juice to taste

Salad
1 cup walnuts
1 tablespoon unsalted butter
1¹/₂ tablespoons sugar
1 teaspoon curry powder
Cayenne pepper to taste
3 tablespoons Worcestershire sauce
Bibb lettuce, Belgian endive or romaine lettuce

For the vinaigrette, whisk the walnut oil, vegetable oil, wine vinegar, salt and lemon juice in a bowl until blended.

For the salad, reserve 2 tablespoons of the walnuts. Coarsely chop the remaining walnuts. Heat the butter in a skillet until melted. Stir in the coarsely chopped walnuts and reserved 2 tablespoons walnuts. Sauté until light brown; do not burn.

Stir in the sugar, curry powder and cayenne pepper. Add the Worcestershire sauce and mix well. Cook over low heat until the walnuts are coated with a thin dark glaze, stirring often. Let stand until cool. Do not chill.

Arrange Bibb lettuce, Belgian endive or romaine on each of 8 salad plates. Spoon the walnut mixture over the greens. Drizzle with the vinaigrette.

Versatile Vinaigrettes

Vinaigrettes have many uses other than dressing salads:

- *Use as a marinade for meats, poultry, or seafood before grilling or broiling.*

- *Pour over sliced or cubed cheese and serve with crackers as an appetizer.*

- *Toss with cooked vegetables and rice or pasta to serve as a cold salad.*

- *Use instead of melted butter as a topping on breads or rolls before baking.*

KENTUCKY CHÈVRE-STUFFED TOMATOES

Serves 4

4 firm ripe tomatoes
4 rounds Capriole goat cheese
Olive oil
Salt and pepper to taste
Rosemary to taste
4 Bibb lettuce leaves

Slice off the top quarter of each tomato and discard. Scoop out the pulp with a grapefruit spoon. Invert the tomatoes on a rack to drain.

Discard the peel from the cheese. Arrange a cheese round in each tomato. Drizzle with olive oil. Sprinkle with salt, pepper and rosemary. Arrange the tomatoes in a baking dish.

Bake at 400 degrees for 15 to 20 minutes. Cover loosely with foil if the cheese appears to be cooking too quickly. Arrange the stuffed tomatoes on the lettuce leaves on each of 4 salad plates. Garnish with sprigs of fresh parsley. Serve immediately with crusty baguettes.

Bibb Lettuce Has "Roots" in Kentucky

"Bibb lettuce was born in Kentucky and named for Judge Jack Bibb, who propagated it around 1865 in his hobby greenhouse in Frankfort. It was called limestone lettuce at first, as the alkaline limestone soil of central Kentucky was credited with helping to produce a superior lettuce. The heads of true Bibb lettuce are compact and exquisitely small—one head is a perfect single serving. The vibrant tones of strong greens and soft yellows are as beautiful as the lettuce is crisp, and its crunchiness never fails to amaze gardeners. But how did Judge Bibb compose and control the size? What strains of lettuce did he cross to achieve these dainty heads of perfect balance in flavor and texture? No one knows. No one has been able to break the code."

CAMILLE GLENN
THE HERITAGE OF SOUTHERN COOKING

Asparagus and Yellow Pepper Frittata
(Photo, pages 78–79)

There are those who will
tell you that real cornbread
has just a little sugar in it.
They'll say it enhances
the flavor or that it's an
old tradition in the South.
Do not listen to them.
If God had meant for
cornbread to have sugar
in it, he'd have called it cake.

Ronni Lundy

BUTTERMILK CHEESE BISCUITS

Makes 10 biscuits

1¼ cups flour	½ cup packed shredded sharp
1½ tablespoons sugar	Cheddar cheese
1 teaspoon baking powder	½ cup packed shredded Monterey
¼ teaspoon baking soda	Jack cheese
⅛ teaspoon salt	½ cup grated Parmesan cheese
3 tablespoons chilled butter,	⅔ cup chilled buttermilk
chopped	

Combine the flour, sugar, baking powder, baking soda and salt in a bowl
and mix well. Cut in the butter until crumbly. Stir in the Cheddar cheese,
Monterey Jack cheese and Parmesan cheese. Add the buttermilk
gradually, stirring constantly until mixed.

Drop the dough by ¼ cupfuls 2 inches apart onto a lightly buttered baking
sheet. Bake at 400 degrees for 16 minutes or until golden brown. Remove
the biscuits to a serving platter. Serve warm or at room temperature.

HAZELNUT SCONES

Makes 12 scones

2½ cups flour	½ cup (1 stick) butter
⅓ cup packed brown sugar	½ cup chopped hazelnuts
1 tablespoon baking powder	½ cup buttermilk
1 teaspoon cardamom	1 egg
½ teaspoon salt	2 to 3 tablespoons cream

Sift the flour, brown sugar, baking powder, cardamom and salt into a bowl
and mix well. Cut in the butter with a pastry blender until crumbly. Stir in
the hazelnuts. Whisk the buttermilk and egg in a bowl until blended. Add
to the flour mixture, stirring until a soft dough forms.

Roll the dough ½ inch thick on a lightly floured surface. Cut into
12 rounds or hearts. Arrange on a lightly greased baking sheet. Brush with
the cream. Bake at 400 degrees for 12 to 15 minutes or until light brown.

Flavored Butters

*For festive occasions, or to
make any morning special,
flavored butters are a
wonderful treat. Top your
toast, scones, pancakes,
French toast or favorite
muffins with one of the
following butters:*

*For Berry Butter, cream
½ cup (1 stick) softened
butter with 1 cup
confectioners' sugar. Stir in
5 ounces thawed frozen
strawberries or raspberries
that have been well drained.*

*For Honey Butter, beat
¼ cup plus 2 tablespoons
softened butter until creamy.
Add ⅔ cup honey gradually,
beating constantly. Add
½ teaspoon grated lemon zest
and beat until blended.*

*Store butters, covered, in the
refrigerator.*

Chipotle Corn Bread

Serves 12

1 cup yellow cornmeal
1 cup flour
1/4 cup sugar
2 teaspoons baking powder
1 teaspoon baking soda
1/2 teaspoon salt
1 cup shredded Monterey Jack cheese
1 cup buttermilk
3 eggs
6 tablespoons butter, melted, cooled
1 to 2 tablespoons minced, seeded canned chipotle chiles
1/8 teaspoon cayenne pepper

Combine the cornmeal, flour, sugar, baking powder, baking soda and salt in a large bowl and mix well. Stir in the Monterey Jack cheese. Whisk the buttermilk, eggs, butter, chiles and cayenne pepper in a medium bowl until blended. Add to the cornmeal mixture and stir until mixed. Spoon the batter into a buttered 5 × 9-inch loaf pan.

Bake at 375 degrees for 35 minutes. Cool in the pan on a wire rack for 10 minutes. Invert onto the wire rack to cool completely.

Strawberry Sparkler

2 strawberries
1 teaspoon simple syrup
1 lemon twist
Korbel Brut Champagne
1 strawberry

Mash 2 strawberries in a bowl. Strain, discarding the seeds. Spoon the strawberry purée into a Champagne flute. Add the simple syrup and lemon twist. Pour in the desired amount of Champagne. Garnish with 1 strawberry. To prepare a simple syrup, boil equal portions of sugar and water until the sugar dissolves.

ZUCCHINI BREAD WITH ZESTY SPREAD

Makes 7 or 8 miniature loaves

Zesty Spread
8 ounces cream cheese,
   softened
1/4 cup orange marmalade

1 teaspoon orange liqueur
   (optional)
1 teaspoon grated orange zest

Zucchini Bread
1/2 cup nonfat dry milk powder
1/2 cup sugar
1/2 cup packed brown sugar
1/2 cup water
3 tablespoons vegetable oil
1 egg, beaten
1/2 teaspoon vanilla extract
1 1/4 cups flour

1/4 cup wheat germ
2 teaspoons baking soda
1/4 teaspoon baking powder
1 teaspoon cinnamon
1/2 teaspoon salt
2 medium zucchini, grated
1/2 cup chopped nuts

For the spread, combine the cream cheese, orange marmalade, liqueur and orange zest in a food processor container fitted with a metal blade. Process until blended. Chill, covered, in the refrigerator.

For the bread, combine the milk powder, sugar, brown sugar, water, oil, egg and vanilla in a food processor container. Process for 3 to 4 seconds. Add the flour, wheat germ, baking soda, baking powder, cinnamon and salt. Process just until moistened. Stir in the zucchini and nuts.

Spoon the batter into 7 or 8 buttered miniature loaf pans. Bake at 325 degrees for 25 to 30 minutes or until a wooden pick inserted in the center comes out clean. Cool in pans for 5 minutes. Remove to a wire rack to cool completely. Serve with the spread. You may bake in a buttered 5 × 9-inch loaf pan at 325 degrees for 50 to 60 minutes or until the loaf tests done.

For Carrot Bread, substitute 1 cup shredded carrot for the zucchini. Serve with Fresh Cranberry Spread. Prepare Cranberry Spread by processing 8 ounces softened cream cheese, 1/2 cup fresh cranberries and 3 tablespoons confectioners' sugar in a food processor until blended.

FOCACCIA

This Italian flatbread is great as an appetizer or as an accompaniment to a meal. Focaccia is especially delicious when dipped in flavored olive oil, so be sure to try the recipes at right.

Serves 8 to 10

1 envelope dry yeast
1 cup lukewarm water
3 tablespoons virgin olive oil
1 teaspoon salt
1 teaspoon sugar
2¹/2 cups bread flour
Olive oil for brushing
Coarse sea salt
¹/2 cup sautéed onion
Freshly grated Parmesan cheese

Combine the yeast with the lukewarm water, 3 tablespoons olive oil, salt and sugar in a mixing bowl and stir until the yeast dissolves. Add the bread flour in 2 or 3 batches, beating until the mixture forms a dough. Remove the dough to a lightly floured surface. Knead for several minutes or until smooth and elastic, adding additional bread flour only if needed to prevent the dough from sticking.

Place the dough in a bowl lightly greased with olive oil, turning to coat the surface. Let rise in a warm place for 30 to 40 minutes or until doubled in bulk. Transfer the dough to a lightly floured surface. Roll ¹/2 inch thick into 1 large or 2 small ovals. Place the oval or ovals on an oiled baking sheet. Brush with olive oil and sprinkle lightly with sea salt. Let rise for 20 minutes. Sprinkle with the sautéed onion and cheese.

Place the baking sheet on the oven rack in top ¹/3 of the oven. Bake at 425 degrees for 20 minutes or until brown. Serve hot with butter if desired.

For variety, substitute or add one of these toppings to the onion and cheese: chopped green olives; chopped, drained oil-pack sun-dried tomatoes added 5 minutes before the end of the baking process; chopped fresh or dried rosemary. The possibilities are endless, so try your hand at creating other topping combinations.

Flavored Olive Oil

For Garlic Oil, warm 1 cup olive oil in a small saucepan over low heat until lukewarm. Stir in 6 garlic cloves, sliced, and ¹/2 teaspoon salt. Let stand at room temperature for about 2 hours to let the flavors marry. Use immediately or refrigerate in a sealed container. Keep oil refrigerated (bring back to room temperature before serving) and use within a week.

For Herb or Spice Oil, combine 1 cup olive oil and ¹/2 cup minced fresh herbs (parsley, sage, rosemary, thyme, cilantro, marjoram, etc., or a combination) or ¹/2 cup ground spice (pepper, curry powder, coriander, ginger, cumin, etc., or a combination) in a heavy skillet. Cook over medium heat until the mixture begins to sizzle, then count to ten and turn off the heat. Let cool. Store in an airtight container in the refrigerator.

CRANBERRY CHRISTMAS CANES

Wrap these cranberry canes in red cellophane and tie with a bow. Place in a holiday mug, along with packets of hot chocolate for a unique gift-giving idea.

Makes 30 canes

Cranberry Filling

1¹/₂ cups cranberries	¹/₃ cup chopped pecans
¹/₂ cup sugar	¹/₃ cup honey
¹/₂ cup raisins	1¹/₂ teaspoons grated orange zest

Christmas Canes

1 envelope dry yeast	1 cup (2 sticks) margarine, melted, cooled
¹/₄ cup lukewarm water	
4 cups flour	2 eggs, beaten
¹/₄ cup sugar	1 teaspoon grated lemon zest
1 teaspoon salt	Lemon Glaze (at right)
1 cup milk, scalded, cooled	

For the filling, combine the cranberries, sugar, raisins, pecans, honey and orange zest in a saucepan and mix well. Cook over medium heat for 5 minutes, stirring frequently. Remove from the heat. Let stand until cool.

For the canes, dissolve the yeast in the lukewarm water in a small bowl. Combine the flour, sugar and salt in a bowl and mix well. Stir in the yeast mixture, milk, margarine, eggs and lemon zest. Chill, tightly covered, for 2 hours or up to 2 days.

Divide the dough into 2 equal portions. Roll one portion into a 15 × 18-inch rectangle on a lightly floured surface. Spread with half the filling. Fold the longside ¹/₃ over the filling. Fold the opposite side over those layers to result in a 3-layered strip 15 inches long. Cut into fifteen 1-inch strips. Hold the ends of each strip and twist lightly, pinching the ends to seal. Shape into candy canes on a nonstick baking sheet. Repeat the process with the remaining dough and filling. Bake at 400 degrees for 10 to 15 minutes or until light brown. Remove to a wire rack to cool. Drizzle Lemon Glaze over the canes.

You may substitute your favorite jam or a mixture of sugar, cinnamon and nuts for the cranberry filling.

LEMON GLAZE

¹/₄ cup (¹/₂ stick) butter, softened

2 tablespoons fresh lemon juice

1 to 2 cups confectioners' sugar

Beat the butter and lemon juice in a mixing bowl until blended. Add the confectioners' sugar gradually, beating constantly until of a glaze consistency.

Southern Comfort Muffins

A great muffin with a little southern tradition.

Makes 1 dozen muffins

Muffins
2 cups flour
1 tablespoon baking powder
1 teaspoon salt
1 cup sugar
1/3 cup butter, softened
1 cup milk
1 egg
1/2 cup chopped pecans
1/3 cup packed brown sugar
1/4 cup flour
1/2 teaspoon cinnamon
3 tablespoons butter

Southern Comfort Glaze
1/2 cup sugar
1/4 cup (1/2 stick) butter
2 tablespoons water
1/2 cup Southern Comfort

For the muffins, mix 2 cups flour, baking powder and salt together.
Beat the sugar and 1/3 cup butter in a mixing bowl until creamy, scraping
the bowl occasionally. Add the milk and egg and beat until blended. Add
the flour mixture, stirring just until moistened. Spoon the batter into
greased muffin cups.

Combine the pecans, brown sugar, 1/4 cup flour and cinnamon in a bowl
and mix well. Cut in 3 tablespoons butter with a pastry blender until
crumbly. Sprinkle over the muffins. Bake at 350 degrees for 30 minutes.

For the glaze, combine the sugar, butter and water in a saucepan. Bring
to a simmer, stirring constantly. Simmer until the sugar dissolves, stirring
constantly. Remove from the heat. Stir in the liqueur. Drizzle over the
hot muffins.

Fruit Smoothie

Serves 1 or 2

1 cup vanilla yogurt
1/2 cup milk
2 tablespoons honey, or to
 taste
1 cup frozen unsweetened
 fruit

Combine the yogurt,
milk, honey and frozen
fruit in the order listed in a
blender container. Process
immediately until smooth.
Pour into 1 or 2 glasses.

BLUE RIBBON YEAST ROLLS

Makes 44 rolls

1 envelope dry yeast
1 cup lukewarm water
2 tablespoons (rounded) shortening
2 cups hot water
$^3/_4$ cup sugar
$^1/_2$ teaspoon salt
7 to 8 cups flour
Melted butter

Dissolve the yeast in the lukewarm water in a bowl and mix well. Combine the shortening and hot water in a bowl, stirring until the shortening dissolves. Stir in the sugar and salt. Add the yeast mixture and mix well. Add enough of the flour to form an easily handled dough.

Knead the dough on a lightly floured surface for 10 minutes or in a bread machine on the knead cycle. Place the dough in a greased bowl, turning to coat the surface. Let rise in a warm place until doubled in bulk. Punch the dough down. Let rise until doubled in bulk. Shape the dough into 1-inch balls. Arrange in a greased 9 × 13-inch baking pan. Let rise until doubled in bulk.

Bake at 450 degrees for 8 minutes or until light brown. Brush with melted butter. Serve immediately.

For a different flavor, add 3 tablespoons (more or less) dillseeds and 2 tablespoons (more or less) sesame seeds with the sugar and salt.

HERB CHEDDAR ROLLS

Makes 1¹/₂ dozen rolls

2 envelopes dry yeast
³/₄ cup lukewarm water
³/₄ cup milk
¹/₄ cup vegetable oil
¹/₄ cup sugar
1 tablespoon salt
4¹/₂ cups flour
3 tablespoons shredded Cheddar cheese
1¹/₂ tablespoons dried herbs (basil, chervil or Italian seasoning)
Grated Romano cheese (optional)

Combine the yeast and lukewarm water in a bowl and mix well. Let stand for 5 minutes or until bubbly. Scald the milk in a saucepan. Cool to 95 degrees. Combine the milk, oil, sugar and salt in a bowl and mix well. Add half the flour and mix well. Stir in the yeast mixture. Add the remaining flour gradually, stirring until the dough forms a ball. Let stand, covered, until doubled in bulk.

Transfer the dough to a lightly floured surface. Knead until smooth and elastic. Roll the dough into a ³/₄-inch-thick rectangle. Sprinkle with the Cheddar cheese, herbs and Romano cheese.

Roll the rectangle into a log. Cut the log into ³/₄-inch slices. Shape each slice into a ball. Arrange the balls in a lightly greased 9 × 13-inch baking pan. Let rise, covered, for 1 hour or until doubled in bulk. Bake at 400 degrees for 15 to 20 minutes or until light brown. Cool in the pan on a wire rack.

Fresh Rolls Anytime

You will always have fresh, homemade rolls on hand with this surefire method.

Prepare rolls as the recipe directs. Bake at 300 degrees for 18 to 20 minutes. Let cool. Store, covered, in the refrigerator or freezer. When ready to use, set the rolls out and bring them to room temperature. Bake at 375 degrees for 10 to 12 minutes.

CANYON VILLA CINNAMON ROLLS

Whispering Winds Inn, Cadiz, Kentucky

Makes 2 dozen rolls

Brown Sugar Filling
1/2 cup packed brown sugar   1/3 cup butter, softened
1 1/2 tablespoons cinnamon

Rolls
1 cup milk   1/2 cup sugar
1 cup water   1 envelope dry yeast
1/2 cup (1 stick) butter   2 teaspoons salt
1 egg, lightly beaten   Melted butter for brushing
6 cups flour   Confectioners' Sugar Glaze (at right)

For the filling, combine the brown sugar and cinnamon in a bowl and mix well. Add the butter, stirring until crumbly.

For the rolls, combine the milk, water and 1/2 cup butter in a saucepan. Heat until the butter melts and a thermometer registers 120 degrees, stirring occasionally. Remove from the heat. Cool slightly. Stir in the egg. Combine 2 cups of the flour, sugar, yeast and salt in a mixing bowl and mix well. Add the milk mixture. Beat at medium speed for 5 to 8 minutes or until smooth and elastic. Add up to 3 1/2 cups of the remaining flour 1 cup at a time until a soft dough forms, beating well after each addition. Place in a greased bowl, turning to coat the surface.

Let rise, covered with a damp tea towel, in a warm place for 1 hour or until doubled in bulk. Punch the dough down. Let rise, covered, for 10 minutes longer. Divide the dough into 2 equal portions. Roll each portion into a 12 × 18-inch rectangle on a hard surface sprinkled with the remaining 1/2 cup flour. Brush the rectangles with melted butter to within 1/2 inch of the edges. Sprinkle each rectangle with half the brown sugar mixture. Roll as for a jelly roll. Cut each roll into 1/2-inch slices.

Arrange the slices cut side down on a greased baking sheet. Let rise, covered with a damp tea towel, in a warm place for 45 to 60 minutes or until doubled in bulk. Bake at 375 degrees for 20 minutes. Drizzle the Confectioners' Sugar Glaze over the warm rolls.

CONFECTIONERS' SUGAR GLAZE

2 tablespoons butter
1 tablespoon milk
2 to 3 cups sifted confectioners' sugar
1 teaspoon vanilla extract

Combine the butter and milk in a saucepan. Heat until the butter melts. Remove from the heat. Add the confectioners' sugar gradually, beating until of a glaze consistency. Stir in the vanilla.

Photo on facing page, Brookside Farm Woodford County, Kentucky

BAKED FRENCH TOAST WITH BERRIES

Serves 4 to 6

This outstanding dish will impress overnight guests.

1 (8-ounce) loaf dry French bread
2¹/4 cups milk
3 eggs, beaten
3 tablespoons sugar
1 tablespoon vanilla extract
1 cup fresh or frozen blueberries

¹/2 cup flour
6 tablespoons brown sugar
¹/2 teaspoon cinnamon
¹/4 cup (¹/2 stick) butter
1 cup sliced strawberries

Cut the bread diagonally into 10 slices. Arrange the slices in a single layer in a 9 × 13-inch baking dish. Whisk the milk, eggs, sugar and vanilla in a bowl until blended. Pour over the bread. Chill, covered, for 8 hours. Sprinkle with the blueberries. Combine the flour, brown sugar and cinnamon in a bowl and mix well. Cut in the butter until crumbly. Sprinkle over the prepared layers. Bake at 375 degrees for 40 to 45 minutes or until set and golden brown. Serve immediately with the strawberries.

BANANA-FILLED FRENCH TOAST

1823 Historic Rose Hill Inn, Versailles, Kentucky

Serves 12

1 unsliced loaf French bread
2 bananas, sliced
5 dozen pecan halves (optional)
12 tablespoons brown sugar

³/4 cup milk or cream
3 eggs
1 teaspoon vanilla extract
¹/4 cup (¹/2 stick) unsalted butter

Slice the ends from the loaf and discard. Cut the loaf into twelve 1-inch slices. Cut each slice to but not through, forming a pocket. Stuff some of the sliced bananas and 5 pecans into each pocket. Spoon 1 tablespoon brown sugar into each pocket. Whisk the milk, eggs and vanilla in a bowl until blended. Dip each stuffed bread slice in the egg mixture. Heat the butter in a skillet until melted. Add the stuffed bread slices. Cook for 5 minutes or until brown on both sides. Serve with confectioners' sugar, maple syrup and/or whipped cream.

CARAMEL PECAN FRENCH TOAST

Kavanaugh House Bed & Breakfast, Lawrenceburg, Kentucky

Serves 6 to 9

 French Toast
1 cup packed brown sugar
¹/₂ cup (1 stick) butter
2 tablespoons light corn syrup
1 cup chopped pecans
12 to 18 slices Italian or French bread
1¹/₂ cups milk
6 eggs
1¹/₂ teaspoons cinnamon
1 teaspoon vanilla extract
¹/₂ teaspoon salt
¹/₄ teaspoon nutmeg

Caramel Sauce
¹/₂ cup packed brown sugar
¹/₄ cup (¹/₂ stick) butter
1 tablespoon light corn syrup

For the French toast, combine the brown sugar, butter and corn syrup in a saucepan. Cook over medium heat until thickened, stirring constantly. Pour into a 9 × 13-inch baking dish. Sprinkle with half the pecans. Arrange 6 to 9 slices of the bread in a single layer over the pecans. Sprinkle with the remaining pecans. Top with the remaining 6 to 9 slices bread.

Process the milk, eggs, cinnamon, vanilla, salt and nutmeg in a blender. Pour over the prepared layers. Chill, covered, for 8 hours. Bake, uncovered, at 350 degrees for 40 to 45 minutes or until light brown.

For the sauce, combine the brown sugar, butter and corn syrup in a saucepan. Cook until thickened, stirring constantly. Drizzle over the toast just before serving.

POTATO PANCAKES WITH APPLE RINGS

This twist on an old favorite is from Burlington's Willis Graves Bed & Breakfast, Burlington, Kentucky.

Serves 4

Apple Topping
4 Granny Smith apples, cored, peeled, sliced into rings
Lemon juice (optional)
3/4 cup packed brown sugar
3 tablespoons flour
1/4 teaspoon cinnamon

Pancakes
3 eggs
2 cups grated potatoes
1 1/2 tablespoons flour
1 1/4 teaspoons salt
1 to 3 teaspoons grated onion
Vegetable oil

Assembly
Fresh blueberries and/or raspberries

For the topping, arrange the apple rings in a microwave-safe dish. Drizzle with lemon juice. Combine the brown sugar, flour and cinnamon in a bowl and mix well. Sprinkle over the apples. Microwave, covered, on High for 4 to 5 minutes or until the apples are tender. Cover to keep warm.

For the pancakes, whisk the eggs in a bowl until blended. Stir in the potatoes. Stir in a mixture of the flour and salt. Add the onion and mix well. Shape the mixture into patties. Brown the patties in hot oil in a skillet until crisp on both sides; drain.

To assemble, arrange the pancakes on a serving platter. Spoon some of the apple topping on each pancake. Sprinkle with blueberries and/or raspberries.

To save time, purchase shredded potatoes in the dairy case at your local supermarket.

HONEY GRANOLA

On the trail or at the breakfast table, this recipe fits the bill for a hearty and healthy meal or snack. From Burlington's Willis Graves Bed & Breakfast, Burlington, Kentucky.

Makes 5 cups

¹/₄ cup canola oil
¹/₄ cup clover honey
¹/₂ teaspoon almond extract, or 1 teaspoon vanilla extract
¹/₈ teaspoon salt
3 cups old-fashioned oats
¹/₂ cup wheat germ
¹/₄ cup coarsely chopped nuts
¹/₄ cup bran
¹/₄ cup sunflower kernels or sesame seeds (optional)
¹/₄ cup dried fruit, such as raisins, dates or figs (optional)

Combine the canola oil, honey, flavoring and salt in a saucepan and mix well. Cook until heated through, stirring frequently. Stir in the oats, wheat germ, nuts and bran in the order listed, mixing well after each addition. Add the sunflower kernels or sesame seeds and mix well.

Spoon into a 9 × 13-inch baking pan. Bake at 300 degrees for 15 minutes; stir. Bake for 15 minutes longer or until golden brown; stir. Stir in the dried fruit.

Measuring Honey

This foolproof method will eliminate the problem of getting all of the honey out of your measuring cup.

Coat the measuring cup with vegetable oil by pouring oil into the cup and then pouring the excess back into the bottle. Next, measure the honey into the empty cup. The thin film of oil will make the honey slide right out of the cup—guaranteeing that all of the honey makes it into the recipe.

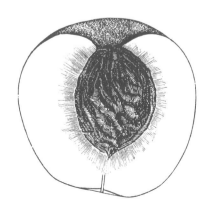

KENTUCKY COUNTRY HAM FRITTATA

Lynn Winter, Lynn's Paradise Cafe

Serves 5 to 8

1/2 cup sliced mushrooms
1/4 cup chopped green bell pepper
1/4 cup chopped red bell pepper
1/4 cup finely chopped white onion
1 to 1 1/2 tablespoons vegetable oil
1/2 cup julienned fresh spinach
1/2 cup chopped cooked potato
1/2 teaspoon thyme
1/2 teaspoon oregano
1/2 teaspoon garlic powder
1/2 teaspoon salt
1/4 teaspoon cayenne pepper
5 eggs
1/4 cup heavy cream
3/4 cup chopped Kentucky country ham
1/2 cup shredded Cheddar cheese
1/2 cup shredded Monterey Jack cheese
3 plum tomatoes, chopped
Hollandaise Sauce (page 166) (optional)

KORBEL MIMOSA

2 parts fresh orange juice
1 part Korbel Champagne

Mix the orange juice and Champagne in a Champagne flute. Garnish with a sprig of fresh mint.

Sauté the mushrooms, bell peppers and onion in the oil in a skillet until tender. Stir in the spinach, potato, thyme, oregano, garlic powder, salt and cayenne pepper. Remove from the heat.

Whisk the eggs with the heavy cream in a large bowl until blended. Stir in the ham, Cheddar cheese, Monterey Jack cheese and tomatoes. Add the sautéed vegetables and mix well. Spoon into a greased 2-quart baking dish.

Bake at 350 degrees for 45 to 60 minutes or until a knife inserted in the center comes out clean. Serve with Hollandaise Sauce. Garnish with additional chopped red bell pepper.

ASPARAGUS AND YELLOW PEPPER FRITTATA

Serves 12

2 pounds thin asparagus spears, trimmed
Salt to taste
1 medium zucchini
3 scallions
2 large yellow bell peppers, cut into $1/4$-inch strips
1 small onion, minced
1 tablespoon unsalted butter
10 eggs
$1/2$ cup heavy cream
3 tablespoons chopped fresh flat-leaf parsley leaves
$1^1/2$ teaspoons salt
$1/2$ teaspoon freshly ground pepper

Cut the asparagus diagonally into $1/4$-inch slices. Blanch the asparagus in boiling salted water in a saucepan for 1 minute; drain. Plunge the asparagus into a bowl of ice water to stop the cooking process. Drain and pat dry. Cut the zucchini lengthwise into halves; cut into diagonal slices. Cut the scallions diagonally into thin slices.

Cook the bell peppers and onion in the butter in a skillet over medium-low heat for 10 minutes or until the bell peppers are tender. Whisk the eggs, heavy cream, parsley, $1^1/2$ teaspoons salt and pepper in a bowl until mixed. Stir in the asparagus, bell pepper mixture, zucchini and scallions.

Pour the egg mixture into a 9×13-inch baking dish. Bake at 350 degrees on the middle oven rack for 35 minutes or until set and golden brown. Cool slightly in the baking dish on a wire rack before serving.

Asparagus "Tips"

- Store fresh asparagus with its cut ends wrapped in damp paper towels in airtight plastic bags.

- Steaming is usually the best method of cooking asparagus. It keeps asparagus crisp and colorful and helps maintain vitamins.

- For an impressive side dish, insert cooked asparagus, warm or chilled, into lemon rings made by slicing a lemon and removing the membrane.

- Asparagus can be used in floral decorations. Stretch a rubber band around any cylindrical container; trim uncooked asparagus to equal lengths and insert them between the container and rubber band. Tie the arrangement with ribbon to hide the rubber band and you have a fresh and colorful container in which you can arrange flowers.

SOUTHWESTERN BREAKFAST BAKE

Go south of the border for breakfast with this tasty, tangy, and tantalizing dish.

Serves 12

2 (7-ounce) cans chopped mild green chiles
6 corn tortillas, cut into $1/2$-inch strips
1 pound Purnell's "Old Folks" Country Sausage, cooked, drained
2 cups shredded Monterey Jack cheese
8 eggs
$1/2$ cup milk
$1/2$ teaspoon salt
$1/2$ teaspoon garlic salt
$1/2$ teaspoon onion salt
$1/2$ teaspoon cumin
$1/2$ teaspoon pepper
2 large tomatoes, sliced
Paprika to taste
Sour cream (optional)
Salsa (optional)

Layer the green chiles, tortillas, sausage and cheese $1/2$ at a time in the order listed in a greased 9 × 13-inch baking dish. Whisk the eggs in a bowl until blended. Stir in the milk, salt, garlic salt, onion salt, cumin and pepper. Pour over the prepared layers.

Arrange the tomato slices over the top. Sprinkle with paprika. Chill, covered, for 8 to 10 hours. Bake, uncovered, at 350 degrees for 45 to 55 minutes or until set and the edges are light brown. Serve with sour cream and salsa.

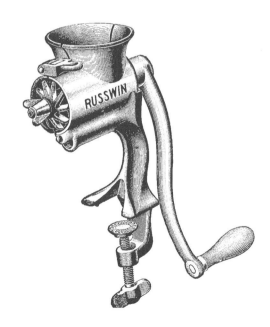

GRITS, CHEESE AND SAUSAGE CASSEROLE

A tasty version of traditional southern grits.

Serves 8 to 10

2 cups water
1/2 cup grits
4 cups shredded sharp Cheddar cheese
1 cup milk
4 eggs
1/2 teaspoon thyme
1 pound Purnell's "Old Folks" Hot Country Sausage, cooked, crumbled

Bring the water to a boil in a saucepan. Stir in the grits. Return to a boil; reduce heat. Cook for 4 minutes, stirring occasionally. Add the cheese, stirring until melted. Remove from the heat.

Whisk the milk, eggs and thyme in a bowl until blended. Stir a small amount of the hot grits mixture into the egg mixture. Stir the egg mixture into the hot grits mixture. Add the sausage and mix well. Spoon into an 8 × 12-inch baking dish sprayed with nonstick cooking spray. Bake at 350 degrees for 30 minutes. Let stand for 5 to 8 minutes before serving.

You may prepare 1 day in advance and store the unbaked casserole, covered, in the refrigerator. Let stand at room temperature for 15 minutes before baking. Bake at 350 degrees for 50 to 55 minutes. Or you can freeze the unbaked casserole for up to 1 week, allowing the casserole to thaw in the refrigerator before baking at 350 degrees for 50 to 55 minutes.

Southern Grits

According to many traditional southern cooks, grits are on the list of what every pantry should have on hand. Grits, or groats as they are sometimes called, refers to coarsely ground grain such as corn, oats, or rice. Grits can be boiled or baked, using either milk or water. They can be made into cereals or side dishes or used in soups. They were originally flavored with red-eye or butter gravy, but over the years gourmet dishes have evolved.

TOMATO AND ONION QUICHE

Aleksander House Bed & Breakfast, Louisville, Kentucky

Serves 6 to 8

1 cup shredded Cheddar cheese
1 cup shredded mozzarella cheese
1 (9-inch) pie shell, partially baked
3 small tomatoes, thinly sliced
1/2 onion, thinly sliced
1 teaspoon basil
1/4 teaspoon garlic salt
Cracked pepper to taste
3/4 cup milk
2 eggs
3 tablespoons grated Parmesan
  cheese

Sprinkle the Cheddar cheese and mozzarella cheese over the bottom of the pie shell. Layer the tomatoes and onion over the cheese. Sprinkle with the basil, garlic salt and cracked pepper.

Whisk the milk and eggs in a bowl until blended. Pour over the prepared layers. Sprinkle with the Parmesan cheese. Bake at 350 degrees for 45 to 50 minutes or until set.

BLT FRIES

Lynn Winter, Lynn's Paradise Cafe

Serves 4

4 cups cooked hash brown potatoes
1 cup fresh spinach, julienned
1/4 cup chopped red onion, sautéed
1/4 cup chopped tomato
1/2 cup crumbled crisp-cooked bacon
1 to 2 cups shredded Monterey
  Jack cheese
1/2 cup sour cream
1 1/2 teaspoons horseradish

Spread the hash brown potatoes in a lightly buttered 8-inch round baking dish. Layer the spinach, onion, tomato, bacon and cheese in the order listed over the potatoes. Bake at 400 degrees for 15 minutes or until golden brown. Combine the sour cream and horseradish in a bowl and mix well. Serve with the fries. For a larger crowd, double the ingredients and bake in a 9 × 13-inch baking dish.

Milano Omelette

Lynn Winter, Lynn's Paradise Cafe

Serves 1 or 2

¹/₄ cup grated carrot
2 tablespoons minced onion
1 garlic clove, minced
1¹/₂ teaspoons olive oil
1¹/₂ teaspoons butter
1 teaspoon brown sugar
¹/₄ cup cream cheese, softened
3 eggs
Salt and pepper to taste
1 cup marinara sauce, heated

Sauté the carrot, onion and garlic in a mixture of the olive oil and butter in a skillet. Stir in the brown sugar. Cook until caramelized. Add the vegetable mixture to the cream cheese in a bowl and mix well.

Whisk the eggs, salt and pepper in a bowl until blended. Pour the eggs into a large nonstick sauté pan. Cook as for an omelet, lifting the edge of the omelet as the eggs set to allow the uncooked egg to flow underneath; do not stir.

Microwave the cream cheese mixture in a microwave-safe dish just until heated through. Spread over the omelet. Top with half the marinara sauce. Fold the omelet over to enclose the filling. Transfer the omelet to a heated plate. Drizzle with the remaining marinara sauce.

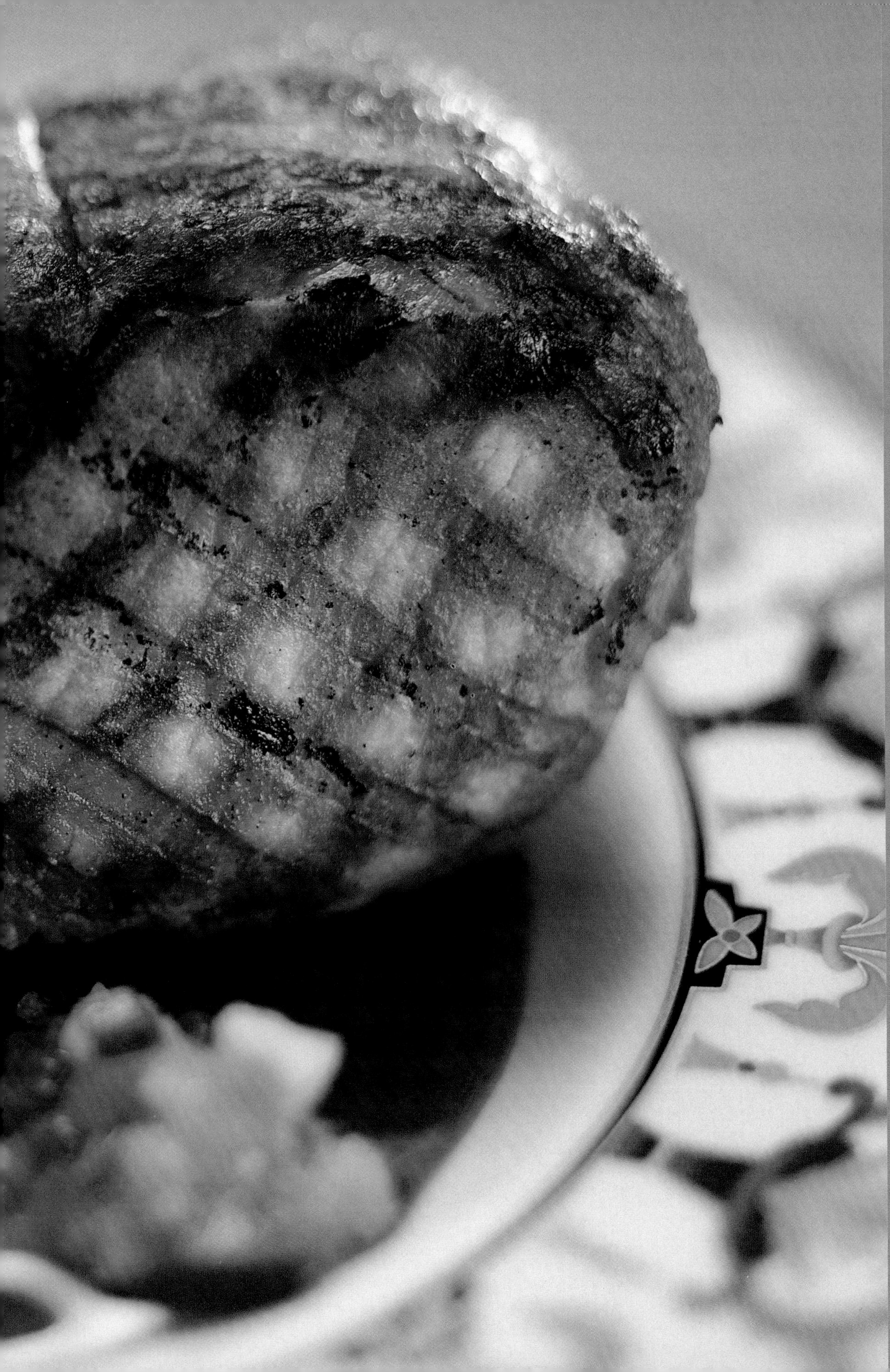

Meats

Woodford Reserve Pork Chops with
Green Tomato and Mango Relish
(Photo, pages 102–103)

Prayer after Eating

I have taken in the light
that quickened eye and leaf.
May my brain be bright with praise
of what I eat, in the brief blaze
of motion and of thought.
May I be worthy of my meat.

Wendell Berry
Collected Poems 1957–1982

Wine-Braised Beef over Cheesy Polenta

The ultimate comfort meal.

Serves 10 to 12

Beef

3 tablespoons olive oil
7 pounds chuck roast, trimmed,
  cut into 1-inch cubes
1 large onion, minced
1/4 cup chopped Italian parsley
3 garlic cloves, chopped
2 bay leaves
1/4 teaspoon each ground cloves,
  cinnamon and allspice
1 cup Bonterra Cabernet Sauvignon

2 1/4 cups beef broth or stock
1 (32-ounce) can Italian plum
  tomatoes, chopped
1/2 cup pitted niçoise olives
4 teaspoons chopped fresh
  rosemary, or 2 teaspoons
  dried rosemary
2 red bell peppers, cut into
  1/4-inch slices
Salt and pepper to taste

Cheesy Polenta

6 cups water
1 1/2 teaspoons salt
1 1/2 cups coarse cornmeal
3 tablespoons butter

3/4 cup grated fresh Parmesan
  cheese
1/4 teaspoon black pepper
Cayenne pepper to taste

For the beef, heat the olive oil in a heavy saucepan over high heat. Add the beef cubes and cook until brown; remove with a slotted spoon. Reduce the heat and add the onion and parsley to the saucepan. Sauté for 10 minutes or until the onion is golden brown. Add the garlic, bay leaves, cloves, cinnamon, allspice and browned beef.

Add the wine and bring to a boil, stirring to deglaze the saucepan. Simmer for 15 minutes. Add the beef broth, undrained tomatoes, olives and rosemary. Cover and reduce the heat to low. Simmer for 1 1/2 hours or until the beef is tender. Add the bell peppers and cook for 15 minutes longer or until the peppers are tender. Season with salt and pepper.

For the polenta, bring the water to a boil in a large saucepan. Add the salt and whisk in the cornmeal. Reduce the heat to low and simmer for 20 to 25 minutes or until smooth, stirring frequently. Remove from the heat and add the butter, cheese, black pepper and cayenne pepper; stir until the cheese melts. To serve, spoon the polenta immediately into heated bowls. Remove the bay leaves from the beef and spoon over the polenta.

GRILLED SIRLOIN IN BOURBON MARINADE

Serves 4 to 6

1 cup beef stock
1/3 cup Old Forester
1/8 cup soy sauce
3 garlic cloves, minced
3 green onions, diced
Fresh ground pepper to taste
2- to 2 1/2-pound sirloin steak,
    1 to 1 1/2 inches thick

Combine the beef stock, bourbon, soy sauce, garlic, green onions and pepper in a bowl and mix well. Pour over the sirloin in a shallow dish. Marinate, covered, for 4 hours, turning once; drain.

Place the steak on a lightly oiled rack over hot coals. Grill for 4 minutes. Turn the steak and grill for 5 minutes longer, or until done to taste.

Remove the steak to a platter and slice diagonally across the grain. Serve with roasted new potatoes and a green salad.

Plentiful Peppercorns

Did you know that the world's most popular spice, pepper, was once considered rare and priceless and used as currency? Today, cooks of all nationalities sprinkle pepper on their prepared food to enhance its flavor. Peppercorn, which grows in clusters on the pepper plant, can be categorized into three different types — black, white, and green. The most common is the black peppercorn that has a pungent hot flavor. White peppercorn, which is less pungent than black, is used by cooks to season light-colored foods or sauces. Green peppercorn is considered the mildest of the three types and has a fresher taste.

CLASSIC BEEF TENDERLOIN

A tried-and-true classic.

Serves 4 to 6

2 tablespoons butter,
  softened
3 tablespoons Dijon mustard
2 teaspoons salt

4 teaspoons mixed peppercorns,
  ground
1 (2-pound) beef tenderloin
Whole mixed peppercorns to taste

Combine the butter, Dijon mustard, salt and ground peppercorns in a
small bowl and mix well. Spread over the tenderloin. Sprinkle with
whole peppercorns. Insert a meat thermometer into the thickest portion
of the tenderloin; place in a roasting pan. Roast at 450 degrees for
35 minutes or to 140 degrees on the meat thermometer for rare.

HERBED AND SPICED BEEF TENDERLOIN

This do-ahead recipe is elegant for any dinner party.

Serves 8

2 tablespoons rosemary leaves
2 tablespoons fresh thyme leaves
4 large garlic cloves
2 bay leaves
1 large shallot, cut into quarters
1 tablespoon grated orange zest
1/2 teaspoon ground nutmeg

1/4 teaspoon ground cloves
1 tablespoon coarse salt
1 teaspoon pepper
2 tablespoons olive oil
2 (2-pound) beef tenderloins, large
  ends only
Red Wine Sauce (page 109)

Combine the first 10 ingredients in a blender container and process until
chopped. Add the olive oil gradually, processing constantly until smooth.
Spread evenly over the tenderloins. Place in a glass dish and cover with
foil. Marinate in the refrigerator for 6 to 24 hours. Place the tenderloins
on a rack in a large roasting pan and insert a meat thermometer into
the thickest portion. Roast at 400 degrees for 35 minutes or to 140 degrees
on the meat thermometer for rare. Cover with foil and let stand for
10 minutes. Slice the beef, reserving pan juices for the Red Wine Sauce.
Serve with the sauce.

RED WINE SAUCE

Serves 8

2¹/₂ cups sliced shallots, about 12 ounces
2 tablespoons minced garlic
2 tablespoons olive oil
1 teaspoon sugar
1 tablespoon flour
2 teaspoons minced fresh rosemary
1 tablespoon minced fresh thyme
1 bay leaf
1 teaspoon grated orange zest
Ground nutmeg and cloves to taste
3¹/₄ cups canned beef broth
1¹/₂ cups Jekel Cabernet Sauvignon
¹/₄ cup Korbel Brandy
¹/₄ cup (¹/₂ stick) unsalted butter, softened
Salt and pepper to taste

Sauté the shallots and garlic in the heated olive oil in a large saucepan over medium-low heat for 10 minutes or until tender. Stir in the sugar and sauté for 15 minutes or until the shallots are golden brown.

Add the flour, rosemary, thyme, bay leaf, orange zest, nutmeg and cloves and cook for 1 minute, stirring constantly. Stir in the beef broth, wine and brandy. Cook for 20 minutes or until the sauce is reduced to 1³/₄ cups. Discard the bay leaf. Pour in any accumulated juices from the beef (page 108). Remove from the heat and whisk in the butter. Season with salt and pepper.

Comfort for the Spirit and Soul

"Wine stimulates the appetite and enhances food. It promotes conversation and euphoria and can turn a mere meal into a memorable occasion."

DEREK COOPER

HOLIDAY RIB-EYE ROAST

A Yuletide tradition.

Serves 8 to 10

Roast
2 garlic cloves, crushed
1 teaspoon dried rosemary leaves, crushed
1 teaspoon salt
1 teaspoon cracked pepper
1 (4-pound) rib-eye roast, trimmed

Holiday Sauce
1^1/$_2$ teaspoons dry mustard
1 teaspoon water
1 (12-ounce) jar brown beef gravy
^{1}/$_4$ cup currant jelly

For the roast, combine the garlic, rosemary, salt and pepper in a small bowl and mix well. Press evenly over the surface of the roast. Place on a rack in a shallow roasting pan and insert a meat thermometer into the thickest portion; do not allow to rest on bone or fat.

Roast at 350 degrees for 18 to 22 minutes per pound or to 140 degrees on the meat thermometer for medium-rare or 155 degrees for medium. Let stand for 15 minutes; internal temperature will continue to rise.

For the sauce, dissolve the dry mustard in the water in a small saucepan. Stir in the gravy and jelly. Cook over medium heat for 5 minutes or until bubbly, stirring constantly. Slice the roast and serve with the sauce.

CHILI RAPHAEL

Serves 12

2 slices bacon, chopped
1¹/₂ cups Mexicorn (optional)
2 pounds sirloin, chopped
20 tomatillos
¹/₄ onion, chopped
1 bunch cilantro
5 serrano chiles
2 garlic cloves
2 tablespoons instant chicken bouillon granules
1 cup water
1 (16-ounce) can black beans
2 (16-ounce) cans pinto beans

Fry the bacon in a large saucepan until crisp. Add the Mexicorn and sauté for several minutes. Add the sirloin and sauté until brown and cooked through.

Combine the tomatillos, onion, cilantro, chiles, garlic, bouillon and water in a blender container and process until smooth. Add to the sirloin mixture in the saucepan. Cook until heated through.

Add the beans and simmer until heated through and of the desired consistency. Serve with rolls or tortillas.

Tomato or Tomatillo?

The tomatillo, also called the Mexican green tomato, belongs to the same family as the tomato. However, it has a thin, papery covering surrounding the fruit. Tomatillos are available sporadically throughout the year and can be found in specialty produce stores and some supermarkets. Choose a firm fruit with dry, tight-fitting husks. Store tomatillos in the refrigerator in a paper bag for up to one month. Remove the husk and wash fruit thoroughly before using.

GRILLED STEAK SANDWICHES ON BAGUETTES

Serves 6

1¹/₂ teaspoons olive oil
1¹/₂ teaspoons herbes de Provence
2 (1-pound) New York strip steaks, ³/₄ to 1 inch thick, trimmed
Salt and pepper to taste
6 (5- to 6-inch) French baguettes
¹/₄ cup olive oil
2 large garlic cloves, cut into halves
3¹/₂ cups arugula
2 large tomatoes, thinly sliced
1 large onion, thinly sliced

Mix 1¹/₂ teaspoons olive oil with the herbes de Provence in a small bowl. Rub evenly over both sides of the steaks; sprinkle with salt and pepper. Grill over medium-hot coals until done to taste. Wrap steaks tightly with foil and chill for up to 24 hours.

Cut the baguettes into halves horizontally. Place cut side up on a broiler pan and brush with ¹/₄ cup olive oil. Broil until golden brown. Rub the toasted sides with garlic.

Slice the steaks ¹/₈ inch thick. Layer the arugula, steak, tomatoes and onion on the bottom halves of the baguettes. Season with salt and pepper and replace the baguette tops. Cut into halves to serve.

Herbes de Provence are an assortment of the dried herbs most commonly used in southern France. The mixture contains basil, fennel seeds, lavender, marjoram, rosemary, sage, summer savory and thyme.

Is a Sandwich Just a Sandwich?

"An English noble bequeathed his name to one of the most popular repasts in the world. In 1762, so the story goes, John Montagu, fourth earl of Sandwich, was so engrossed in one of his many all-night gambling sessions that he refused to break for a meal. Instead, he ordered an underling to bring him slices of cold roast and cheeses between two pieces of bread so he could keep one hand free for gambling. The incident became such a notorious example of the earl's excesses that soon people were referring to such handy snacks as sandwiches."

MARTHA BARNETTE
LADYFINGERS AND NUN'S TUMMIES

*Photo on facing page,
Labrot & Graham Distillery
Woodford County, Kentucky*

GRILLED LEG OF LAMB

Serves 8 to 10

1 (5- to 6-pound) leg of lamb, boned, butterflied
6 garlic cloves, minced
1/4 cup fresh rosemary sprigs or dried rosemary
1 tablespoon salt
1 cup Woodford Reserve Bourbon
Jalapeño Jelly (below)

Remove any membrane covering the fat on the lamb. Rub the lamb with the garlic, rosemary and salt. Place in a shallow dish and pour the bourbon over the top. Marinate, covered with plastic wrap, in the refrigerator for 8 hours or longer.

Remove the lamb from the marinade and place 2 skewers into the leg to hold its shape during grilling. Place on a heated grill and grill for 15 minutes on each side or until 140 degrees on meat thermometer for rare.

Serve with Jalapeño Jelly and thinly sliced French bread.

JALAPEÑO JELLY

Makes 6 1/2 pints

3/4 cup ground seeded jalapeño chiles, or to taste
3/4 cup ground red and green bell peppers and banana peppers
1 1/2 cups vinegar
6 1/2 cups sugar
1 bottle of liquid pectin

Combine the chiles, bell pepper and banana pepper mixture, vinegar and sugar in a saucepan. Bring to a rolling boil and boil for 3 to 4 minutes. Stir in the pectin and boil for 1 minute longer.

Cool slightly and pour into sterilized jars, leaving 1/2 inch headspace; seal with 2-piece lids. Serve with meats or on cream cheese as a spread for crackers.

Hazelnut Racks of Lamb

Serves 4

1 cup olive oil
2 tablespoons chopped fresh
   rosemary
1 tablespoon chopped garlic
2 (1$\frac{1}{3}$- to 1$\frac{1}{2}$-pound) racks of
   lamb, trimmed, Frenched
Salt and pepper to taste
2 cups bread crumbs

$\frac{1}{2}$ cup chopped fresh parsley
$\frac{1}{4}$ cup hazelnuts, toasted, skins
   removed
1 large shallot, cut into quarters
3 tablespoons olive oil
3 tablespoons Dijon mustard
Tomato Ragout (at right)

Combine 1 cup olive oil, rosemary and garlic in a shallow dish and mix well. Sprinkle the lamb with salt and pepper and add to the dish, turning to coat well. Marinate, covered, in the refrigerator for 8 hours or longer, turning occasionally.

Combine the bread crumbs, parsley, hazelnuts and shallot in a food processor container and process until finely ground. Add 2 tablespoons olive oil gradually and process until the mixture begins to stick together. Remove to a bowl and toss with salt, pepper and the remaining tablespoon of olive oil.

Heat a large heavy skillet over high heat. Add 1 rack of lamb at a time, allowing some marinade to adhere. Cook for 4 minutes on each side or until brown; remove to a roasting pan and let stand for 15 minutes.

Spread the Dijon mustard over the rounded side of each rack and press the bread crumb mixture firmly into the mustard. Insert a meat thermometer into the center of the lamb. Roast for 25 minutes or to 135 degrees on the meat thermometer for medium-rare. Let stand for 15 minutes. Carve into chops. Serve with the Tomato Ragout.

Tomato Ragout

1 tablespoon chopped garlic
$\frac{1}{2}$ teaspoon crushed dried
   red pepper
1 tablespoon olive oil
2 cups chopped fresh
   fennel bulb
1 (28-ounce) can Italian
   tomatoes
$\frac{1}{2}$ cup kalamata olives,
   cut into halves
$\frac{1}{4}$ cup chopped fresh basil
1 tablespoon butter
Salt and black pepper to taste

Sauté the garlic and red pepper in the heated olive oil in a heavy skillet over medium-low heat for 5 minutes. Add the fennel and sauté for 3 minutes or until translucent. Add the undrained tomatoes and olives. Increase the heat and bring the ragout to a gentle boil. Cook for 18 minutes or until of the desired consistency, stirring to break up the tomatoes. Stir in the basil and butter. Season with salt and black pepper.

WOODFORD RESERVE PORK CHOPS

This recipe for Woodford Reserve Pork Chops with Green Tomato and Mango Relish was created by Chef Jim Gerhardt, The Oakroom at The Seelbach Hilton.

Serves 4

Pork Chops
1/4 cup maple syrup
1/4 cup Kentucky sorghum molasses
2 tablespoons (or more) Woodford Reserve Bourbon
2 tablespoons sweet chili sauce
1 1/2 teaspoons garlic chile paste
4 (14-ounce) Frenched center-cut pork rib chops

Country Ham Jus
8 ounces Kentucky country ham bones or smoked pork bones
4 cups water
1 small onion, chopped
1 rib celery, chopped
1 small carrot, chopped
1 sprig of fresh thyme, or 1/2 teaspoon dried thyme
1 bay leaf
1 tablespoon whole peppercorns
2 cups demi-glace or very rich veal stock
Kosher or sea salt to taste
1/2 cup Green Tomato and Mango Relish (page 117)
8 slices Fried Plantains (page 117)

To marinate the pork chops, combine the maple syrup, molasses, bourbon, chili sauce and chile paste in a shallow dish and mix well. Add the pork chops, turning to coat well. Marinate, covered, in the refrigerator for 8 hours or longer.

For the country ham jus, combine the ham bones, water, onion, celery, carrot, thyme, bay leaf and peppercorns in a large stockpot. Simmer, uncovered, for 3 hours or until reduced to 1 cup; strain. Combine with the demi-glace in the stockpot and cook until reduced by 1/2. Season with the salt. Store in the refrigerator.

To grill the pork chops, drain, reserving the marinade. Insert a meat thermometer into the thickest portion of 1 chop. Grill the chops over medium coals for 10 minutes on each side or to 150 degrees on the meat thermometer and the juices run clear when the centers are pressed.

To serve, reheat the country ham jus and spoon 1/4 cup onto each serving plate. Place the chops on the plates and add a generous spoonful of Green Tomato and Mango Relish. Top with 2 slices of Fried Plantains.

Green Tomato and Mango Relish

Makes 3 cups

Juice of 1 small lime
1 tablespoon honey
2 tablespoons chopped fresh cilantro
1/2 teaspoon cumin
1 green tomato, peeled, seeded
1 mango, peeled, pitted
1/2 roasted red bell pepper, peeled, seeded
1/2 small red onion
Kosher or sea salt to taste

Combine the lime juice, honey, cilantro and cumin in a bowl and mix well. Cut the green tomato, mango, bell pepper and onion into 1/4-inch squares. Add to the lime juice mixture. Season with salt and toss to mix well. Let stand at room temperature for 30 minutes or store, tightly covered, in the refrigerator for 8 hours or longer.

Fried Plantains

Makes 4 (2-slice) garnishes

1 large or 2 small plantains
1 cup peanut oil, corn oil or safflower oil for deep-frying

Slice the plantain 1/8 inch thick. Deep-fry in the heated oil until light brown. Drain on paper towels. These may be prepared in advance and allowed to stand uncovered for 8 hours or more to crisp.

"I would describe my relationship to food as spiritual. It sounds a little extreme but you need that kind of reverence to really take this line of work to the top of the pack. No love of food and your quality standard is compromised before you start."

Chef Jim Gerhardt
The Oakroom at
The Seelbach Hilton

PORK CROWN ROAST

Fit for a king's banquet.

Serves 10

1 cup golden raisins
1 pound Purnell's "Old Folks" Country Sausage
5 cups cooked rice
2 teaspoons seasoned salt
1¹/2 teaspoons pepper
1/2 teaspoon garlic powder
1 (10-rib) crown pork roast
Seasoned salt and pepper to taste
Garlic cloves, cut into slivers

Rinse the raisins in hot water and drain. Combine with the sausage, rice, 2 teaspoons seasoned salt, 1¹/2 teaspoons pepper and garlic powder in a bowl and mix well. Chill in the refrigerator for 2 to 8 hours.

Rub the roast with seasoned salt and pepper to taste. Cut slits at 1¹/2-inch intervals around the thickest portion of the crown and insert the garlic slivers.

Place the roast in a roasting pan and insert a meat thermometer into the thickest portion. Pack the center of the roast lightly with some of the rice mixture; cover with foil. Place the remaining rice mixture in a buttered baking dish; cover.

Place the roast in an oven preheated to 450 degrees and reduce the temperature to 350 degrees. Roast for 25 to 30 minutes per pound or to 180 degrees on the meat thermometer, removing the foil during the last 30 minutes of baking time to brown.

Place the rice casserole in the oven when the foil is removed from the roast and bake for the remaining 30 minutes of the roasting time.

If time is of the essence, remember that many local butcher shops will assemble the crown for you.

A Crowning Glory

To prepare the crown, you will need a boning knife to trim the rib bones, a larger knife, cotton kitchen twine to thread the racks together and a barding needle for the threading.

Start by cutting the rack into 2 equal portions. Make an indentation perpendicular to the bone of the first rack, about 1¹/2 to 2 inches from the end of the bone, with the larger knife. Continue with the second rack by lining it up with the indentation of the first rack so that they will be even. Cut away the excess meat between the incisions and the ends of the bone, cutting deep enough to expose the bones. Reserve excess meat for another use.

(continued at right)

KENTUCKY SWEET-AND-SOUR RIBS

Succulent ribs easily prepared in the oven.

Serves 4

1 cup ketchup
1/2 cup white vinegar
1/4 cup dark unsulfered molasses
1/4 cup honey
1/4 cup currant jelly
2 tablespoons soy sauce
1/2 sweet yellow onion, chopped
1 tablespoon chopped garlic
1 teaspoon dry mustard
1 teaspoon ground ginger
3 to 3 1/2 pounds baby back ribs

Combine the ketchup, vinegar, molasses, honey, jelly, soy sauce, onion, garlic, dry mustard and ginger in a large heavy saucepan. Bring to a boil over medium-high heat, stirring occasionally. Reduce the heat to medium and simmer for 5 minutes.

Cut the ribs into 2-rib sections and add to the sauce. Simmer for 45 to 60 minutes, rearranging the ribs in the sauce occasionally. Remove the ribs to a baking sheet. Place in a 350-degree oven. Bake for 10 minutes.

Boil the sauce remaining in the saucepan for 10 minutes or until reduced to 2 cups. Spoon enough sauce over the ribs to coat well. Bake for 20 minutes longer. Serve with the remaining sauce.

Use the boning knife to cut the rest of the meat away between the incisions and the ends of the bones, leaving 1 1/2 to 2 inches of bones exposed. Lay the rack down with the meaty side up. Make an incision between every chop, about 1/3 of the way through. This will give you the flexibility to bend the chops into a circle. Stand the racks up, chop sides down, and bend them into a circle. Join the two chops together with two separate ties, one about 1 inch below the exposed bone and the second 2 to 3 inches below that, using the needle and twine. Tighten the twine until the chops are evenly spaced and tie-off with a simple knot. Repeat at the opposite side of the crown. You are now ready to roast!

PORK TENDERLOIN WITH CRANBERRY SAUCE

Serves 2

1 (14-ounce) can chicken broth
$1/4$ cup sherry
$1/3$ cup dried cranberries
$1/3$ cup balsamic vinegar
1 pound pork tenderloin
Salt and pepper to taste
1 tablespoon olive oil

Combine $1^1/4$ cups of the chicken broth with the sherry in a small saucepan. Simmer over low heat for 15 minutes or until reduced to 1 cup. Add the cranberries and vinegar. Simmer for 20 minutes longer or until reduced to $2/3$ cup.

Cut the pork crosswise into 4 portions. Flatten with the palm and sprinkle with salt and pepper. Sauté in the heated olive oil in a medium skillet over medium-high heat for 2 minutes on each side or until brown. Add the remaining chicken broth to the skillet and reduce the heat to low.

Cook, covered, for 6 minutes or until the pork is cooked through and no longer pink in the center. Remove to a serving plate and tent with foil to keep warm.

Pour the cranberry mixture into the skillet, stirring to deglaze. Bring to a boil and reduce the heat. Simmer for 5 minutes or until reduced to $2/3$ cup. Season with salt and pepper and spoon over the pork.

SOUTHERN COMFORT PORK TENDERLOIN

Serves 4 to 6

1/4 cup Southern Comfort
2 tablespoons soy sauce
1 tablespoon hoisin sauce
3 tablespoons plum sauce
1/2 teaspoon chile garlic sauce
1 teaspoon minced gingerroot
2 (1-pound) pork tenderloins
1 cup reduced-sodium chicken broth
3 tablespoons Southern Comfort
2 tablespoons plum sauce

Combine 1/4 cup liqueur, soy sauce, hoisin sauce, 3 tablespoons plum sauce, chile garlic sauce and gingerroot in a shallow dish and mix well. Remove the silver membrane from the pork and add the pork to the marinade, turning to coat well. Marinate in the refrigerator for 5 hours or longer, turning several times.

Drain, reserving the marinade. Place the pork in a small roasting pan sprayed with nonstick cooking spray; tuck under the narrow ends. Roast at 400 degrees for 20 to 25 minutes or until the juices run clear. Remove to a warm plate.

Add the chicken broth, 3 tablespoons liqueur, 2 tablespoons plum sauce and the reserved marinade to the roasting pan, stirring to deglaze the pan. Bring to a boil and cook for 5 minutes or until reduced to the desired consistency. Cut the pork into 1/2-inch slices and serve with the sauce.

A Cut Above the Rest

"Get a sharp knife. If you dislike cooking, you'll get out of the kitchen faster. If you like cooking, you'll like it more with a sharp knife. They are expensive, but they are a once-in-a-lifetime expense that will improve your quality of life."

SARAH FRITSCHNER
EXPRESS LANE COOKBOOK

No kitchen should go without six basic kitchen knives. These essential culinary tools will make any task easier — 10-inch chef's knife, 10-inch slicer, 8-inch chef's knife, 8-inch bread knife, 3 1/2-inch paring knife, and a 6-inch boning knife. A good-quality knife should not be too heavy or too light, with most of the weight balanced in the blade.

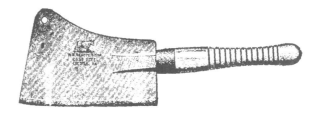

SOUTHERN SWEET AND SPICY PORK CHOPS

Serves 4 to 8

1/3 cup chili sauce
1/4 cup vegetable oil
1/4 cup hoisin sauce
1/4 cup all-fruit apricot preserves
1 tablespoon red wine vinegar

Louisiana-style hot sauce to taste
1 teaspoon dry mustard
2 garlic cloves, minced
1/2 cup Southern Comfort
8 pork loin chops

Combine the chili sauce, vegetable oil, hoisin sauce, apricot preserves, red wine vinegar, hot sauce, dry mustard, garlic and liqueur in a small bowl. Whisk until well blended.

Dip the pork loin chops into the sauce mixture. Place the pork loin chops on a rack 4 to 6 inches from hot coals. Grill for 4 minutes on each side or until light brown and cooked through, basting frequently.

OLD KENTUCKY BOURBON MARINADE

This Bluegrass favorite is great for beef, pork, or chicken.

Makes enough for 2 pounds of meat

1/2 cup Old Forester
3/4 cup soy sauce
1/4 cup canola oil or corn oil
1/4 cup water
1/4 cup Worcestershire sauce
2 tablespoons brown sugar

4 garlic cloves, minced
1 tablespoon brown mustard
1/2 teaspoon ground ginger
1 teaspoon white pepper
3 tablespoons coarsely ground
   black pepper

Combine the bourbon, soy sauce, oil, water, Worcestershire sauce, brown sugar, garlic, mustard, ginger, white pepper and black pepper in a jar with a tight-fitting lid. Cover and shake to mix well. Use to marinate 2 pounds of beef, pork or chicken.

Marinades

Most marinades contain an acid such as lemon juice, vinegar, spirits, herbs, or spices. The acid ingredient is important for tough cuts of meat because it serves as a tenderizer. Marinating should be done in a glass, ceramic, or stainless steel container — never in aluminum.

KENTUCKY COUNTRY HAM

Serves 25

1 Kentucky country ham
4 cups cola

Place the ham in a large container with water to cover it and scrub with a brush. Drain and cover with fresh water. Let stand overnight. Repeat the process twice; drain.

Arrange 2 layers of heavy-duty foil in a large roasting pan and place the ham in the center. Add the cola and seal the foil tightly. Roast the ham at 350 degrees for 15 minutes per pound. Remove from the oven and let stand, still sealed, until it comes to room temperature. Remove from the foil and trim.

KENTUCKY COUNTRY HAM BALLS

Makes 8 dozen

2 pounds Kentucky country ham, ground
1 pound Purnell's "Old Folks" Country Sausage
2 cups dry bread crumbs
2 eggs
1^1/$_2$ to 2 cups milk
2 cups packed brown sugar
1 cup water
1 cup white vinegar
1 tablespoon prepared mustard

Combine the ham, sausage, bread crumbs and eggs in a large bowl and mix well. Add enough milk gradually to moisten and mix well. Shape into small balls and place in a single layer in a baking dish.

Combine the brown sugar, water, vinegar and mustard in a saucepan and mix well. Bring to a boil and pour over the ham balls.

Bake the ham balls at 350 degrees for 45 minutes, basting after 25 minutes.

Delicious Ham Gravy

Brown ^{1}/$_3$ cup flour in a skillet over medium heat, stirring constantly. Stir in 3 tablespoons butter to form a paste. Add 2^1/$_2$ cups milk or half-and-half gradually, whisking constantly. Whisk in ^{1}/$_2$ cup pan juices from a baked country ham. Bring to a boil; reduce the heat. Cook until desired consistency, whisking occasionally. Remove from the heat; gravy will thicken as it cools. You may add additional milk or pan juices if needed. Season with salt and pepper to taste.

ITALIAN TORTA

Outstanding presentation!

Serves 8

1/2 (32-ounce) package frozen bread
    dough, thawed
2 (10-ounce) packages frozen
    chopped spinach, thawed
1 (14-ounce) can artichoke hearts,
    cut into quarters
1 (12-ounce) jar marinated red
    peppers, chopped
16 ounces small fresh mushrooms

1 tablespoon olive oil
8 ounces thinly sliced salami
1 (3-ounce) can chopped black
    olives
8 ounces thinly sliced provolone
    cheese
8 ounces thinly sliced cooked ham
1 egg
1 tablespoon water

Cut 1 loaf of dough into halves crosswise. Roll 1 half into a 10-inch circle on a lightly floured surface. Cover and set aside.

Press the remaining dough together and roll into a 12-inch circle. Fit into a greased 9-inch springform pan, allowing the edges to overhang.

Drain the spinach, artichokes and red peppers, pressing the spinach and red peppers with paper towels to remove as much moisture as possible. Sauté the mushrooms in the olive oil in a nonstick skillet for 8 minutes; drain.

Layer half the salami in the prepared springform pan. Layer the sautéed mushrooms, olives, half the cheese slices and half the ham over the salami. Continue layering with the spinach, red peppers, remaining salami and remaining ham. Top with the artichokes and remaining cheese slices.

Mix the egg and water in a small bowl. Brush on the overhanging dough edges. Top with the remaining dough circle, fold the overhanging edges over the top and press or crimp to seal. Brush with the remaining egg wash.

Place on the lower oven rack and bake at 350 degrees for 45 to 55 minutes or until golden brown, covering with foil during the last 15 to 20 minutes if necessary to prevent overbrowning. Cool in the pan on a wire rack. Place on a serving plate and remove the side of the pan. Cut into wedges to serve.

Torta (TOHR-tub) is the Italian word for "tart," "pie," or "cake." This Mediterranean delight creates an irresistible main course for a casual gathering with friends.

GRILLED VEAL CHOPS WITH CABERNET SAUCE

This recipe for Grilled Veal Chops with Cabernet-Wild Mushroom Sauce is from John Ash, From the Earth to the Table.

Serves 6

Cabernet-Wild Mushroom Sauce

1/2 cup sliced shallots

1/2 cup chopped shiitake
  mushrooms

1 tablespoon chopped garlic

2 tablespoons olive oil

1/2 ounce dried porcini
  mushrooms

1 cup chopped seeded tomatoes

5 cups rich beef or chicken stock

2 cups Fetzer Valley Oaks Cabernet
  Sauvignon

2 bay leaves

2 teaspoons fresh thyme, or
  1 teaspoon dried thyme

1 tablespoon Dijon mustard

2 teaspoons minced fresh mint

Salt and freshly ground pepper
  to taste

Veal Chops

1/2 cup chopped onion

2 tablespoons minced garlic

3 tablespoons minced fresh basil

1 1/2 tablespoons minced fresh mint

1/4 cup Bel Arbor Chardonnay

2 tablespoons white wine vinegar

1 teaspoon salt

1 teaspoon cracked pepper

1/3 cup olive oil

6 veal loin chops, 1 1/4 inches thick

For the sauce, sauté the shallots, shiitake mushrooms and garlic in the heated olive oil in a saucepan until light brown. Add the porcini mushrooms, tomatoes, stock, wine, bay leaves, thyme and mustard and bring to a boil. Reduce the heat to medium and simmer for 40 to 60 minutes or until reduced to a light sauce consistency. Strain through a fine-mesh strainer, pressing to remove the liquid. Add the mint, salt and pepper. Store, covered, in the refrigerator for up to 2 days.

For the veal chops, combine the onion, garlic, basil, mint, wine, vinegar, salt and pepper in a food processor container. Pulse 3 or 4 times to chop. Combine with the olive oil in a bowl, whisking to mix well. Add the veal chops, turning to coat evenly. Marinate, covered, in the refrigerator for 2 hours or longer; drain. Grill or broil the chops for 5 to 6 minutes on each side or just until still slightly pink and juicy. Remove to a serving plate. Reheat the sauce and spoon around the chops. Garnish with grilled shiitake or other wild mushrooms and fresh herb sprigs.

Poultry

Herbed Chicken and Sausage Skewers
(Photo, pages 126–127)

At every Sunday dinner,
in the middle of the table,
in a bowl of water,
floated a single magnolia
blossom, cut from the
tree in our front yard.
Its perfume, layered
between the chicken and
the kale, is still what
Sundays smell like.

Frederick Smock
"One Writer's Beginning"
Savory Memories

ROASTED CHICKEN WITH GARLIC CREAM

Serves 4

1 (4-pound) chicken
Salt and freshly ground pepper to taste
4 teaspoons chopped fresh rosemary
8 medium garlic cloves, thinly sliced
3 shallots, minced
1 tablespoon unsalted butter
1 tablespoon vegetable oil
3/4 cup Bolla Pinot Grigio
1/2 cup heavy cream
1 tablespoon unsalted butter

Sprinkle the chicken inside and out with salt and pepper. Place the rosemary, garlic and shallots in the cavity. Heat 1 tablespoon butter with the oil in a Dutch oven over medium-high heat. Place the chicken breast side down in the Dutch oven and cover. Roast at 475 degrees for 50 minutes. Turn the chicken breast side up and roast for 20 minutes longer or until the juices run clear when the thigh is pierced. Remove to a platter. Cover to keep warm.

Skim the fat from the drippings in the Dutch oven. Add the wine and bring to a boil. Cook for 5 minutes or until the liquid is reduced by 1/2, stirring constantly. Add any collected juices from the chicken. Stir in the heavy cream and cook for 5 minutes or until thick enough to coat a wooden spoon. Whisk in 1 tablespoon butter and season with salt and pepper. Serve with the chicken.

Serve with Garlic Gruyère Mashed Potatoes (page 180).

Garden Chicken

Serves 4 to 6

1 cup flour
1 teaspoon salt
1 teaspoon pepper
2¹/₂ to 3 pounds chicken pieces, skinned
¹/₄ cup (¹/₂ stick) butter
³/₄ cup chicken broth

³/₄ cup dry sherry
1 (16-ounce) can artichoke hearts, drained
2 tomatoes, cut into wedges
1 medium onion, sliced
¹/₂ medium green bell pepper, sliced

Combine the flour, salt and pepper in a nonrecycled brown paper bag. Add the chicken and shake to coat. Brown the chicken in the butter in a skillet over medium-high heat, turning occasionally. Reduce the heat. Stir in the chicken broth and sherry.

Simmer, covered, for 45 minutes. Add the artichokes, tomatoes, onion and bell pepper. Cook, covered, for 15 minutes longer or until the chicken is cooked through and the vegetables are of the desired crispness.

Simmer the remaining liquid for 10 minutes longer to create a sauce that can be served over hot cooked rice.

Herb-Baked Chicken

Serves 2 to 4

1 to 2 pounds chicken pieces, skinned
3 to 4 tablespoons olive oil
¹/₄ cup teriyaki sauce
1 teaspoon chopped fresh gingerroot

¹/₂ teaspoon salt
¹/₄ teaspoon oregano
¹/₄ teaspoon rosemary
¹/₈ teaspoon pepper
1 lemon, thinly sliced

Brush the chicken with the olive oil. Arrange in a single layer in a baking dish. Drizzle with the teriyaki sauce. Sprinkle with a mixture of the gingerroot, salt, oregano, rosemary and pepper. Top with the lemon slices. Bake at 350 degrees for 1 hour.

KORBEL CHAMPAGNE CHICKEN

Serves 2

2 boneless skinless chicken breasts
1¹/₂ teaspoons extra-virgin olive oil
1¹/₂ cups Korbel Brut Champagne
3 shallots, thinly slivered

¹/₃ cup heavy cream
1 bunch fresh tarragon,
   coarsely chopped
Salt and pepper to taste

Brown the chicken in the heated olive oil in a heavy skillet over medium heat for 5 minutes on each side. Remove to a platter. Add ¹/₂ cup of the Champagne, stirring constantly to deglaze.

Add the shallots and cook for 8 or 9 minutes or until translucent. Stir in the remaining 1 cup Champagne and cook until reduced by ¹/₂. Return the chicken to the skillet and stir in the cream and tarragon. Cook until the chicken is cooked through. Season with salt and pepper.

Serve on rice or fettuccini with steamed asparagus or broccoli.

EARLY TIMES MUSTARD CHICKEN

Serves 4 to 6

¹/₂ cup Early Times
¹/₂ cup Dijon mustard
¹/₂ cup packed brown sugar
1 teaspoon Worcestershire sauce
4 scallions, thinly sliced

1 teaspoon salt
4 to 6 boneless skinless chicken
   breasts
1 tablespoon butter
1 tablespoon vegetable oil

Combine the whisky, Dijon mustard, brown sugar, Worcestershire sauce, scallions and salt in a dish and mix well. Pound the chicken ¹/₄ inch thick. Add to the mustard mixture, turning to coat well. Marinate, covered, in the refrigerator for 1 hour. Drain, reserving the marinade.

Heat the butter and oil in a heavy skillet over medium-high heat. Add the chicken and sauté for 3 to 4 minutes on each side or until golden brown. Remove to a warm platter. Drain the skillet and add the reserved marinade. Bring to a boil, stirring constantly. Drizzle over the chicken.

CHEESES AND CHICKEN IN PHYLLO

Serves 8

8 boneless skinless chicken breasts
Salt and pepper to taste
4 cups chopped fresh spinach or drained frozen spinach
1 cup chopped shallots
2 tablespoons olive oil
4 ounces cream cheese, cubed, softened
1 cup shredded mozzarella cheese
1/2 cup crumbled feta cheese
1/2 cup shredded Cheddar cheese
1 egg yolk, beaten
1 tablespoon flour
1/2 teaspoon nutmeg
1/2 teaspoon cumin
16 sheets frozen phyllo dough, thawed
2/3 cup butter, melted, or clarified butter

Pound the chicken 1/8 inch thick between sheets of heavy plastic wrap with the flat side of a meat mallet. Season with salt and pepper.

Sauté the spinach and shallots in the heated olive oil in a skillet until the shallots are tender. Remove from the heat and stir in the cream cheese until melted. Add the mozzarella cheese, feta cheese, Cheddar cheese, egg yolk, flour, nutmeg and cumin. Spoon about 1/2 cup of the spinach mixture onto each chicken breast and roll to enclose the filling.

Layer 2 sheets of the phyllo on a work surface, brushing or spritzing each with butter; keep the remaining dough moist by covering with waxed paper topped with a damp towel. Place 1 chicken roll on the phyllo; roll once to cover the chicken. Fold in the long sides and continue to roll from the narrow side to enclose the chicken. Repeat the process with the remaining phyllo, chicken rolls and butter. Arrange the rolls in a shallow 11 × 13-inch baking pan. Brush with additional butter. Bake at 350 degrees for 30 to 35 minutes or until the chicken is cooked through.

To make this dish more festive, cut the chicken rolls into 1-inch slices and arrange them on serving plates. Garnish with endive, Greek olives, and roasted peppers.

Phyllo "Phacts"

Phyllo is Greek for the word leaf. For cooks, the term refers to very thin layers of pastry dough, similar to strudel dough, used primarily in Greek and eastern food preparation. Many cooks become frustrated working with phyllo because of its thinness and tendency to dry out. Remember to keep the phyllo moist by covering with waxed paper and placing a damp paper towel over the unused portion. Phyllo is available, either fresh or frozen, in large supermarkets. Phyllo dough can be stored in the refrigerator for up to two weeks if unopened. Once opened, it must be used within two to three days.

133

CHICKEN AND ROASTED TOMATO SAUCE

Serves 4

Chicken
1 tablespoon chopped fresh basil
4 ounces Capriole goat cheese
4 boneless skinless chicken breasts
¹/₄ cup fresh or commercial pesto
¹/₃ cup bread crumbs
Olive oil

Roasted Tomato Sauce
2 large tomatoes
¹/₂ onion
2 tablespoons balsamic vinegar
2 tablespoons olive oil
1 garlic clove, minced

For the chicken, mix the basil and goat cheese in a bowl. Flatten the chicken between sheets of plastic wrap. Spread the pesto evenly on the chicken and sprinkle with the cheese mixture. Fold the chicken to enclose the filling.

Coat the chicken with the bread crumbs and arrange in a baking dish. Drizzle with olive oil. Bake at 350 degrees for 30 to 45 minutes or until cooked through.

For the sauce, arrange the tomatoes and onion on a baking sheet. Roast at 400 degrees until the tomato skins split; remove the skins. Combine the tomatoes, onion, balsamic vinegar, olive oil and garlic in a food processor container and process until smooth.

To serve, remove the chicken to a heated platter and serve with the warm sauce. Garnish with fresh basil leaves.

For a fresh pesto recipe, refer to page 202.

CREAMY GORGONZOLA CHICKEN

Serves 6

6 boneless skinless chicken breasts
2 tablespoons olive oil
1/2 cup finely chopped green onions
1 garlic clove, minced
3 tablespoons butter
1/4 cup flour
1/4 teaspoon pepper
1 cup chicken broth
3/4 cup heavy cream
2 teaspoons Fetzer Sundial Chardonnay
2 teaspoons Worcestershire sauce
1/4 cup crumbled Gorgonzola cheese

Cook the chicken in the olive oil in a skillet over medium heat for 8 to
10 minutes or until cooked through and brown, turning frequently.
Remove the skillet from heat. Cover to keep warm.

Sauté the green onions and garlic in the butter in a saucepan until the
green onions are tender. Stir in the flour and pepper. Add the broth,
heavy cream, cooking wine and Worcestershire sauce and mix well.

Cook over medium heat until thickened and bubbly, stirring constantly.
Transfer the mixture to the skillet and mix well. Bring to a boil. Cook for
2 minutes, stirring constantly. Stir in the Gorgonzola cheese. Remove the
chicken to a platter with a slotted spoon. Drizzle with the sauce. Garnish
with parsley or chives.

Guadalajara Chicken Olé

Serves 6 to 8

1¹/₂ cups chopped onions
1 medium green bell pepper, chopped
¹/₄ cup (¹/₂ stick) butter
¹/₄ cup flour
2 cups milk
1¹/₂ cups chicken broth
1 cup sour cream
2 teaspoons cumin
2 (4-ounce) cans chopped green chiles, drained
¹/₄ cup chopped jalapeño chiles
2 (2-ounce) cans sliced black olives, drained
2 teaspoons seasoned salt
6 boneless skinless chicken breasts, cooked, coarsely chopped
8 flour tortillas, cut into bite-size pieces
1 pound sharp Cheddar cheese, shredded
8 ounces Monterey Jack cheese, shredded

Sauté the onions and bell pepper in the butter in a saucepan until tender. Stir in the flour and cook for 1 minute. Add the milk, chicken broth, sour cream and cumin. Cook until thickened, stirring constantly. Add the green chiles, jalapeño chiles, olives and seasoned salt.

Alternate layers of the chicken, tortillas, sauce, Cheddar cheese and Monterey Jack cheese in a greased 3-quart baking dish until all the ingredients are used, ending with the cheeses. Bake at 375 degrees for 1 hour.

You may prepare ahead and freeze until ready to use. Thaw and bake for 45 minutes longer.

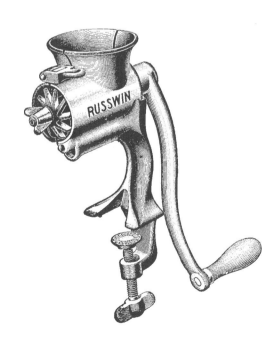

FETA CHICKEN WITH MUSHROOMS AND HERBS

Serves 4

Chicken
1/2 cup crumbled feta cheese
1/4 cup minced green onions
Freshly ground pepper to taste
4 boneless skinless chicken breasts

Mushroom and Tomato Sauce
1 small onion, minced
3 small garlic cloves, minced
1 cup sliced mushrooms
2 tablespoons chopped fresh parsley or basil
1 teaspoon oregano
3 tablespoons butter
1 tablespoon flour
1/3 cup Bolla Chardonnay
1/2 cup chicken broth
1/2 cup chopped plum tomatoes
1 tablespoon feta cheese

For the chicken, mix the feta cheese, green onions and pepper in a bowl. Pound the chicken with the flat side of a meat mallet. Spoon the cheese mixture evenly over the chicken and fold to enclose the filling. Arrange in a shallow baking dish. Bake at 350 degrees for 35 to 40 minutes or until cooked through.

For the sauce, sauté the onion, garlic, mushrooms, parsley and oregano in the butter in a skillet for 2 to 3 minutes. Add the flour gradually and mix well. Stir in the wine gradually. Cook until thickened, stirring constantly. Add the chicken broth, tomatoes and feta cheese. Simmer for 10 minutes, stirring occasionally. Serve over the chicken.

SOUTHERN SPICY CHICKEN WITH COMFORT

Serves 6

Chicken
2 tablespoons butter
2 tablespoons vegetable oil
6 boneless skinless chicken breasts
Salt and cayenne pepper to taste
1/2 cup flour

Comfort Sauce
1/4 cup Southern Comfort
2 cups chicken broth
2 teaspoons green peppercorns in brine, drained
Cayenne pepper to taste
2 tablespoons butter
2 tablespoons Southern Comfort

For the chicken, heat the butter and oil in a large sauté pan over medium-high heat. Season the chicken with salt and cayenne pepper and coat with the flour. Add to the sauté pan and cook until golden brown on both sides and cooked through. Remove to a warm platter and drain the skillet.

For the sauce, add 1/4 cup liqueur, chicken broth, peppercorns and cayenne pepper to the same skillet and simmer until reduced by half. Whisk in the butter and 2 tablespoons liqueur.

Return the chicken to the sauté pan and cook just until heated through, stirring frequently. Garnish with chopped fresh parsley.

Photo on facing page,
Stone fence on Pisgah Pike
Woodford County, Kentucky

SUMMERTIME BASIL CHICKEN

This is also good with the Cucumber Mustard Sauce on page 162 or the Lime Watercress Sauce on page 154. Pack the chilled slices in an insulated cooler for transport to a picnic.

Serves 6

¹/₂ teaspoon paprika	2 teaspoons vegetable oil
¹/₂ teaspoon salt	¹/₃ cup chicken broth
¹/₄ teaspoon pepper	¹/₃ cup Fetzer Echo Ridge Fumé Blanc
6 medium boneless skinless	1 tablespoon chopped fresh basil
chicken breasts	Creamy Lemon Basil Sauce (below)

Mix the paprika, salt and pepper in a small dish. Sprinkle on both sides of the chicken. Sauté the chicken in the oil in a 12-inch skillet over medium heat until brown, turning once. Add the chicken broth, wine and chopped basil. Cook, covered, over medium-low heat for 10 minutes or just until the chicken is tender.

Place the chicken and cooking juices in a covered container and chill in the refrigerator for 4 to 24 hours. Cut diagonally into ³/₄-inch slices and arrange on a platter. Garnish with basil leaves. Serve with Creamy Lemon Basil Sauce.

CREAMY LEMON BASIL SAUCE

This is also delicious over vegetables, salmon, or shrimp.

Makes 1¹/₄ cups

¹/₄ cup fresh lemon juice	1 teaspoon sugar
¹/₂ cup fresh basil leaves	¹/₂ teaspoon salt
¹/₄ cup fresh parsley leaves	1 cup mayonnaise
1 garlic clove, chopped	

Combine the lemon juice, basil, parsley, garlic, sugar and salt in a food processor container and process until smooth. Whip the mayonnaise in a small mixing bowl until creamy. Stir in the basil mixture. Chill, covered, until serving time.

ZESTY LEMON CHICKEN

Serves 6

Chicken
6 boneless skinless chicken breasts
Salt and pepper to taste
1/4 cup (1/2 stick) butter, melted

Lemon Cream Sauce
2 tablespoons Noilly Prat Dry Vermouth
2 tablespoons fresh lemon juice
2 teaspoons grated lemon zest
3/4 cup heavy cream
1/2 cup reduced-sodium chicken broth
1/2 cup freshly grated Parmesan cheese
Salt and pepper to taste
Chopped fresh parsley to taste

For the chicken, pound the chicken breasts 1/2 inch thick between sheets of plastic wrap with a meat mallet. Season with salt and pepper. Sauté in the butter in a large heavy skillet over medium heat for 3 minutes on each side or until cooked through. Remove to a warm platter and cover with foil; drain the skillet.

Add the vermouth, lemon juice and lemon zest to the same skillet and cook for 1 minute, stirring to deglaze the skillet. Add the cream, chicken broth and any juices which have accumulated from the chicken. Cook for 8 minutes or until reduced to a sauce consistency, stirring frequently. Add half the cheese, salt and pepper, stirring until the cheese melts.

Spoon the sauce over the chicken and sprinkle with the remaining cheese and parsley. Garnish with lemon wedges.

Lemons, Lemons Everywhere

Lemons not only add zest to many recipes, they are also versatile kitchen helpers.

- *To get the most juice from a fresh lemon, bring it to room temperature and roll it under your palm against a hard, flat surface, then cut the lemon and squeeze.*

- *Squeeze fresh lemons on your hands after handling garlic and onions to help eliminate the odor.*

- *Grind lemon rinds in the garbage disposal to give it a fresh smell.*

- *Place whole lemons in a glass vase before arranging fresh, cut flowers for a creative and beautiful centerpiece.*

PECAN AND SAUSAGE-STUFFED CHICKEN

Serves 4

$^1/_3$ **pound Purnell's "Old Folks" Country Sausage**
$^1/_3$ **cup butter**
$^1/_3$ **cup finely chopped celery**
$^1/_3$ **cup finely chopped green bell pepper**
2 small shallots, finely chopped
$^1/_3$ **cup chopped pecans**
$^1/_8$ **teaspoon salt**
$^1/_4$ **teaspoon pepper**
3 cups ($^1/_4$-inch) dry bread cubes
1 egg, lightly beaten
1$^1/_2$ tablespoons milk
4 whole boneless skinless chicken breasts
1$^1/_2$ tablespoons butter, melted
3 tablespoons chopped pecans
3 tablespoons fine dry bread crumbs

Brown the sausage in a heavy saucepan, stirring until crumbly. Remove to a bowl with a slotted spoon and drain the saucepan. Melt $^1/_3$ cup butter in the saucepan over medium-high heat and add the celery, bell pepper and shallots. Sauté until the vegetables are tender.

Add $^1/_3$ cup pecans, salt and pepper. Cook for 3 minutes, stirring constantly. Remove from the heat and stir in the sausage, bread cubes, egg and milk.

Place the chicken between sheets of plastic wrap and pound $^1/_4$ inch thick with a meat mallet. Spoon the sausage mixture evenly down the center of each piece of chicken and fold the long sides over to enclose the filling; secure with wooden picks. Arrange seam side down in a foil-lined baking pan.

Mix 1$^1/_2$ tablespoons melted butter with 3 tablespoons pecans and the bread crumbs in a bowl. Press evenly over the chicken rolls. Bake at 350 degrees for 30 minutes or until cooked through and golden brown. Garnish with chopped fresh parsley.

Herbed Chicken and Sausage Skewers

Serves 8

8 mild Italian sausages
8 boneless skinless chicken breasts
2 cups olive oil
²/3 cup fresh lemon juice
1/2 cup red wine vinegar
6 garlic cloves, minced
1/4 cup Dijon mustard
1/4 cup herbes de Provence
1 teaspoon salt
1 teaspoon pepper
2 lemons, thinly sliced
16 bay leaves
1 (16-ounce) loaf dry French bread, cut into 1-inch slices
24 to 32 cherry tomatoes

Combine the sausages with cold water to cover in a large saucepan. Cook, loosely covered, for 12 to 15 minutes or until the sausages are cooked through and firm; drain and cool.

Cut each sausage and chicken breast crosswise into quarters and combine in a shallow dish. Mix the olive oil, lemon juice, vinegar, garlic, Dijon mustard, herbes de Provence, salt and pepper in a bowl. Pour half the mixture over the chicken and sausage, reserving the remaining mixture for basting. Add the lemon slices and bay leaves and mix gently. Marinate, covered, in the refrigerator for 1 to 2 hours, stirring occasionally.

Remove the chicken, sausage, lemon slices and bay leaves from the marinade and discard the marinade. Thread the chicken, sausage, bread slices, tomatoes, lemon slices and bay leaves alternately onto skewers.

Grill for 10 to 15 minutes or until the chicken is cooked through, turning occasionally and basting with the reserved marinade. Remove to a platter, discarding the bay leaves. Serve with rice or orzo.

Grill additional skewers of cherry tomatoes, squash, zucchini, and bell peppers to make a colorful accompaniment to the main course.

Bay Leaf Traditions

The bay leaf is one of America's most commonly used herbs, but southern families have a unique set of bay leaf traditions similar to the New Orleans King Cake tradition. The family member served the bay leaf, thought to be the recipient of good luck, wins an extra serving of dessert, is rewarded the task of clearing the dinner table, or can make and receive a special wish. Whatever your family tradition, bay leaves are a flavorful addition to marinades, sauces, or soups. Remember to crack the leaves before immersing them into liquid. If they break, they are old and should be discarded.

BLUEGRASS FREE-RANGE CHICKEN

Created by Chef Jim Gerhardt, The Oakroom at The Seelbach Hilton

Serves 4

Chicken

4 (6- to 7-ounce) free-range
   chicken breasts
1/4 cup Three-Herb Pesto (at right)
4 (1-ounce) slices Kentucky
   country ham

Salt and pepper to taste
1/4 cup olive oil or peanut oil

Old Forester Bourbon Sauce

1 tablespoon chopped shallot
1/2 teaspoon olive oil
1/2 cup Old Forester
12 ounces The Oakroom Demi-Glace
   (page 145)

2 ounces gastrique (page 145)
1/2 ounce cornstarch
2 tablespoons cold water

For the chicken, remove the tenderloins from the chicken breasts and reserve. Cover the chicken with plastic wrap and pound to an even thickness with a meat mallet. Place skin side down on a work surface and spread 1 tablespoon of the pesto on each. Layer 1 slice country ham and the reserved tenderloins over the pesto. Fold the sides of the chicken over to enclose the filling and secure with wooden picks. Season with salt and pepper. Heat the olive oil in an ovenproof sauté pan over high heat. Add the chicken skin side down and sauté until golden brown. Turn the chicken and place the pan in a 400-degree oven. Bake for 15 to 20 minutes or to 160 degrees on a meat thermometer.

For the sauce, sweat the shallot in the heated olive oil in a small saucepan over medium heat for 2 minutes. Remove from heat and add the bourbon. Cook until reduced by 3/4; keep cover available in case the bourbon should flame. Stir in the demi-glace and gastrique and bring to a boil. Boil for 3 to 5 minutes, stirring occasionally. Blend the cornstarch and water in a small bowl. Drizzle slowly into the boiling mixture, whisking constantly. Bring to a slow boil and cook for 2 to 3 minutes or until thickened, stirring constantly. To serve, spoon the sauce onto serving plates. Slice each chicken roll into 5 medallions and arrange in the sauce.

THREE-HERB PESTO

1 bunch fresh basil
1/2 bunch fresh tarragon
1/2 bunch fresh cilantro
1 tablespoon chopped garlic
2 ounces toasted pine nuts
1 ounce Parmesan cheese
4 ounces extra-virgin olive oil
Salt and pepper to taste

Combine the basil, tarragon, cilantro, garlic, pine nuts and Parmesan cheese in a food processor and process until minced, gradually adding the olive oil. Season with salt and pepper. Store in an airtight container in the refrigerator.

THE OAKROOM DEMI-GLACE

Makes 1 quart

2 pounds veal shank bones, cut into 2-inch pieces
1 cup water
2 carrots, peeled, chopped
3 ribs celery, chopped
1 onion, chopped
6 garlic cloves
2 tablespoons tomato paste
3 sprigs of thyme
3 bay leaves
12 black peppercorns
1 gallon water
2 tablespoons cornstarch
1/4 cup water
Salt and pepper to taste

Roast the veal bones in a roasting pan at 400 degrees until the bones are a rich brown color. Transfer the bones to a large stockpot. Add 1 cup water to the roasting pan and stir to dislodge any brown particles. Add the pan drippings to the stockpot. Stir in the carrots, celery, onion, garlic, tomato paste, thyme, bay leaves, peppercorns and 1 gallon water. Bring to a boil over medium heat. Boil for 30 minutes, stirring occasionally. Reduce the heat to low.

Simmer for 4 to 6 hours, stirring occasionally and adding additional water if the stock reduces too quickly. Strain, discarding the solid materials. Return the liquid to the stockpot. Whisk in a mixture of the cornstarch and 1/4 cup water. Bring to a boil over medium heat. Boil for 2 to 3 minutes, stirring frequently. Season with salt and pepper.

You may thicken two 12-ounce cans of double-strength beef stock with a paste of cornstarch and water as a substitute for demi-glace. To make gastrique, combine 3 tablespoons sugar with 2 ounces white vinegar and cook to a medium caramel stage.

CHICKEN AND KENTUCKY COUNTRY HAM POT PIE

Serves 8 to 10

4 refrigerator pie pastries
6 cups chicken stock
2 cups water
2¼ pounds boneless skinless
   chicken breasts
3 large russet potatoes, peeled,
   cut into ½-inch pieces
3 large carrots, peeled, cut into
   ½-inch pieces, or 1 cup
   baby carrots
2 fennel bulbs, cut lengthwise into
   halves, cored, thinly sliced
2 onions, chopped

6 tablespoons unsalted butter
6 tablespoons flour
2 cups milk
2 teaspoons fennel seeds
2 teaspoons chopped fresh thyme,
   or ¼ teaspoon dried thyme
½ teaspoon salt
2 tablespoons fresh lemon juice
4 ounces Kentucky country ham,
   julienned
Salt and pepper to taste
1 egg, beaten

Roll 2 of the pastries if necessary to fit two 9-inch deep-dish pie plates; trim the edges. Line the pastry with foil and fill with dried beans or pie weights. Bake at 425 degrees for 10 minutes. Remove the foil and beans and bake for 5 minutes longer or just until light brown.

Bring the stock and water to a boil in a saucepan. Add the chicken and simmer for 10 minutes or until tender; remove and cut into ½-inch pieces.

Add the potatoes, carrots and fennel to the stock in the saucepan and cook just until tender. Remove the vegetables to a bowl with a slotted spoon. Cook the stock for 20 minutes longer or until reduced to 2 cups.

Sauté the onions in the butter in a large heavy saucepan over medium heat for 8 minutes or until tender. Add the flour and cook for 2 minutes or until golden brown, stirring constantly. Whisk in the reduced stock, milk, fennel seeds, thyme and ½ teaspoon salt. Cook for 10 minutes or until thickened, stirring constantly. Stir in the lemon juice. Add the chicken, country ham and vegetables and mix well. Season with salt and pepper.

Spoon into the prepared pie plates. Top with the remaining pastries and crimp the edges; cut 4 vents in each. Brush with the beaten egg. Bake at 425 degrees for 25 minutes or until golden brown. Let stand for 5 to 10 minutes before serving. Serve with Cold Asparagus Vinaigrette (page 175).

Serve with Cold Asparagus Vinaigrette (page 175).

Kentucky Hospitality

Many of us have relatives, usually an aunt or grandmother, whose hostessing style is reminiscent of the following memory of Richard Taylor, the 1999–2001 Kentucky Poet Laureate.

"One principle that Cousin Mony and Cousin Lucy both shared was an insistent hospitality that bordered on the militant. It was unthinkable for anyone to leave the premises without taking in a few calories. Just as in the Civil War when what began as a skirmish often heated up as a battle, in Cousin Mony's kitchen what began as a snack would quickly take on the dimensions of a meal."

RICHARD TAYLOR
"GUINEAS AND GRIDDLE CAKES"
SAVORY MEMORIES

KENTUCKY COUNTRY HAM-STUFFED CHICKEN

Country Cured Ham

Serves 4

4 boneless skinless chicken breasts, trimmed
4 thin slices Kentucky country ham
3 ounces Gouda cheese, shredded
1/4 cup olive oil
1 garlic clove, chopped
2 tablespoons chopped fresh parsley
2 tablespoons chopped fresh basil
1 tablespoon green peppercorns, crushed
Salt and freshly ground pepper to taste
16 fresh mushrooms
1/2 cup chicken stock
1 tablespoon chopped fresh parsley

Flatten the chicken to 1/4-inch thickness between sheets of waxed paper with a rolling pin. Place 1 slice of country ham on each piece.

Combine the cheese, olive oil, garlic, 2 tablespoons parsley, basil, peppercorns, salt and pepper in a small bowl and mix well. Spoon 1 tablespoon of the mixture onto the ham slices and roll the chicken to enclose the filling; secure each with 2 wooden picks.

Arrange seam side down in a baking dish. Arrange the mushrooms around the rolls and spoon the remaining cheese mixture over the top.

Bake at 350 degrees for 15 minutes. Heat the chicken stock in a small saucepan. Pour into the baking dish and baste the chicken and mushrooms. Bake for 20 to 25 minutes longer or until the chicken is tender, basting frequently.

Remove the chicken and mushrooms to a warm serving platter and spoon the pan juices over the top. Sprinkle with 1 tablespoon parsley.

Ham is a flavorful companion to poultry in many dishes. Kentuckians prefer country cured ham over the ordinary wet, cured product. Kentucky country ham is dry-cured in a mixture of salt, sugar, and seasonings and then slowly smoked over hardwood fires for 6 to 12 months. It is distinguished from its "poor cousins" by its dark red color, firm, salty tasting meat, and by the fact that it does not require refrigeration until separated from its plastic wrapper. America's most famous country cured hams come from Kentucky.

GRILLED BOURBON TURKEY

Serves 2

1 to 2 tablespoons Woodford
  Reserve Bourbon
1 teaspoon soy sauce
1 tablespoon Worcestershire sauce
1 tablespoon vegetable oil

$1/4$ teaspoon thyme
$1/8$ teaspoon salt
1 large onion, cut into $1/4$-inch slices
2 (8-ounce) turkey breast steaks
$3/4$ teaspoon ground pepper

Combine the bourbon, soy sauce, Worcestershire sauce, oil, thyme and salt
in a shallow medium bowl and mix well. Add the onion and turkey steaks
and turn to coat. Marinate in the refrigerator for 30 minutes or longer.
Drain, reserving the turkey and onion slices. Press the coarse ground
pepper firmly over both sides of the turkey.

Grill or broil the turkey 5 to 6 inches from the heat source for 3 to
5 minutes on each side or until the juices run clear when the turkey is
pierced. Place the reserved onion on the grill just before the turkey is
done and grill for 2 to 3 minutes. Serve the onion with the steaks.

CREOLE FRIED TURKEY

Serves 8 to 10

$1/2$ cup (1 stick) margarine or
  butter, melted
$1/4$ cup onion juice
$1/4$ cup garlic juice
$1/2$ cup soy sauce

$1/2$ cup Worcestershire sauce
1 (14- to 15-pound) turkey
Creole seasoning to taste
1 medium onion, cut into quarters
Peanut oil for deep-frying

Combine the margarine, onion juice, garlic juice, soy sauce and Worcestershire sauce in a bowl and mix well. Inject the mixture evenly into the entire
turkey, adding slightly more to the breast portion. Sprinkle inside and out
with Creole seasoning. Place in a sealable plastic bag and marinate in the
refrigerator for 8 hours. Place the onion in the turkey cavity.

Add enough peanut oil to a large outdoor cooker to completely cover the
turkey and heat to 400 degrees. Add the turkey and deep-fry for 3 minutes
per pound plus 5 to 10 additional minutes. Drain well.

MARINATED CORNISH HENS

Serves 2

2 Cornish game hens
Salt and pepper to taste
1 onion, chopped
1 garlic clove, minced
1/2 cup (1 stick) butter

1 (10-ounce) can beef broth
2 tablespoons sherry
1 bay leaf
1/4 teaspoon thyme
16 ounces fresh mushrooms

Season the game hens with salt and pepper and place in a shallow baking dish. Sauté the onion and garlic in the butter in a skillet. Add the broth, sherry, bay leaf and thyme and mix well. Cook until heated through. Pour over the hens. Chill, covered, for 8 hours or longer. Add the mushrooms to the baking dish. Bake at 350 degrees for 1 hour, basting frequently. Remove the bay leaf and serve with rice.

HERBED QUAIL STROGANOFF

Serves 4

8 quail, dressed
1 medium onion, chopped
8 ounces fresh mushrooms, sliced
2 tablespoons butter
1 (10-ounce) can cream of
  celery soup

1/2 cup Fetzer Sundial Chardonnay
1/2 teaspoon oregano
1/2 teaspoon rosemary
1/4 teaspoon pepper
1 cup sour cream

Arrange the quail in a 9 × 13-inch baking dish sprayed with nonstick cooking spray. Sauté the onion and mushrooms in the butter in a skillet until tender. Add the soup, wine, oregano, rosemary and pepper and mix well. Cook until heated through, stirring occasionally. Pour over the quail. Bake, covered, at 350 degrees for 45 minutes. Remove the quail to a platter with a slotted spoon and stir the sour cream into the pan juices. Return the quail to the baking dish and bake, uncovered, for 10 minutes longer or until the quail are cooked through. Serve over wild rice.

You may substitute bone-in chicken breasts or split Cornish game hens for the quail if you prefer.

Garnishing Ideas

Give your culinary creations a special finishing touch. Garnishes enhance presentation and take food from everyday fare to extraordinary cuisine. Follow these garnishing guidelines:

• A garnish should be edible and a complement to your dish. For example, Herbed Quail Stroganoff can be served with small bunches of fresh rosemary or green onion tops tied with ribbon. Chicken and Roasted Tomato Sauce (page 134) can be garnished with cherry tomato halves and fresh basil leaves.

• Arrange food, especially vegetables, to give each plate an artistic presentation. Cheeses and Chicken in Phyllo (page 133) can be sliced in 1-inch portions and shingled on a bed of fresh spinach. Don't be afraid to be creative.

Seafood

Wok-Seared Asian Salmon with Spicy
Shrimp Fried Rice
(Photo, pages 150–151)

Eating is the most intimate
and at the same time the
most public of biological
functions. Going from
dinner table to dinner table
is the equivalent of going
from one culture to another,
even within the same family.

Guy Davenport

SPICY CATFISH WITH LIME WATERCRESS SAUCE

Serves 6

Lime Watercress Sauce
1 egg yolk
1/2 cup minced watercress leaves
1/4 cup chopped scallions
2 tablespoons fresh lime juice
1 tablespoon Dijon mustard
1/2 teaspoon salt
Pepper to taste
3/4 cup vegetable oil
2 teaspoons grated lime zest

Catfish
1/2 cup dry bread crumbs
1 tablespoon grated lemon zest
2 teaspoons paprika
2 teaspoons oregano
2 teaspoons salt
1 teaspoon red pepper flakes
1 egg
1/4 cup half-and-half
1/4 teaspoon sugar
6 (31/2-ounce) skinless catfish fillets

For the sauce, combine the egg yolk, watercress, scallions, lime juice, Dijon mustard, salt and pepper in a food processor container and process until smooth. Add the oil gradually, processing constantly until thick and smooth. Combine with the lime zest in a bowl and mix well. Chill, covered, in the refrigerator.

For the catfish, toss the bread crumbs, lemon zest, paprika, oregano, salt and red pepper flakes in a shallow dish. Beat the egg with the half-and-half and sugar in a shallow dish.

Dip the fillets in the egg mixture and coat with the crumbs. Arrange on a lightly greased baking sheet. Bake at 450 degrees for 12 to 14 minutes or until the fish is sizzling and flakes easily with a fork. Serve with the sauce.

Blacken Fish Instantly

A variety of commercial products are available to instantly "blacken" fish and seafood. These may be found at the seafood counter or in the spice section in your grocery store.

CURRIED HALIBUT WITH CHUTNEY

Halibut has a dense white flesh and a mild sweet flavor. This lean fish can easily become too dry if overcooked.

Serves 4

2 tablespoons flour
2 tablespoons curry powder
1/2 teaspoon salt
Freshly ground pepper to taste

4 (8-ounce) halibut steaks
3 tablespoons butter
Peach or mango chutney

Mix the flour, curry powder, salt and pepper together. Coat the halibut steaks on both sides with the mixture. Melt the butter in a cast-iron or nonstick skillet over medium-high heat and add the steaks. Cook just until brown on both sides.

Remove to a baking sheet. Bake at 400 degrees for 10 minutes or until the fish flakes easily with a fork. Serve with chutney.

Chutney is a combination of fruits, vegetables, honey, vinegar and spices; it can be sweet, tart and sometimes spicy. Mango and peach chutneys are good complements to fish and can be purchased at most supermarkets.

KENTUCKY TROUT WITH ALMONDS

Serves 4

8 (4-ounce) trout fillets
Juice of 1 lemon
Salt to taste

1 egg, beaten
1 cup dry bread crumbs
1/2 cup sliced almonds

Sprinkle the fleshy sides of the fillets with the lemon juice and salt. Dip in the egg and coat the fleshy sides with a mixture of the bread crumbs and almonds. Arrange the fillets skin side down on a baking sheet. Bake at 400 degrees for 10 minutes or just until the fish flakes easily with a fork.

PECAN CRUNCH GROUPER

Serves 4

4 (6- to 8-ounce) grouper, salmon or
   amberjack fillets
1/4 cup fresh lemon juice
1/4 teaspoon salt
1/4 teaspoon freshly ground pepper
2 tablespoons Dijon mustard

2 tablespoons butter, melted
1 1/2 tablespoons honey
1/4 cup soft bread crumbs
1/4 cup finely chopped pecans
2 teaspoons chopped fresh parsley

Sprinkle the fillets with the lemon juice, salt and pepper and arrange in a
lightly greased 9 × 13-inch baking pan. Combine the Dijon mustard, butter
and honey in a small bowl and brush on the fillets. Mix the bread crumbs,
pecans and parsley in a small bowl and spoon evenly over the fillets. Bake
at 450 degrees for 10 minutes or until the fish flakes easily with a fork.
Garnish servings with fresh parsley sprigs and/or lemon slices.

PARMESAN DILL GROUPER

Serves 4

1 cup freshly grated Parmesan
   cheese
1/2 cup (1 stick) butter, softened
3 tablespoons mayonnaise
2 scallions, chopped
1 tablespoon chopped fresh
   dillweed

4 (6- to 8-ounce) grouper fillets
1/4 cup fresh lemon juice
1/4 teaspoon salt
1/4 teaspoon freshly ground pepper

Combine the cheese, butter, mayonnaise, scallions and dillweed in a bowl
and mix well. Arrange the fillets in a broiler pan sprayed with nonstick
spray; sprinkle with the lemon juice, salt and pepper. Broil for 8 to
10 minutes or until the fish flakes easily with a fork. Spread with the
cheese mixture. Broil for 2 minutes longer or until the topping is brown.
Garnish with chives tied in the middle and arranged on top of the fillets.

When Is Fish Cooked Just Right?

*Fish should be cooked 10
minutes for every inch of
thickness. Follow this rule
whether the cooking method
you choose is grilling,
broiling, frying, poaching, or
baking. Fresh fish turns
opaque when done. Test by
inserting a knife into the
thickest part of the fish. The
fish should flake easily, and
the juices should run clear.
Or, insert a meat thermometer
at an angle in the thickest
portion of the flesh. Internal
temperature should be at
140 degrees.*

*Seafood is delicate, and
should not be overcooked. It
should be cooked quickly or it
will be tough. When the fish
is done, remove it from the
heat at once.*

GRILLED MAHIMAHI WITH SHERRY SAUCE

Serves 4

4 (8-ounce) mahimahi fillets
2 to 3 tablespoons olive oil
2 medium red onions, thinly sliced
Freshly ground pepper to taste
2 to 3 tablespoons olive oil
1/2 cup cream sherry
1 cup heavy cream
6 tablespoons butter, cut into quarters, softened
Salt to taste

Combine the fish with 2 to 3 tablespoons olive oil in a shallow dish and turn to coat well, ending with the skin side down. Arrange a few slices of red onion on the top and sprinkle with pepper. Marinate, covered, in the refrigerator for 2 to 3 hours.

Sauté the remaining onions in 2 to 3 tablespoons olive oil in a skillet over medium heat until light brown but still crisp. Add the sherry and heavy cream and bring to a boil. Remove from the heat and whisk in the butter 1/4 at a time. Season with salt and pepper.

Remove the fish from the marinade and season both sides with salt. Grill over medium coals until the fish flakes easily with a fork. Reheat the sauce over low heat and drizzle over the fish on a serving platter. Serve with wild rice.

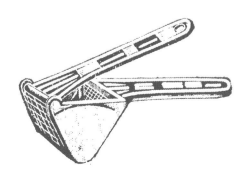

Fish Substitutions

The following substitutions can be used in seafood recipes:

Grouper recipes: Substitute tuna, halibut, or sea bass.

Red snapper recipes: Substitute sea bass, grouper, halibut, or scrod.

Mahimahi recipes: Substitute grouper, halibut, or sea bass.

FILLET OF RED SNAPPER ROQUEFORT

Serves 6 to 8

3/4 cup (1 1/2 sticks) butter, softened
3/4 cup crumbled Roquefort cheese
3/4 cup freshly grated Parmesan cheese
1/3 cup toasted bread crumbs
1 1/2 tablespoons tomato paste
1 1/2 tablespoons lemon juice
1 1/2 teaspoons Worcestershire sauce
1 1/2 teaspoons chopped fresh parsley
2 onions, sliced
3 pounds red snapper fillets
Juice of 1 lemon
Salt and pepper to taste
5 pink peppercorns
3 small dried red peppers
1 bay leaf

Combine the butter, Roquefort cheese, Parmesan cheese, bread crumbs, tomato paste, 1 1/2 tablespoons lemon juice, Worcestershire sauce and parsley in a bowl and mix well.

Scatter the onions in a shallow saucepan. Cut the fish into 6 to 8 portions and sprinkle with the juice of 1 lemon, salt and pepper. Arrange over the onions. Add the peppercorns, dried red peppers, bay leaf and just enough water to cover.

Cover the saucepan with foil and punch several holes in the foil to allow steam to escape. Simmer for 5 minutes; fish will be slightly underdone.

Remove the fish to an ovenproof serving dish. Spread with the cheese mixture. Broil until the topping is brown and bubbly and the fish flakes easily with a fork. Discard the bay leaf, peppercorns and red peppers and serve immediately.

Marinating snapper or any other strong-flavored fish in either Bel Arbor Chardonnay or milk for about one hour minimizes the fishy taste. Adding 1/2 teaspoon of pink peppercorns adds zip to seafood recipes.

*Photo on facing page,
Bonnie Bell Riverboat
on the Ohio River near
the Big Four Bridge
Louisville, Kentucky*

Louisiana Grilled Salmon

Serves 6 to 8

¹/2 cup chopped onion
1 large garlic clove
¹/4 cup Worcestershire sauce
1 teaspoon Tabasco sauce
2 teaspoons dry mustard
1 teaspoon paprika
2 teaspoons salt
1 tablespoon cracked pepper
¹/2 cup olive oil
³/4 cup Southern Comfort
6 to 8 salmon steaks, 1 inch thick

Combine the onion, garlic, Worcestershire sauce, Tabasco sauce, dry mustard, paprika, salt and pepper in a food processor container and pulse until the onion is finely chopped. Add the olive oil and process until mixed. Pour into a bowl and whisk in the liqueur.

Arrange the salmon in a single layer in a shallow nonreactive dish. Pour the marinade over the salmon, turning to coat well. Marinate, covered with plastic wrap, in the refrigerator for 3 to 4 hours, turning once.

Drain, reserving the marinade. Heat the marinade in a small saucepan. Grill the fish 4 to 6 inches from hot coals for 6 to 8 minutes. Turn the fish and baste with the marinade. Grill for 6 to 10 minutes longer or until the fish flakes easily with a fork. Bring the remaining marinade to a boil. Boil for 1 minute. Serve with the salmon.

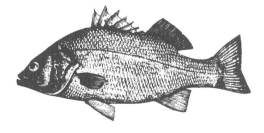

The Magic of Cooking Without Recipes

There are actually cooks who successfully prepare food without recipes, as evidenced by this Kentucky author in her book about her lifelong friend and family cook.

"Annie's cozy kitchen is the heart of her house, which is situated in a quiet and well-tended section of Louisville. An old wooden china cabinet full of beautiful dishes is the focal point of the kitchen. Bright, patterned curtains frame the windows that overlook her deck and backyard. In the center of the room, a large oval table has a lazy Susan as its centerpiece. The kitchen cabinet holds four or five cookbooks, mostly from local churches and clubs. A few of Annie's hand-written recipes are held there between the pages, in no particular order.

(continued at right)

SEARED SPICED SALMON

Serves 6

Black Bean Salsa
4 ounces dried black beans
1 medium red onion, chopped
1/2 cup chopped, seeded, skinned
    tomato
1 red chile, seeded, chopped

1 tablespoon chopped cilantro
1 tablespoon extra-virgin olive oil
Juice of 2 limes
1/2 teaspoon salt

Salmon
3 large garlic cloves
2 teaspoons rock salt
1/2 ounce fresh cilantro leaves
1 (1 1/2-inch) piece of gingerroot,
    chopped
Grated zest of 2 limes

Cinnamon and cumin to taste
Freshly ground pepper to taste
1 tablespoon light olive oil
6 (5- to 6-ounce) salmon steaks
1 tablespoon light olive oil

For the salsa, soak the black beans in enough cold water to cover
overnight; drain and rinse. Combine the beans with enough water to cover
in a saucepan and bring to a boil. Boil for 10 minutes; reduce the heat.
Simmer for 30 minutes or until tender; drain. Let cool. Combine the cooled
beans with the onion, tomato, chile, cilantro, olive oil, lime juice and salt in
a bowl and mix well. Let stand, covered, for several hours to allow the
flavors to marry.

For the salmon, crush the garlic and rock salt with a pestle in a mortar.
Reserve 6 sprigs of the cilantro for garnish and chop the remaining
cilantro. Add the chopped cilantro, gingerroot, lime zest, cinnamon, cumin,
pepper and 1 tablespoon olive oil to the mortar and mix well. Wipe the
salmon with damp paper towels and remove any visible bones. Place on a
platter. Spread the spice mixture over the salmon and cover with plastic
wrap. Marinate in the refrigerator for several hours. Brush a baking sheet
with 1 tablespoon olive oil and place under the preheated broiler until very
hot. Place the salmon on the baking sheet. Broil 3 inches from the heat
source for exactly 7 minutes. Remove the skin with a sharp knife and place
the salmon on a heated serving platter. Garnish with the reserved cilantro
sprigs and serve with the salsa.

CUCUMBER MUSTARD SMOKED SALMON

Serves 8

Salmon
8 (1- to 1¹/₂-inch) salmon steaks with skin
2 cups water
¹/₂ cup packed brown sugar
1 tablespoon salt
1 teaspoon red pepper

Cucumber Mustard Sauce
³/₄ cup sour cream
¹/₂ cup chopped peeled cucumber
¹/₄ cup mayonnaise
¹/₄ cup prepared mustard
1 tablespoon chopped fresh chives
¹/₂ teaspoon chopped fresh parsley
¹/₄ teaspoon salt
¹/₄ teaspoon dillweed

For the salmon, arrange the salmon in a single layer in 2 large shallow dishes. Combine the water, brown sugar, salt and red pepper in a bowl and mix well. Pour over the salmon, turning to coat. Marinate, covered, in the refrigerator for 6 hours, turning occasionally.

Prepare a charcoal fire in a smoker. Let burn for 10 to 15 minutes. Sprinkle hickory chips over the hot coals. Fill the water pan in the smoker with hot water. Arrange the salmon steaks on a rack in the smoker. Smoke, covered, for 1 to 1¹/₂ hours or to the desired degree of doneness, adding additional charcoal as needed. Transfer the salmon to a serving platter. Garnish with sprigs of fresh chives.

For the sauce, combine the sour cream, cucumber, mayonnaise, prepared mustard, chives, parsley, salt and dillweed in a bowl and mix well. Chill, covered, for 1 hour or longer. Serve with the salmon.

"Smoke" Marinade

If you do not have a smoker, or do not want to go to the effort of smoking fish, you can achieve a "smoky" taste by marinating the fish prior to cooking. The following recipe is a marinade for any fish that benefits from this flavoring, such as salmon, halibut, trout, swordfish, bluefish, or butterfish.

Process 2 chopped cloves of garlic, ¹/₂ cup olive oil, 2 tablespoons fresh lemon juice, 1 teaspoon commercial smoke flavoring (available in a number of flavors, including mesquite and hickory) and ¹/₂ teaspoon salt in a blender. Marinate fish in the refrigerator for 1 hour before cooking.

WOK-SEARED ASIAN SALMON

This recipe for Wok-Seared Asian Salmon with Spicy Shrimp Fried Rice was created by Chef Jim McKinney, Club Grotto.

Serves 1

1 (4- to 5-ounce) salmon fillet
1/2 teaspoon minced shallot
1/4 teaspoon minced gingerroot
1/4 teaspoon minced garlic
1 teaspoon sesame oil
1 teaspoon peanut oil
1 ounce finely chopped carrot
1 ounce finely chopped onion
1 pinch each minced serrano and Thai chiles
3 to 4 ounces jasmine rice, cooked
1 tablespoon rice wine
3 (21- to 25-count) shrimp, peeled, deveined
1 1/2 teaspoons soy sauce or reduced-sodium soy sauce
1 tablespoon green peas, blanched

Sear the salmon fillet in a heated wok. Remove to a baking pan and place in a 350-degree oven while the rice is prepared.

Stir-fry the shallot, gingerroot and garlic in the sesame oil and peanut oil in the wok. Add the carrot, onion and chiles. Stir-fry until tender-crisp. Add the rice and stir-fry until brown. Add the rice wine and shrimp. Cook just until the shrimp are pink and opaque. Stir in the soy sauce and peas.

Mound the rice and shrimp mixture on a plate and top with the salmon.

To garnish, make a paste of hot mustard and soy sauce and spoon around the edge of the plate. Boil teriyaki sauce to a syrupy consistency and use to drizzle Chinese characters on top. Finish with crisp-fried leeks if desired.

"I am a very passionate person about my family, friends and cooking! My goal is to create food that is not only stimulating to one's palate, but is also visually pleasing to one's eye."

CHEF JIM MCKINNEY
CLUB GROTTO

SWORDFISH WITH GRAPEFRUIT SALSA

Serves 4

Grapefruit Salsa
4 to 6 ruby or pink grapefruit
1 lime
1/2 green chile, seeded, thinly sliced
1/3 cup chopped scallions
2 tablespoons chopped fresh cilantro
1 tablespoon sugar
3 tablespoons Pepe Lopez Tequila

Swordfish
4 teaspoons fresh lime juice
2 tablespoons olive oil
Freshly ground pepper to taste
4 (8-ounce) swordfish steaks

For the salsa, grate the zest from the grapefruit and lime with a zester and combine in a bowl. Squeeze the juice from the lime into the bowl. Section the grapefruit, discarding all the pith, and add to the bowl. Add the green chile, scallions, cilantro, sugar and tequila and mix well.

For the swordfish, combine the lime juice, olive oil and pepper in a shallow dish or sealable bag. Add the swordfish and coat well. Marinate in the refrigerator for 1 hour; drain.

Grill over medium-high heat for 4 to 5 minutes on each side or until cooked through, or broil for 4 minutes on each side. Serve with the salsa.

As an alternative to the salsa, serve the swordfish with Ginger Cilantro Butter. Combine 2 tablespoons softened butter, 2 teaspoons chopped fresh cilantro, 2 minced garlic cloves and 1 teaspoon grated gingerroot and mix well. Spread over the hot swordfish and garnish with cilantro sprigs and lime slices.

Grilling Fish

Preparing fish on the grill can enhance the flavor, particularly if you use mesquite or hickory chips or some of the new "flavored" charcoal briquettes. Try throwing a few bay leaves on the briquettes. Generally, firm or compact fish can be placed directly on the preheated grill. These varieties include halibut, grouper, tuna, swordfish, and mahimahi.

More delicate varieties may fall apart if placed directly on the grill and will fare better if placed in a basket. These include salmon, trout, whitefish, cod, or sea bass.

Another grilling technique is threading the fish on a skewer. Tuna, swordfish, and shellfish such as scallops and shrimp can be grilled using this method.

(continued at right)

OLIVE VINAIGRETTE SAUTÉED TUNA

Serves 4

1 garlic clove, minced
1 teaspoon Dijon mustard
2 teaspoons balsamic vinegar
1 tablespoon water
3 tablespoons olive oil
5 kalamata olives, chopped
2 teaspoons drained capers, chopped
1 plum tomato, seeded, chopped
4 (1-inch) tuna steaks
Salt and pepper to taste
1 tablespoon olive oil
2 tablespoons finely chopped roasted red bell pepper
1 tablespoon finely chopped green onions

Combine the garlic, Dijon mustard, balsamic vinegar and water in a bowl and whisk until well mixed. Whisk in 3 tablespoons olive oil gradually. Add the olives, capers and tomato and mix well.

Pat the tuna steaks dry and season with salt and pepper. Heat 1 tablespoon olive oil in a heavy nonstick skillet over medium-high heat until hot but not smoking. Add the tuna and cook for 4 to 5 minutes on each side or just until cooked through. Remove to a warm platter and wipe the skillet.

Add the vinaigrette mixture to the skillet and cook over medium heat until heated through. Stir in the roasted bell pepper and green onions. Spoon over the tuna. Garnish with additional roasted bell pepper and green onions. Serve with lemon wedges.

If the fish has not been marinated, spread vegetable or olive oil on both sides prior to grilling so that the fish does not stick to the grill or grilling basket. You can also spray the basket or skewers with a nonstick cooking spray.

Be careful not to overcook the fish.

Fish that are good for grilling are:

Bass	*Pompano*
Cod	*Redfish*
Crappie	*Red Snapper*
Flounder	*Salmon*
Freshwater Bass	*Scrod*
	Sole
Grouper	*Swordfish*
Halibut	*Trout*
Mackerel	*Tuna*
Mahimahi	*Whitefish*

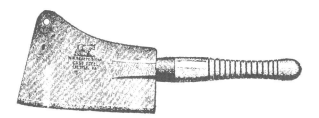

TROPICAL TUNA

Serves 4

Pineapple Pepper Salsa
1 green bell pepper, chopped
1 red bell pepper, chopped
1 (8-ounce) can juice-pack crushed pineapple
1 medium red onion, chopped
$1/2$ cup orange juice

Tuna
4 (8-ounce) tuna steaks
Salt and pepper to taste

Hollandaise Sauce
$1/2$ cup (1 stick) butter
2 egg yolks
2 tablespoons fresh lemon juice
$1/2$ teaspoon salt
Cayenne pepper to taste

For the salsa, combine the bell peppers, undrained pineapple, onion and orange juice in a bowl and mix well.

For the tuna, season the steaks with salt and pepper. Grill over hot coals until the steaks flake easily with a fork.

For the sauce, melt the butter in a small saucepan and heat to bubbling. Combine the egg yolks, lemon juice, salt and cayenne pepper in a blender container and pulse twice. Set the blender to high speed and add the butter gradually, blending constantly until thickened and smooth.

To serve, place the tuna steaks on serving plates. Spoon the salsa onto the steaks. Drizzle with the warm sauce.

Tuna Tips

Tuna is available as whole loins or steaks. All tuna has dark red streaks of meat running down both sides that is oilier and stronger-tasting. Trimming off this part of the tuna before cooking will result in a milder taste. Tuna meat tends to be soft before cooking but firms up and becomes meaty when cooked. Fresh tuna is best when cooked to a succulent medium-rare. Avoid overcooking tuna; it makes the meat dry and tasteless.

Savory Seafood Torta

Serves 6 to 8

$1/2$ cup sherry
$1/2$ cup water
Red pepper flakes to taste
4 ounces plaice, sole or codfish fillets
8 ounces peeled cooked shrimp
4 ounces flaked crab meat
2 tablespoons butter
2 tablespoons flour
1 garlic clove, crushed
1 refrigerator pie pastry
2 egg yolks
$1/2$ cup heavy cream
Chopped fresh parsley to taste
Salt and black pepper to taste
$1/4$ cup grated Parmesan cheese

Combine the sherry, water and red pepper flakes in a saucepan and add the fish. Cook for 10 minutes or until the fish flakes easily and is firm to the touch. Drain, reserving the cooking liquid. Flake the fish into a bowl and add the shrimp and crab meat. Strain the reserved liquid.

Melt the butter in a small saucepan and stir in the flour. Cook for several minutes, stirring constantly. Stir in the reserved liquid gradually and add the garlic. Bring to a boil over high heat, stirring constantly. Reduce the heat and cook for 1 minute longer, stirring constantly. Pour over the seafood mixture and mix gently. Let stand until cool.

Roll the pastry on a lightly floured surface to fit a 10-inch springform pan. Press the pastry into the pan and trim the edge. Prick the bottom and cover with waxed paper. Fill with dried beans or pie weights. Chill for 10 minutes. Bake at 375 degrees for 15 minutes; remove the beans or weights.

Combine the egg yolks, heavy cream and parsley in a bowl and mix well. Stir into the seafood mixture. Season with salt and black pepper. Spoon the seafood mixture into the prepared pastry and top with the cheese. Bake for 25 minutes. Cool slightly and place on a serving plate. Remove the side of the pan and slice into wedges to serve.

CRAB CAKES WITH HORSERADISH SAUCE

Serves 6 to 8

1 pound fresh lump crab meat
1/4 cup dry bread crumbs
3 green onions, chopped
1/4 cup chopped fresh parsley
1/4 teaspoon salt
1/4 teaspoon cayenne pepper

1/4 teaspoon freshly ground
  black pepper
1/4 to 1/2 cup mayonnaise
Bread crumbs for coating
2 to 3 tablespoons vegetable oil
Horseradish Sauce (at right)

Combine the crab meat, 1/4 cup bread crumbs, green onions, parsley, salt, cayenne pepper and black pepper in a bowl and mix well. Add 1/4 cup mayonnaise, or enough to bind, and mix well. Shape into 6 to 8 patties. Coat with additional bread crumbs. Fry in the heated oil in a nonstick skillet over medium heat for 2 to 3 minutes on each side or until golden brown. Drain on paper towels. Serve with Horseradish Sauce.

GRILLED BOURBON SHRIMP SKEWERS

Serves 6 to 8

3 tablespoons Old Forester
3 tablespoons honey
1 tablespoon soy sauce
2 tablespoons Creole mustard

3 tablespoons minced onion
1/2 teaspoon freshly ground pepper
2 pounds deveined peeled shrimp

Soak 6 to 8 wooden skewers in water for 1 hour. Combine the bourbon, honey, soy sauce, mustard, onion and pepper in a bowl and mix well. Add the shrimp and mix well. Marinate, covered, in the refrigerator for 1 to 2 hours, stirring every 15 to 20 minutes.

Spray the grill with nonstick cooking spray and let stand for 5 minutes. Preheat the grill on medium for 10 minutes. Drain the shrimp, reserving the marinade. Thread the shrimp onto the skewers.

Grill the shrimp for 3 to 4 minutes on each side or until pink and opaque, basting occasionally with the reserved marinade.

HORSERADISH SAUCE

1/2 cup sour cream
1/4 cup mayonnaise
2 tablespoons prepared
  horseradish

Combine the sour cream, mayonnaise and prepared horseradish in a bowl and mix well. Store, covered, in the refrigerator until serving time.

BARBECUED SHRIMP

Serves 6

2¹/₂ pounds large or jumbo fresh shrimp in shells
1 medium onion, thinly sliced
2 lemons, thinly sliced
1 cup (2 sticks) butter, melted
³/₄ cup lemon juice
³/₄ cup Worcestershire sauce
2 to 3 teaspoons hot sauce
3 medium garlic cloves, chopped
1 teaspoon rosemary leaves
1 tablespoon salt
¹/₈ teaspoon ground red pepper
1 tablespoon coarsely ground black pepper

Rinse the shrimp and drain well. Layer the shrimp, onion and lemons in a 9 × 13-inch baking dish.

Combine the butter, lemon juice, Worcestershire sauce, hot sauce, garlic, rosemary, salt, red pepper and black pepper in a bowl and mix well. Pour over the prepared layers.

Bake at 400 degrees for 20 to 25 minutes or until the shrimp are pink and opaque. Serve the shrimp with the cooking sauce and French bread for dipping. Garnish with sprigs of fresh rosemary.

Tomato, Cheese and Herb Tart
(Photo, pages 170–171)

Freshness is at the heart
of all fine vegetable cookery,
and that freshness must
be guarded jealously.

Camille Glenn
The Heritage of Southern Cooking

GREEN BEAN BUNDLES

This colorful arrangement is the perfect complement to Sunday brunch.

Serves 8

8 ounces haricots verts or any tiny young green beans
1 yellow squash, about 1¹/₂ inches in diameter
2 tablespoons extra-virgin olive oil
2 garlic cloves, minced
1 tablespoon finely chopped shallots
¹/₂ teaspoon tarragon, crushed
Salt and pepper to taste

Snap off the stem end of each bean. Arrange the beans in 8 stacks, about 10 to 12 beans per stack. Cut the squash into eight ¹/₂-inch slices. Hollow out each slice to within ¹/₄ inch of peel. Thread the bean stacks through the squash rings.

Place the bean bundles in a steamer basket in a large saucepan. Add enough water to measure 1 inch; the water should not touch the bottom of the basket. Cover the saucepan. Bring to a boil over high heat. Steam for 4 minutes or until the beans turn bright green and are tender-crisp, adding additional water as needed to prevent the pan from boiling dry.

Heat the olive oil in a skillet over medium-high heat. Add the garlic, shallots and tarragon and mix well. Cook until the garlic is tender but not brown, stirring constantly. Remove from the heat.

Transfer the bean bundles to a serving platter. Drizzle with the garlic oil. Sprinkle with salt and pepper. Garnish with sprigs of fresh herbs and/or sliced cherry tomatoes. Serve immediately.

Are You from Beans?

"I am from beans—green, lima and pea—picked, strung, snapped and shelled into pans, and put on the stove to simmer for hours."

MARIE BRADBY
MOMMA, WHERE ARE YOU FROM?

174

COLD ASPARAGUS VINAIGRETTE

A festive dish for your holiday buffet.

Serves 3 or 4

1 bunch asparagus
¼ cup gourmet Italian salad dressing
2 tablespoons balsamic vinegar
2 tablespoons finely chopped red bell pepper
½ teaspoon whole sesame seeds

Discard the tough ends of the asparagus. Blanch the asparagus in boiling water in a saucepan. Plunge the asparagus into ice water in a bowl to stop the cooking process. Drain and pat dry.

Arrange the asparagus on a serving platter. Drizzle with the salad dressing and balsamic vinegar. Sprinkle with the bell pepper and sesame seeds.

You may prepare in advance by blanching the asparagus and storing in the refrigerator. Add the salad dressing, balsamic vinegar, bell pepper and sesame seeds 20 minutes before serving.

Seasonal Menus

"Let the seasons guide your menu planning. Fix asparagus in the spring (and let the kids eat it with their fingers), tomatoes in the summer, squash in the fall. Don't worry about being repetitive. Many growing seasons are short and you'll be through it and on to the next vegetable in the blink of an eye."

SARAH FRITSCHNER
EXPRESS LANE COOKBOOK

Frazier's Corn Pudding

This recipe will add a touch of comfort to your next brunch, tailgate party, or barbecue.

Serves 6 to 8

1 (14-ounce) can cream-style corn
1 (11-ounce) can whole kernel corn
1 (8-ounce) package corn bread mix
1/2 cup (1 stick) butter, melted
2 eggs, lightly beaten
1 cup sour cream

Combine the cream-style corn, undrained whole kernel corn, corn bread mix, butter, eggs and sour cream in a bowl and mix well. Spoon into a 1-quart baking dish. Bake at 350 degrees for 35 to 40 minutes or until golden brown.

Fresh Dill and Green Bean Stir-Fry

Serves 4 to 6

11/2 pounds fresh green beans, trimmed
2 tablespoons water
4 teaspoons vegetable oil
6 scallions, sliced
1/4 cup chopped fresh dillweed
3 tablespoons red wine vinegar
1/2 teaspoon salt

Combine the green beans and water in a microwave-safe dish. Microwave, covered, on High for 5 minutes; drain. Heat the oil in a large skillet over high heat until hot. Add the beans.

Stir-fry for 4 minutes or until brown specks appear on the beans. Stir in the scallions, dillweed, wine vinegar and salt. Reduce the heat to medium.

Stir-fry for 8 minutes longer. Spoon onto a serving platter. Serve immediately.

EGGPLANT ROULADE

Try this vegetarian version of the French roulade, which is traditionally a thin slice of meat rolled around a filling.

Serves 4

1 large eggplant, peeled
Salt to taste
Olive oil
1 cup ricotta cheese
1/2 medium onion, chopped
1/2 red or green bell pepper, chopped
1/4 cup chopped assorted fresh herbs (basil, thyme, oregano, parsley, chervil)
Freshly ground pepper
2 cups homemade or prepared tomato sauce
4 ounces mozzarella cheese, shredded

Cut the eggplant lengthwise into eight 1/4-inch slices. Sprinkle the slices with salt. Drain in a colander for 30 to 60 minutes. Pat the slices dry with paper towels.

Brush both sides of the eggplant slices with olive oil. Arrange the slices in a single layer on an oiled baking sheet. Broil 4 to 5 inches from the heat source for 3 to 4 minutes per side or until tender; do not brown.

Combine the ricotta cheese, onion, bell pepper and fresh herbs in a bowl and mix well. Season with salt and pepper. Spoon 1 heaping tablespoon of the ricotta mixture on the large end of each eggplant slice and roll to enclose the filling. Arrange the rolls seam side down in an oiled 9 × 13-inch baking dish. Drizzle the rolls with the tomato sauce. Sprinkle with the mozzarella cheese.

Bake at 350 degrees for 30 minutes or until the sauce is bubbly and the cheese melts.

Eggplant Essentials

Eggplant belongs to the potato family and surprisingly originated not with eggplant Parmesan but in India and Asia thousands of years ago. British traders brought this vegetable to the London market in the seventeenth century. Due to their unusual color and size, eggplant are a bit intimidating for some people to work with. Here are some tips to make fresh eggplant recipes turn out great:

- *When purchasing eggplant look for those that are heavy and firm and have a shiny, uniform color*

- *After peeling and slicing, salt each slice and place slices in a colander for 20 to 30 minutes to allow excess moisture to drain*

- *After slicing, rub each slice with lemon to help retain the white color*

MUSHROOM TART

A real treat for the mushroom lover.

Serves 10

$1/2$ **(15-ounce) package refrigerated pie pastry**
1 cup chopped fresh shiitake mushrooms
1 cup sliced fresh brown or white mushrooms
1 cup chopped fresh oyster mushrooms
$1/2$ **teaspoon snipped fresh marjoram, or** $1/8$ **teaspoon dried marjoram**
2 tablespoons butter
$3/4$ **cup shredded Gruyère cheese**
$3/4$ **cup shredded Swiss cheese**
$1/2$ **cup chopped Canadian bacon**
$1/2$ **cup milk**
2 eggs, lightly beaten
1 tablespoon snipped fresh chives

Fit the pastry into a 9-inch tart pan with a removable bottom. Press the pastry into the flutes and trim even with the top edge; do not prick the pastry. Line the pastry with 2 sheets of foil. Bake at 450 degrees for 8 minutes. Remove the foil. Bake for 4 to 5 minutes longer or until set and dry. Reduce the oven temperature to 375 degrees.

Sauté the shiitake mushrooms, brown or white mushrooms, oyster mushrooms and marjoram in the butter in a skillet over medium-high heat for 4 to 5 minutes or until the mushrooms are tender and the liquid has been absorbed. Remove from the heat.

Combine the Gruyère cheese, Swiss cheese and Canadian bacon in a bowl and mix well. Stir in the mushroom mixture, milk, eggs and chives. Pour into the partially baked tart shell.

Bake at 375 degrees for 20 minutes or until set and golden brown. Cool in the pan on a wire rack for 10 to 15 minutes. Remove from the pan. Cut into wedges. Garnish with Canadian bacon wedges and sprigs of fresh marjoram.

SWEET ONION, OLIVE AND BACON TART

Serves 6 to 8

Pastry
1¼ cups unbleached flour
1 tablespoon chopped fresh thyme
¼ teaspoon salt

½ cup (1 stick) unsalted butter, chilled, cut into 8 pieces
⅓ cup sour cream

Tart
4 slices bacon
3 tablespoons olive oil
1½ pounds sweet onions, thinly sliced

¾ cup chopped kalamata olives
Freshly grated nutmeg
Salt and pepper to taste

For the pastry, combine the flour, thyme and salt in a food processor container. Process until mixed. Add the butter. Process until crumbly. Spoon the sour cream in dollops around the inside of the food processor container. Pulse just until a firm ball gathers around the blade. Remove the dough and shape into an oval. Roll into a 12- to 14-inch circle ⅛ inch thick on a lightly floured surface. Place on a lightly floured baking sheet or pizza pan. Chill, covered, until ready to bake.

For the tart, fry the bacon in a heavy skillet over medium heat until crisp. Drain, discarding the bacon drippings. Crumble the bacon into bite-size pieces. Add the olive oil to the skillet. Heat over medium-low heat until hot. Add the onions. Sauté for 30 to 45 minutes or until tender. Stir in the olives and bacon. Season with nutmeg, salt and pepper. Let stand until cool.

Remove the pastry from the refrigerator. Let stand at room temperature until slightly softened. Spread the onion mixture evenly over the surface of the pastry, leaving a 2-inch border. Fold the uncovered edge of the pastry over the onion mixture. Bake at 375 degrees for 30 minutes or until the pastry is brown. Let stand for 10 minutes before serving. Serve warm or at room temperature with fresh tomato slices.

If time is of the essence, substitute the homemade pastry with commercially prepared pie pastry.

No More Tears

Preparing onions for cooking can literally bring tears to your eyes. Here are a few hints to keep those tears away:

- *Cut onions under running water. The water will neutralize the sulfuric acid, therefore eliminating the tears*

- *Begin slicing at the top of the onion. Sulfuric acid is found in greater amounts in the root end of the onion*

- *Refrigerate onions before cutting to reduce the release of sulfuric acid*

- *Mince or dice onions in the food processor or garlic press*

CARAMELIZED ONION PUDDING

Created by Chef Kathy Cary of Lilly's, onions never tasted so good.

Serves 4 to 6

3 cups sliced onions
1/4 cup (1/2 stick) butter
3 eggs
1 cup heavy cream
2 tablespoons sugar

2 tablespoons flour
1 teaspoon salt
1 teaspoon baking powder
4 ounces Capriole goat cheese, crumbled (optional)

Cook the onions in the butter in a skillet over low heat for 20 to 30 minutes or until tender, stirring occasionally.

Whisk the eggs in a bowl until blended. Add the heavy cream, sugar, flour, salt and baking powder and mix well. Beat in the goat cheese. Stir in the onion mixture. Pour into a greased 7 × 10-inch baking dish. Bake at 350 degrees on the middle oven rack for 25 minutes or until set. Serve with pork dishes.

May be prepared 1 day in advance, refrigerated overnight, and baked just before serving. Bring to room temperature before baking. This recipe is easily doubled. Bake in a 9 × 13-inch baking dish for 35 minutes or until set.

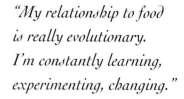

"My relationship to food is really evolutionary. I'm constantly learning, experimenting, changing."

CHEF KATHY CARY
LILLY'S

GARLIC GRUYÈRE MASHED POTATOES

Serves 6 to 8

6 medium potatoes, peeled
3/4 cup milk, heated
1/2 cup sour cream
1/4 cup (1/2 stick) butter, softened

1 garlic clove, minced
1/2 teaspoon salt
1/8 teaspoon ground red pepper
3 ounces Gruyère cheese, shredded

Cut the potatoes into 1-inch cubes. Combine the potatoes with enough water to cover in a saucepan. Bring to a boil. Boil for 15 minutes or until tender; drain. Beat the potatoes in a mixing bowl until smooth. Stir in the hot milk, sour cream, butter, garlic, salt and red pepper. Add the cheese and mix well. Serve immediately.

ROSEMARY AND GARLIC RED POTATOES

Serves 6 to 8

1 1/2 pounds small red potatoes, cut into quarters
1 tablespoon unsalted butter
1 tablespoon extra-virgin olive oil
3 garlic cloves, minced
4 teaspoons chopped fresh rosemary, or 2 teaspoons dried rosemary
Salt and freshly ground pepper to taste

Arrange the potatoes in a microwave-safe dish. Microwave, covered, just until tender-crisp or firm when pierced with a fork.

Heat the butter and olive oil in a cast-iron skillet or skillet over medium-high heat until the butter melts; do not scorch. Add the potatoes, garlic and rosemary. Sauté until light brown; reduce the heat to medium-low. Cook, covered, for 10 to 12 minutes, stirring occasionally. Season with salt and pepper. Serve immediately.

TENDER PEAS WITH PARMESAN

Serves 6

2 (10-ounce) packages frozen baby green peas
1/4 cup freshly grated Parmesan cheese
2 tablespoons butter, softened
1 tablespoon fresh lemon juice
1/2 teaspoon salt
1/4 teaspoon tarragon
1/8 teaspoon freshly grated lemon zest

Cook the peas using package directions; drain. Combine the peas, Parmesan cheese, butter, lemon juice, salt, tarragon and lemon zest in a bowl and mix well. Serve immediately with additional Parmesan cheese.

SPINACH TIMBALES

Serves 6 to 8

Melted butter
1 (10-ounce) package frozen chopped spinach
1/4 cup chopped onion
2 tablespoons butter
2 eggs
1 teaspoon salt
1/8 teaspoon pepper
1/8 teaspoon coriander or nutmeg
1 cup bread crumbs
1/2 cup half-and-half
1/2 cup milk
1/2 cup shredded Swiss cheese

Coat the inside of 6 to 8 individual timbale molds with melted butter, tilting the molds to coat completely. Cook the spinach in boiling water in a saucepan just until tender; drain. Press the spinach to remove the excess moisture.

Sauté the onion in 2 tablespoons butter in a skillet until tender. Stir in the spinach. Cook for 3 minutes, stirring frequently. Process the eggs in a food processor for 3 to 4 seconds. Add the spinach mixture, salt, pepper and coriander. Process until mixed. Add the bread crumbs, half-and-half, milk and cheese. Process until mixed.

Fill the prepared timbale molds 2/3 full. Place the molds in a baking pan. Add enough water to the baking pan to measure 1/4 inch. Bake at 350 degrees for 35 to 40 minutes or until set.

To save time, prepare the timbales 1 to 2 weeks in advance and store, tightly wrapped, in the freezer. Thaw in the refrigerator for 2 hours before baking. Most any green vegetable can be substituted for the spinach. When substituting artichokes, use Parmesan cheese in place of the Swiss cheese.

Photo on facing page,
Goddard Bridge
Fleming County, Kentucky

BUTTERNUT SQUASH CASSEROLE

Harvest gold for the autumn table and almost as good as dessert from the Pinecrest Cottage Bed & Breakfast in Louisville, Kentucky.

Serves 8 to 10

1¹/₂ to 3 pounds butternut squash
6 tablespoons butter, softened
³/₄ cup sugar
1 (5-ounce) can evaporated milk
2 eggs
1 teaspoon vanilla extract
1 cup crisp rice cereal
¹/₂ cup packed brown sugar
¹/₂ cup chopped pecans
¹/₄ cup (¹/₂ stick) butter, melted

Cut the squash lengthwise into halves; discard the seeds. Arrange the halves cut side down in a microwave-safe dish or place directly on the carousel plate in the microwave. Microwave for 20 to 35 minutes or until tender. Scoop the pulp into a bowl, discarding the peel. Mash enough of the squash to measure 2 cups.

Beat 6 tablespoons butter and sugar in a mixing bowl until creamy. Add 2 cups squash, evaporated milk, eggs and vanilla. Beat until mixed. Spoon the squash mixture into a 9 × 13-inch baking dish. Bake at 350 degrees for 1 hour or until a knife inserted in the center comes out clean.

Combine the cereal, brown sugar, pecans and ¹/₄ cup butter in a bowl and mix well. Sprinkle over the top of the squash mixture. Bake for 5 to 10 minutes longer or until bubbly.

For variety, dot with pecan halves and omit the chopped pecans.

Perfect Squash

Squash can generally be divided into two categories — summer and winter. Summer squash consists of zucchini, yellow squash, summer squash, and crooknecks. Winter squash includes acorn and butternut. A good squash of the summer variety is no longer than eight inches with a diameter of no more than two inches. It should be firm and rigid with a smooth, dry, vibrantly colored skin. A good winter squash is heavier than it looks and has deep, vibrant color. It should have a smooth surface free of any gouges, cracks, or soft spots.

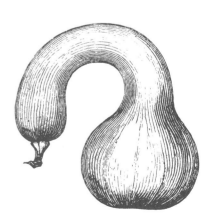

BOURBON-SPIKED SWEET POTATOES

Enjoy a splash of Kentucky history during Thanksgiving dinner.

Serves 8

5 pounds unpeeled medium sweet potatoes
1/4 cup heavy cream
1 tablespoon fresh lemon juice
1/2 teaspoon finely grated lemon zest
Salt and freshly ground pepper to taste
1/3 cup Woodford Reserve Bourbon
1/4 cup packed dark brown sugar

Pierce the sweet potatoes with a fork. Arrange in a large roasting pan. Roast at 450 degrees for 1 hour or until tender and brown on the bottom. Let stand for 15 minutes.

Peel the sweet potatoes, reserving as much of the caramelized pulp as possible. Cut into large chunks. Combine the sweet potatoes, heavy cream, lemon juice, lemon zest, salt and pepper in a food processor container. Process until puréed.

Combine the bourbon and brown sugar in a large nonreactive saucepan. Bring just to a boil, stirring occasionally. Stir in the sweet potato mixture. Cook over low heat just until heated through, stirring occasionally. Spoon into a serving bowl. Serve immediately.

You may prepare the sweet potato purée in advance and store, covered, in the refrigerator. Reheat over low heat.

CREOLE CORN-STUFFED TOMATOES

Serves 4

4 tomatoes
Salt to taste
2 slices bacon
1 red onion, chopped
1 green bell pepper, chopped
2 green onion bulbs, chopped
1 bay leaf
Kernels of 2 ears of corn
$1/4$ teaspoon salt
$1/8$ teaspoon black pepper
Cayenne pepper to taste

Slice off the top quarter of each tomato. Scoop the pulp from the tomatoes into a bowl. Sprinkle the inside of each tomato shell with salt to taste. Invert the shells onto paper towels. Drain for 20 minutes.

Fry the bacon in a skillet until crisp. Drain, reserving the bacon drippings. Crumble the bacon. Sauté the red onion, bell pepper and green onions in the reserved bacon drippings over medium heat for 8 minutes. Add the tomato pulp and bay leaf and mix well.

Simmer for 10 minutes, stirring occasionally. Stir in the corn. Simmer for 10 minutes longer, stirring occasionally. Discard the bay leaf. Stir in the bacon, $1/4$ teaspoon salt, black pepper and cayenne pepper. Spoon into the tomato shells.

Arrange the stuffed tomatoes in nonstick muffin cups. Bake at 400 degrees for 30 minutes.

You may prepare the stuffed tomatoes in advance and store, covered, in the refrigerator until ready to bake.

Elegant Broccoli

More than 75 years ago, no one outside the Italian community ate broccoli. But a few enterprising Italian farmers in California shipped crates of broccoli to Boston and sparked an interest in broccoli as a commercial crop.

Consider these finishing touches to serve with or over 4 cups steamed broccoli—

- *With Crumbs—heat 6 tablespoons butter in a sauté pan, add $1/2$ cup fresh (or Italian seasoned) bread crumbs and sauté until crumbs are light brown.*

- *With Garlic—melt $1/4$ cup butter in a sauté pan until brown, add 2 teaspoons finely chopped garlic and mix (do not brown garlic). Serve immediately.*

(continued at right)

TOMATO, CHEESE AND HERB TART

Put your bumper crop of summer tomatoes to good use in this easy recipe.

Serves 8

Pastry
1¹/4 cups flour
¹/4 teaspoon salt
¹/2 cup (1 stick) butter, chilled, cut into 8 pieces
¹/4 cup (about) ice water

Tomato Filling
4 medium tomatoes, cut into ¹/4-inch slices
9 ounces Emmentaler or Gruyère cheese, sliced
3 tablespoons chopped mixed fresh herbs (basil, thyme or oregano)
3 tablespoons grated Parmesan cheese

For the pastry, combine the flour and salt in a food processor container. Add the butter. Pulse until crumbly. Add the water 1 tablespoon at a time, processing constantly until a moist dough forms. Shape the dough into a ball; flatten into a disk. Chill, wrapped in plastic wrap, for 30 minutes.

Roll the dough into a 13-inch circle on a lightly floured surface. Fit into an 11-inch tart pan with removable bottom. Trim the edge. Freeze for 15 minutes. Line the pastry with foil. Weight down with dried beans or pie weights. Bake at 375 degrees for 15 minutes. Remove the beans and foil. Bake for 15 minutes longer or until light golden brown. Let stand until cool. May be prepared 1 day in advance and stored, covered, at room temperature.

For the filling, cut each tomato slice into halves. Drain on paper towels for 45 minutes. Sprinkle the Emmentaler cheese over the bottom of the baked layer. Arrange the tomatoes over the cheese, overlapping slightly. Sprinkle with the herbs and Parmesan cheese. Bake at 375 degrees for 35 minutes or until the cheese melts and the tomatoes are tender. Cool slightly. Remove the side of the pan. Cut the tart into wedges.

Serve as an appetizer, side dish or on top of a baby lettuce salad tossed with balsamic vinaigrette. You may substitute a commercially prepared pie pastry for the homemade pastry.

- *With Pine Nuts — melt ¹/4 cup of butter in a sauté pan until light brown, add ¹/2 cup toasted pine nuts and mix.*

- *With Lemon Zest and Almonds — melt ¹/4 cup of butter in a sauté pan, add ¹/4 cup sliced almonds, 2 tablespoons fresh lemon juice and ¹/2 teaspoon lemon zest and mix well.*

GRILLED VEGETABLES OVER RICE

Raid your garden for this heavenly vegetarian summer fare.

Serves 4

Lemon Herb Dressing
1/2 cup fresh lemon juice
1/2 cup olive oil
1/4 cup vegetable oil

3 garlic cloves
1/8 teaspoon salt
1 tablespoon chopped fresh basil

Grilled Vegetables
1 cup long grain rice
2 cups chicken stock or water
2 medium yellow squash
2 medium zucchini
4 medium carrots
1 medium red onion

2 portobello mushroom caps,
   cut into halves
Olive oil
1/4 cup freshly grated Parmesan
   cheese
Freshly ground pepper

For the dressing, combine the lemon juice, olive oil, vegetable oil, garlic and salt in a food processor or blender container. Process until the garlic is minced. Pour into a jar with a tight-fitting lid. Add the basil. Cover and shake to mix. Store in the refrigerator.

For the vegetables, cook the rice using package directions and substituting the stock for the water. Slice the squash, zucchini and carrots lengthwise into 3 long strips. Cut the onion into 4 slices.

Pour 1/4 cup of the dressing into a bowl large enough to hold all of the vegetables. Spray both sides of each vegetable with olive oil. Grill, covered, over hot coals for 2 minutes per side or until al dente; the onion may take a little longer. Place the vegetables in the bowl containing the dressing and toss gently to coat.

Spoon the rice onto a serving platter. Arrange the grilled vegetables over the top. Sprinkle with the Parmesan cheese and pepper. Serve with the remaining dressing.

Grilling Onions Easily

Onion slices can be difficult to cook evenly on the grill. To solve this problem, cut 1/2-inch-thick slices of onion and skewer each slice horizontally all the way through with a bamboo or thin metal skewer. The skewered onions remain intact during grilling and can be easily flipped with tongs.

LE TIAN

Serves 8

4 garlic cloves	2 tablespoons olive oil
2 small eggplant	1/4 teaspoon salt
3 medium onions	8 ounces sliced mozzarella cheese
6 medium tomatoes	1 tablespoon olive oil
2 large zucchini	2 tablespoons chopped fresh thyme

Cut garlic cloves into halves and vegetables into 1/4-inch slices. Make the circumference of vegetables equal. Sprinkle the garlic over the bottom of an oiled 9 × 12-inch baking dish. Starting at one long side of the dish, arrange alternating slices of the eggplant, onions, tomatoes and zucchini on edge to create 3 lengthwise rows. Brush with 2 tablespoons olive oil. Sprinkle with the salt.

Bake at 400 degrees for 45 to 55 minutes or until the eggplant is very tender. Insert thin cheese slices randomly between the vegetables. Brush with 1 tablespoon olive oil. Sprinkle with the thyme. Bake for 12 to 15 minutes longer or until the cheese melts. Let stand for 10 minutes before serving. Garnish with sprigs of fresh thyme.

VEGETARIAN FAJITAS

Created by Chef Anoosh Shariat, Shariat's

Serves 4

2 tablespoons olive oil	1 medium red onion, sliced
1 tablespoon taco seasoning mix	2 tablespoons fresh cilantro
1 pound mushrooms, sliced	2 tablespoons fresh lemon juice
2 medium red bell peppers, roasted, peeled, seeded, cut into strips	4 (10-inch) tortillas, heated
	Salsa

Mix the oil and seasoning mix in a bowl. Add the mushrooms, bell peppers and onion and toss to coat. Marinate at room temperature for 10 to 15 minutes. Grill the vegetables over hot coals or sauté in a skillet until tender. Heat the vegetables, cilantro and lemon juice in a saucepan. Place 2 spoonfuls of the mixture on each tortilla; roll to enclose. Top with salsa.

SANTA FE VEGGIE LASAGNA

Created by Chef Anoosh Shariat, Shariat's

Serves 2

4 tomatillos or tomatoes
1 small onion, cut into halves,
   thinly sliced
1 teaspoon taco seasoning mix
1 to 2 tablespoons vegetable oil
1 zucchini, thinly sliced
1 yellow squash, thinly sliced
8 ounces fresh spinach, trimmed
1/8 teaspoon salt

1 jalapeño chile, seeded, finely
   chopped (optional)
2 tablespoons chopped fresh
   cilantro
1 garlic clove, minced
8 (6-inch) corn tortillas
4 ounces soy cheese or mozzarella
   cheese, shredded

Roast the tomatillos in the oven in a roasting pan or grill over hot coals until the pulp separates from the peel easily. Peel the tomatillos. Process in a blender until puréed. Cook the onion and 1/4 teaspoon of the seasoning mix in the oil in a sauté pan until dark brown in color and caramelized, stirring frequently. Remove to a bowl. Sauté the zucchini and 1/4 teaspoon of the seasoning mix in a nonstick sauté pan until tender. Remove to a bowl. Sauté the squash and 1/4 teaspoon of the seasoning mix in a nonstick sauté pan until tender. Remove to a bowl. Sauté the spinach, 1/4 teaspoon seasoning mix and salt in a nonstick sauté pan until wilted. Remove to a bowl. Combine the tomatillo purée, chile, cilantro and garlic in a bowl and mix well.

Layer 2 tortillas, zucchini, 1/3 of the onion mixture, 2 tablespoons of the tomatillo sauce and 1 ounce of the cheese in a 8-inch round baking dish. Layer with 2 more tortillas, the spinach mixture, 1/2 of the remaining onion, 2 tablespoons of the tomatillo sauce and 1 ounce of the cheese. Layer with 2 more tortillas, squash, remaining onion mixture, 2 tablespoons of the tomatillo sauce and 1 ounce of the cheese. Top with remaining 2 tortillas, sauce and cheese. Bake at 350 degrees for 10 to 12 minutes or until bubbly.

You may substitute mushrooms and eggplant for the zucchini and yellow squash. Be sure the tortillas are completely covered by the vegetables and/or sauce so they will not become crisp during the baking process.

"You have to have a passion for cooking, and naturally, cooking is an art. Cooking is a unique and distinctive art form because you're using all of your senses and it all comes together on a plate."

CHEF ANOOSH SHARIAT
SHARIAT'S

Garden Vegetable Sandwich

Serves 4

1 (10-ounce) package frozen
  chopped spinach, cooked,
  drained
1/2 cup chopped onion
1/2 cup chopped green bell pepper
1/2 cup chopped scallions
2 tablespoons sour cream
2 tablespoons mayonnaise
1 teaspoon Dijon mustard

Cayenne pepper to taste
Salt to taste
2/3 cup shredded mozzarella cheese
1/3 cup shredded Swiss cheese
1/3 cup shredded Cheddar cheese
8 slices pumpernickel bread
1/4 cup sunflower kernels
1 cup sliced mushrooms
Sprouts

Press the spinach to remove the excess moisture. Combine the spinach, onion, bell pepper and scallions in a bowl and mix well. Stir in a mixture of the sour cream, mayonnaise, Dijon mustard, cayenne pepper and salt. Toss the mozzarella cheese, Swiss cheese and Cheddar cheese in a bowl.

Place the cheese mixture on 1/2 of the bread slices. Sprinkle with the sunflower kernels and mushrooms. Arrange on a baking sheet. Broil until the cheese melts. Remove from the oven. Top with sprouts.

Spread the spinach mixture on the remaining bread slices. Place filling side down on top of the sprouts. Cut into quarters. Serve immediately.

Spread the mixtures on party pumpernickel bread and serve as an appetizer.

Aunt Sally's Pickles

A crowd-pleasing hostess gift, sure to get you invited back!

Makes 8 to 10 pints

1 gallon whole dill pickles
  in jar
5 cups sugar
1 large garlic bulb, chopped
1 small bottle Tabasco sauce

Drain the pickles, reserving the juice. Cut the pickles into thin slices or into 1/2-inch slices. Return 1/5 of the pickles to the jar. Sprinkle with 1 cup of the sugar, 1/5 of the garlic and 1/5 of the Tabasco sauce. Repeat the process 4 more times. After all 5 layers are complete, fill the jar to the top with reserved pickle juice. Seal the jar and invert. Let stand at room temperature for 5 days, shaking the jar each day. Pack the pickles into hot sterilized 1-pint jars; seal with 2-piece lids. Store in the refrigerator.

HOT CRANBERRY CASSEROLE

Serves 8

3 cups chopped unpeeled green
    apples
2 cups cranberries
1¼ cups sugar
1½ cups quick-cooking oats

½ cup packed brown sugar
⅓ cup flour
⅓ cup chopped pecans
½ cup (1 stick) butter, melted

Combine the green apples, cranberries and sugar in a bowl and mix well.
Spoon into a 2-quart baking dish. Combine the oats, brown sugar, flour
and pecans in a bowl and mix well. Add the butter, stirring until crumbly.
Sprinkle over the prepared layer. Bake at 325 degrees for 1 hour or until
light brown and bubbly. Serve immediately.

You may top with vanilla ice cream and serve as a dessert.

SCALLOPED PINEAPPLE

Rosedale Bed & Breakfast, Paris, Kentucky

Serves 6 to 8

1 (20-ounce) can juice-pack
    pineapple tidbits
3 tablespoons flour
1 cup shredded sharp Cheddar
    cheese

⅓ cup sugar
18 butter crackers, crushed
3 tablespoons butter, melted

Drain the pineapple, reserving 3 tablespoons of the juice. Combine the
reserved juice and flour in a bowl and mix well. Stir in the pineapple,
cheese and sugar. Spoon into an 8 × 8-inch baking pan.

Combine the cracker crumbs and butter in a bowl and toss to mix.
Sprinkle over the prepared layer. Bake at 350 degrees for 25 to 30 minutes
or until bubbly. Serve for breakfast or brunch or as a side dish with pork
or Kentucky country ham.

CRANBERRY AND PEAR RELISH

Makes 3 cups

1 unpeeled orange, cut into eighths
1/2 cup walnuts, toasted
1 large unpeeled Bosc pear, cut into eighths
12 ounces cranberries
1/2 cup sugar

Combine the orange and walnuts in a food processor container. Process until coarsely chopped. Add the pear and cranberries. Process until coarsely chopped. Spoon into a bowl. Stir in the sugar. Chill, covered, until serving time. You may freeze for future use.

Serve with your Thanksgiving turkey or ham.

KENTUCKY TOMATO RELISH

This unique hostess gift is excellent on beef.

Makes about 6 cups

2 quarts fresh tomatoes, peeled, seeded, chopped (about 4 pounds)
2 large or 4 medium onions, chopped
2 cups chopped green bell peppers
2 cups chopped celery
1 3/4 cups sugar
1 cup cider vinegar
2 tablespoons salt
1/2 teaspoon ground cloves
1/2 teaspoon cinnamon
1/2 teaspoon allspice
1/2 teaspoon pepper

Combine the tomatoes, onions, bell peppers, celery, sugar, vinegar, salt, cloves, cinnamon, allspice and pepper in a stockpot and mix well. Bring to a boil; reduce heat. Simmer over low heat for 3 to 3 1/2 hours or until thickened, stirring occasionally. Spoon the relish into hot sterilized jars; seal with 2-piece lids. Store in the refrigerator.

Tomato Basics

First, core the tomatoes. Then for a quick and easy way to peel, place the tomatoes in boiling water. Boil until skins split and begin to curl around the cored area of the tomatoes—about 15 seconds for very ripe tomatoes. Remove tomatoes from water with a slotted spoon and place in a bowl of ice water until cool enough to handle. Peel the skins away with a paring knife, using the curled edges as your point of departure. Halve the tomatoes and scoop out the seeds and the gelatinous material with a small spoon. To chop the tomatoes, lay each tomato half cut side down on the cutting board. With a chef's knife held parallel to the work surface, slice into the lower portion of each tomato half, using a wide sawing motion. Stack the slices and cut into strips. Turn the strips and cut crosswise into cubes.

Penne con Pomodoro e Pescespada
(Photo, pages 194–195)

Food was the center of
our lives. Everything we
did and thought revolved
around it. We planted it,
grew it, harvested it,
peeled it, cooked it,
served it, consumed it —
endlessly, day after day,
season after season.
This was life on a farm —
as it had been time
out of mind.

Bobbie Ann Mason
Clear Springs

FUSILLI WITH ASIAGO CHEESE AND SPINACH

A perfect entrée for a summer luncheon or a twilight gathering on the patio with friends.

Serves 8

3 cups boiling water
4 ounces dry-pack sun-dried tomatoes
12 ounces uncooked fusilli
2 tablespoons extra-virgin olive oil
2 garlic cloves, crushed
10 ounces fresh spinach, torn
1/8 teaspoon salt
1/8 teaspoon freshly ground pepper
3/4 cup grated asiago cheese
1/2 cup finely grated Romano cheese

Pour the boiling water over the sun-dried tomatoes in a bowl and let stand for 30 minutes. Drain and chop the sun-dried tomatoes. Cook the pasta al dente using the package directions; drain.

Combine the sun-dried tomatoes and pasta in a bowl. Add the olive oil, garlic, spinach, salt and pepper and mix gently. Add the cheeses and toss to mix well. Serve immediately.

You may substitute farfalle, penne, cavatappi or any other medium pasta for the fusilli.

JALAPEÑO ORANGE PASTA WITH SHRIMP

Serves 4

24 jumbo shrimp, peeled, deveined
1/4 cup (1/2 stick) unsalted butter
1 garlic clove, chopped
1/4 cup chopped onion
1 jalapeño chile, seeded, thinly sliced
1/2 cup Fetzer Echo Ridge Fumé Blanc
1 1/2 cups orange juice
1/2 cup heavy cream
Salt and pepper to taste
10 ounces uncooked angel hair pasta

Sauté the shrimp in the butter in a large heavy skillet over medium-high heat for 1 minute on each side or just until pink. Remove the shrimp to a plate with a slotted spoon. Add the garlic, onion and jalapeño chile to the skillet and sauté for 1 minute.

Stir in the wine and bring to a boil. Add the orange juice and heavy cream. Cook for 8 to 10 minutes or until reduced to a thin sauce, stirring occasionally. Season with salt and pepper.

Cook the pasta al dente using the package directions. Add the shrimp to the sauce and cook just until heated through. Drain the pasta and add to the sauce; toss to mix well. Garnish with chopped fresh parsley.

Reducing a Liquid

Many recipes call for a liquid (usually stock, wine, or sauce mixture) to be "reduced." In its simplest form, reducing means to boil a liquid rapidly until the volume is reduced by evaporation, thus thickening the consistency and intensifying the flavor. It is essential to reduce the jalapeño orange sauce (at left) because the contrasting flavors of the jalapeño and the orange juice are intensified to create an extremely flavorful and unique sauce.

PRIMAVERA PASTA WITH ASPARAGUS

Primavera means springtime in Italian and this dish is bursting with flavor from fresh asparagus, flavorful cheeses, and zesty lemon.

Serves 4 to 6

1/2 cup (1 stick) butter
1 1/2 cups heavy cream
1 1/2 tablespoons grated lemon zest
3/4 cup grated Parmesan cheese
1/4 cup grated Romano cheese
1 1/2 cups coarsely chopped prosciutto
Salt to taste
1/8 teaspoon pepper
16 ounces uncooked penne
1 pound fresh asparagus, trimmed, cut into 1/2-inch pieces

Combine the butter, heavy cream and lemon zest in a small saucepan. Cook over medium heat for 5 minutes, stirring frequently. Stir in the Parmesan cheese, Romano cheese, prosciutto, salt and pepper. Cook until heated through, stirring frequently.

Cook the pasta using the package directions and adding the asparagus 3 minutes before the end of the cooking time; drain. Combine with the sauce in a bowl and toss to coat well. Serve immediately with additional grated fresh Parmesan cheese.

Add Some Zest

The zest is the perfumy, outermost layer of citrus fruit. Only the colored portion of the skin (not the white pith) is considered the zest. The aromatic oils in citrus zest are what add so much flavor to the food.

How to zest a citrus fruit:

- *Using a zester or fine shredder, draw its thick, sharp-edged holes along the surface of the fruit to remove the zest in fine shreds*

- *Alternatively, using a vegetable peeler or a paring knife, remove the zest (in big pieces), then cut into thin strips*

- *For finely grated zest, use a fine handheld grater*

Roasted Red Pepper Lasagna

A wonderful, unique meatless lasagna that makes an ideal entrée for entertaining.

Serves 8 to 10

16 ounces uncooked lasagna noodles
20 to 22 ounces Capriole goat cheese
3 scallions
3 garlic cloves
1/2 to 3/4 cup heavy cream
1/2 cup fresh basil leaves
1/2 cup fresh parsley leaves
1/2 cup fresh oregano leaves
2 (20- to 24-ounce) jars marinara sauce
6 large red bell peppers, roasted, chopped, or 2 small jars roasted red peppers, drained, chopped
1/2 cup grated Parmesan cheese

Cook the pasta al dente using the package directions; drain.

Combine the goat cheese, scallions, garlic, 1/2 cup heavy cream, basil, parsley and oregano in a food processor container and process until smooth. Add additional cream if necessary for a spreadable consistency.

Spread a thin layer of the marinara sauce over the bottom of a greased 9 × 13-inch baking dish. Layer the noodles, cheese mixture, roasted bell peppers, remaining marinara sauce and Parmesan cheese in the order listed 1/4 at a time in the prepared dish.

Bake, covered with foil, at 375 degrees for 35 to 40 minutes. Bake, uncovered, for 10 to 15 minutes longer or until bubbly. Let stand for 10 minutes before serving.

Roasting Peppers

Gas Burner — Turn the burner to high. Pierce a bell pepper with a long-handled fork and hold over high heat. Turn to char skin evenly. When skin is brown and cracking, immediately plunge pepper in a bowl of ice water; the skin will fall away. Seed pepper and chop.

Oven Broiler — In a preheated broiler, place whole peppers on the rack 4 to 6 inches from the heat source with oven door slightly ajar. Turn the peppers one quarter each time to blacken evenly on all sides. When peppers are blackened, remove from oven and place in a plastic bag; seal tightly. Let stand for ten minutes. Peel skin, seed, and chop.

Roasted peppers can be placed in a plastic container with wax paper between the layers and frozen for several months. If you plan to use the peppers within one to two weeks, place in a small container, cover with olive oil, and refrigerate.

PENNE CON POMODORO E PESCE SPADA

This dish for Pasta with Tomato and Swordfish was created by Chef Agostino Gabriele, Vincenzo's.

Serves 4

 2 quarts water
1 tablespoon salt
16 ounces uncooked penne
12 ounces swordfish, cut into medium cubes
1/2 cup extra-virgin olive oil
1/4 cup Bolla Soave
6 tomatoes, peeled, seeded, chopped

1 small eggplant, cut into medium cubes
2 tablespoons Fresh Pesto (below)
Salt and pepper to taste
1 tablespoon grated Parmigiano-Reggiano cheese
1 tablespoon chopped Italian parsley

"From my perspective, cooking is both an art and a passion. Without the desire or passion to create, the cuisine cannot become a work of art."

CHEF AGOSTINO GABRIELE
VINCENZO'S

Combine the water and 1 tablespoon salt in a large saucepan and bring to a boil. Add the pasta and cook for 4 to 5 minutes or until al dente.

Sauté the swordfish in the olive oil in a large sauté pan. Add the wine and stir to deglaze. Add the tomatoes, eggplant and pesto. Season with salt and pepper to taste. Cook until the eggplant is cooked through, stirring occasionally.

Drain the pasta and add to the sauté pan. Add the cheese and toss to mix well. Sprinkle with the parsley. Serve immediately.

FRESH PESTO

Makes 2 1/2 cups

2 cups fresh basil leaves
1/2 cup olive oil
2 tablespoons pine nuts, toasted

2 garlic cloves
1 teaspoon salt
1/2 cup grated Romano cheese

Process the basil, olive oil, pine nuts, garlic and salt in a food processor until well blended. May be frozen at this point. Before using, bring to room temperature and stir in the cheese.

THREE-CHEESE PENNE WITH GRILLED CHICKEN

Serves 8

8 boneless chicken breasts
1 (16-ounce) bottle Italian salad dressing
16 ounces uncooked penne
2 cups heavy cream
8 ounces fresh spinach leaves, trimmed, coarsely chopped
1/2 cup grated Parmesan cheese
1/2 cup shredded Bel Paese cheese
1/4 cup mascarpone cheese
1 teaspoon minced fresh rosemary
Salt to taste
2 tablespoons butter, chopped
4 ounces pancetta, chopped

Combine the chicken with the salad dressing in a shallow dish, turning to coat well. Marinate in the refrigerator for several hours, turning occasionally.

Cook the pasta al dente using the package directions; drain. Add the heavy cream, spinach, cheeses and rosemary. Season with salt and mix well. Spoon into a buttered 3-quart baking dish. Dot with butter and sprinkle with the pancetta. Bake at 400 degrees for 15 to 20 minutes or until heated through.

Drain the chicken and place on a rack on the grill. Grill over hot coals until cooked through, turning occasionally. Serve with the pasta.

For a more elegant presentation, slice the chicken and fan on top of the pasta.

Perfect Pasta

Bring 1 gallon (16 cups) of water per pound of pasta to a boil. This may sound like a lot of water but the pasta should have enough space to turn comfortably in the pot when you stir it. Add all of the pasta and stir frequently while boiling. Always taste the pasta to determine doneness — it should be firm but tender. As soon as the pasta is done, drain well and serve. Don't let it sit in hot water or rinse with cold water (unless making a cold pasta dish).

Helpful hint: It is often a good idea to reserve some of the pasta cooking water before you drain the pasta so it can be used to thin the sauce if it is too thick.

PENNE ALLA VODKA E PROSCIUTTO

Pasta and Prosciutto with Vodka Sauce

Serves 4

1 cup chopped onion
4 garlic cloves, minced
1/2 cup chopped prosciutto
1 teaspoon extra-virgin olive oil
1/2 cup Jekel Cabernet Sauvignon
1/3 cup Finlandia Vodka
1 tablespoon sugar
2 tablespoons tomato paste

2 (14-ounce) cans diced tomatoes
1/4 teaspoon freshly ground pepper
1/2 cup fat-free half-and-half
2 tablespoons chopped fresh
  parsley
12 ounces penne or rigatoni,
  cooked, drained

Sauté the onion, garlic, and prosciutto in the olive oil in a saucepan
for 5 minutes. Stir in the wine, vodka, sugar, tomato paste, undrained
tomatoes and pepper. Simmer for 20 minutes, stirring occasionally.
Remove the sauce from the heat and stir in the half-and-half and parsley.
Spoon the pasta onto serving plates and top with the sauce.

FRESH TUNA WITH BOW TIE PASTA

Serves 2

1/4 cup chopped fresh basil
2 garlic cloves, minced
6 teaspoons fresh lemon juice
1/4 teaspoon freshly ground pepper
12 ounces tuna steaks
2 cups bow tie pasta, cooked

1 (7-ounce) jar roasted red bell
  peppers, drained, coarsely
  chopped
3/4 cup crumbled feta cheese
1 (4-ounce) can sliced black olives,
  drained

Combine the basil, garlic, lemon juice and pepper in a medium bowl and
whisk to mix well. Spray a medium nonstick skillet with nonstick cooking
spray and heat over medium-high heat. Add the tuna steaks and cook for
5 to 6 minutes on each side. Cut into bite-size pieces.

Return the tuna to the skillet and add the pasta, roasted bell peppers,
cheese, olives and basil mixture. Cook until heated through, tossing to
mix well.

Pasta alla penne

"The short, diagonally cut
tubes of Italian pasta called
penne *take their name from
Latin* penna *which means
'feather' and, by extension,
'quill pen.'"*

MARTHA BARNETTE
LADYFINGERS AND NUN'S TUMMIES

CRAWFISH TORTELLINI

Serves 6 to 8

16 ounces uncooked cheese tortellini
1 small onion, chopped
2 or 3 garlic cloves, minced
5 or 6 green onions, chopped
1/2 cup chopped fresh parsley
2 tablespoons butter
2 tablespoons flour
2 to 3 cups milk or cream
2 tablespoons fresh lemon juice
1/4 cup Fetzer Sundial Chardonnay
1 teaspoon Worcestershire sauce
16 ounces fresh crawfish tails
Salt, cayenne pepper and black pepper to taste

Cook the tortellini using the package directions; drain.

Sauté the onion, garlic and half the green onions and half the parsley in the butter in a large skillet just until the onion is tender. Stir in the flour. Cook for several minutes, stirring constantly; do not allow to brown.

Add 2 cups milk gradually and simmer for 5 to 10 minutes or until thickened, stirring constantly and adding additional milk if needed for the desired consistency.

Stir in the lemon juice, wine, Worcestershire sauce, undrained crawfish tails, pasta, salt, cayenne pepper and black pepper. Sprinkle with the remaining green onions and remaining parsley. Simmer for 15 minutes, stirring occasionally.

Frozen crawfish tails are available at most large grocery stores and seafood markets. You may also substitute shrimp for the crawfish.

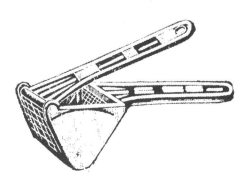

RAGIN' CAJUN PASTA

Serves 6 to 8

1^{1}/$_{2}$ cups water
8 ounces medium shrimp
2 boneless skinless chicken breasts
8 ounces andouille or smoked Cajun sausage, sliced
^{1}/$_{2}$ cup chopped onion
1 garlic clove, minced
1 tablespoon olive oil
^{1}/$_{2}$ cup Fetzer Sundial Chardonnay
1 teaspoon flour
^{1}/$_{2}$ cup chicken broth
1 cup heavy cream
2 tablespoons tomato paste
1 tablespoon Cajun seasoning
1 teaspoon cracked pepper, or to taste
1 green bell pepper, cut into thin strips
1 red bell pepper, cut into thin strips
16 ounces fettuccini, cooked

Bring the water to a boil in a saucepan. Add the shrimp and cook for 3 to 5 minutes or until pink; rinse with cold water and drain. Peel and devein the shrimp.

Cut the chicken into ^{1}/$_{4}$-inch strips. Sauté the chicken and sausage with the onion and garlic in the olive oil in a large skillet over medium-high heat until the chicken is light brown, stirring frequently. Remove the mixture to a bowl with a slotted spoon.

Add the wine to the skillet, stirring to deglaze. Bring to a boil, reduce the heat and simmer for 3 to 5 minutes. Blend the flour into the chicken broth in a cup. Add to the skillet with the heavy cream, tomato paste, Cajun seasoning and pepper. Bring to a boil, reduce the heat and simmer for 20 minutes, stirring occasionally.

Return the chicken mixture to the skillet and add the bell peppers. Cook until the bell peppers are tender, stirring frequently. Combine with the pasta and shrimp in a bowl and toss gently to mix well.

Portioning Tomato Paste

Many recipes call for only one or two tablespoons of tomato paste. Unfortunately, the rest of the tomato paste ends up wasted. With this handy way to store it, tomato paste will never go to waste again.

Open both ends of the tomato paste can. Remove the lid from one end and use the other end to push the paste out onto a sheet of plastic wrap. Wrap the paste in the plastic wrap and place it in the freezer. Once the paste is frozen, cut off as much as you need for the recipe. Return the frozen paste to the freezer for the next time.

Green Chile and Cheese Polenta

Serves 4 as a main dish or 8 as a side dish

3/4 cup yellow cornmeal
3 garlic cloves, minced
2 cups milk
1 cup water
1/2 tablespoon garlic salt
1 teaspoon salt
1/2 cup grated Parmesan cheese
Salt and pepper to taste

1 (7-ounce) can whole green
  chiles, drained
1 cup drained canned corn
2/3 cup chopped cilantro
2 cups shredded Monterey Jack
  cheese
1/2 cup heavy cream or 2% milk

Mix the cornmeal, garlic, milk, water, garlic salt and 1 teaspoon salt in
a heavy saucepan and bring to a simmer over medium heat, whisking
constantly. Cook for 12 minutes or until thickened, stirring frequently.
Stir in the Parmesan cheese and season with salt and pepper to taste.

Layer the cornmeal mixture, green chiles, corn, cilantro and Monterey
Jack cheese 1/2 at a time in a buttered 8 × 8-inch baking dish, pouring
half the cream over each cheese layer. Bake at 400 degrees for 25 minutes
or until puffed and light brown. Cut into squares to serve. May be
prepared and chilled until baking time; increase baking time to 30 minutes.

Grits Gruyère

Serves 8 to 10

4 cups milk
1/2 cup (1 stick) butter
1/2 teaspoon salt
1 cup quick-cooking grits

6 ounces shredded Gruyère cheese
Tabasco sauce or cayenne pepper
  to taste
1/2 cup grated Parmesan cheese

Bring the milk, butter and salt almost to a boil in a heavy saucepan and
stir in the grits. Cook until thickened, stirring constantly. Remove from the
heat and stir in the Gruyère cheese and Tabasco sauce; beat with a mixer
for creamier grits. Spoon into a buttered 2-quart baking dish and sprinkle
with the Parmesan cheese. Bake at 350 degrees for 15 to 30 minutes or
until set. Broil for 5 minutes to brown the top.

Pass the Polenta

*A staple of northern Italy,
polenta is a mush made
from cornmeal that has
been stirred until all the
liquid is absorbed. It can be
eaten hot with butter or
cooled until firm for grilling,
broiling, frying, or simply
cutting into squares.
Polenta is a wonderful
vegetarian entrée or
substitute for potatoes.*

VEGETABLE HARVEST COUSCOUS

This dish packs a lot of punch with a wide variety of vegetables and spices and an abundance of flavor that will satisfy any meat-lover's soul.

Serves 4 as a main dish or 8 as a side dish

1/2 cup chopped red onion
3 garlic cloves, minced
2 tablespoons olive oil
4 red potatoes, cut into 1/2-inch pieces
3 carrots, cut diagonally into 1/2-inch pieces
2 small zucchini, cut into 1-inch slices
1 tablespoon chili powder
1 teaspoon paprika
1 teaspoon curry powder
1/2 teaspoon cumin
1/2 teaspoon turmeric
Cinnamon to taste
1 (15-ounce) can tomato sauce
1/2 cup water
Salt and pepper to taste
10 ounces uncooked couscous
1 cup crumbled feta cheese

Sauté the onion and garlic in the olive oil in a large heavy skillet over medium-high heat for 4 minutes or until tender. Add the potatoes and carrots and sauté for 5 minutes. Add the zucchini, chili powder, paprika, curry powder, cumin, turmeric and cinnamon. Sauté for 1 minute or until the spices are fragrant.

Stir in the tomato sauce and water. Bring to a boil and reduce the heat. Simmer, covered, for 10 minutes or until the potatoes are tender and the sauce is slightly thickened, stirring occasionally. Season with salt and pepper. You may prepare to this point 1 day in advance and store, covered, in the refrigerator.

Cook the couscous using the package directions. Combine with the vegetable mixture and cheese in a bowl and mix gently. Garnish with chopped fresh parsley.

The Spices of Life

"Look on your pantry shelf. Salt, pepper and sugar are likely to be there already. Pasta, potatoes and beans all need some salt to be flavorful. Freshly ground pepper is worth more than any exotic seasoning when it comes to flavoring vegetarian food. And a pinch of sugar can bring out the flavor of foods like tomatoes or spice mixtures."

SARAH FRITSCHNER
*VEGETARIAN EXPRESS
LANE COOKBOOK*

Photo on facing page, Farmer in Western Kentucky

Easy Oven-Baked Mushroom Risotto

The earthiness of Italy's beloved dried porcini mushrooms gives this dish a hearty, rich flavor that teams perfectly with roasted meats and complements any fall meal.

Serves 6

$1/2$ ounce dried porcini mushrooms
2 cups boiling water
1 medium onion, finely chopped
5 tablespoons butter
8 ounces fresh dark-gilled mushrooms
6 ounces uncooked arborio or canaroli rice
5 ounces dry madeira
Salt and freshly ground pepper to taste
2 tablespoons grated Parmesan cheese
2 ounces Parmesan cheese, shaved

Soak the dried mushrooms in the boiling water in a bowl for 30 minutes. Drain the mushrooms and chop into $1/2$-inch pieces. Place in a paper-towel-lined sieve over a bowl and press to remove the excess moisture, reserving the mushrooms and liquid. Chop the mushrooms fine.

Sauté the onion in the butter in a saucepan over low heat for 5 minutes. Add the fresh mushrooms and chopped porcini mushrooms. Sweat for 20 minutes. Stir in the rice, wine, reserved mushroom liquid, salt and pepper. Bring to a simmer.

Spoon into a 9-inch baking dish that has been warmed in a 300-degree oven. Place on the center rack of the oven and bake for 20 minutes. Stir in the grated Parmesan cheese. Bake for 15 minutes longer. Remove from the oven. Cover with a tea towel until serving time. Sprinkle with the shaved Parmesan cheese.

BAY SCALLOP RISOTTO WITH HERBS

Serves 4

1 garlic bulb
1 teaspoon olive oil
1/2 cup chopped onion
2 tablespoons olive oil
2 cups uncooked arborio rice
1 cup Fetzer Sundial Chardonnay
4 1/2 cups chicken broth, heated
1 tablespoon butter or margarine
1 pound bay scallops
1/4 cup Fetzer Sundial Chardonnay
1 tablespoon minced fresh rosemary
2 tablespoons minced fresh parsley
2 tablespoons minced fresh basil
1/2 teaspoon freshly ground pepper

Cut a 1/4-inch slice from the top of the garlic bulb to expose the cloves and place on a square of foil. Drizzle with 1 teaspoon olive oil and fold the foil to enclose the garlic. Roast at 350 degrees for 30 minutes. Open the foil and cool to room temperature. Press the garlic cloves from the skins and cut into slivers.

Sauté the onion in 2 tablespoons olive oil in a saucepan over medium-high heat for 3 minutes. Stir in the rice and sauté for 1 minute. Stir in 1 cup wine and reduce the heat to medium.

Stir in the heated chicken broth 1/2 cup at a time, cooking until the liquid is nearly absorbed after each addition; the rice should be creamy but still slightly firm.

Heat the butter in a sauté pan and add the scallops. Sauté for 3 minutes or until opaque. Drain, reserving both the scallops and the pan drippings. Stir the reserved pan drippings and 1/4 cup wine into the rice and cook until the liquid is nearly absorbed.

Add the scallops, garlic, rosemary, parsley, basil and pepper to the rice and mix gently. Cook until heated through, stirring frequently. Serve with freshly grated Parmesan cheese and chopped seeded tomato.

Roasted Garlic Dressing

Blend 2 tablespoons raspberry vinegar, 1 small shallot, 1 small clove roasted garlic and 2 tablespoons water in a food processor. With machine running, add 6 tablespoons walnut oil and 2 tablespoons vegetable oil. Season with salt.

Delicious over unusual mixed greens with dried cherries and feta or pears and Brie.

ASIAN RICE PILAF

Serves 6 to 8

2 cups chicken stock or Korbel Brut Champagne
2 tablespoons orange liqueur
2 tablespoons soy sauce
1 tablespoon sesame oil
$1/2$ teaspoon Chinese chile sauce
2 teaspoons grated orange zest
$1/2$ teaspoon salt
$1^1/2$ cups uncooked long grain rice
3 garlic cloves, minced
3 tablespoons unsalted butter
$1/2$ cup currants
$1/2$ cup chopped green onions
$1/4$ cup chopped fresh basil
$1/2$ cup chopped red bell pepper
$1/3$ cup pine nuts, toasted

Combine the chicken stock, liqueur, soy sauce, sesame oil, chile sauce, orange zest and salt in a bowl and mix well.

Rinse the rice under cold water until the water runs clear; drain well. Sauté the garlic in the butter in a saucepan over medium-low heat. Add the rice and sauté until heated through, stirring to coat well. Stir in the currants and stock mixture. Bring to a low boil, stirring constantly.

Spoon into a 2-quart baking dish. Bake, covered, at 350 degrees for 30 to 35 minutes or until the liquid is absorbed and the rice is tender. Stir in the green onions, basil, bell pepper and pine nuts at serving time.

You may prepare up to 2 days in advance and store, covered, in the refrigerator. Reheat before serving.

WILD RICE AND PINE NUT CASSEROLE

Serves 6

1/4 cup chopped fresh parsley
1/2 teaspoon dried thyme
1 bay leaf
1 1/2 cups chicken broth
1 cup uncooked wild rice
1/2 cup uncooked long grain rice
1/3 cup chopped onion
1/2 cup (1 stick) butter
8 ounces fresh mushrooms, sliced
1/2 teaspoon pepper
3/4 cup pine nuts, toasted
3 tablespoons flour
1 cup milk
1/2 cup seasoned bread crumbs
2 tablespoons butter, melted

Tie the parsley, thyme and bay leaf in a cheesecloth bag. Combine with the chicken broth, wild rice and long grain rice in a saucepan and bring to a boil. Reduce the heat and simmer, covered, for 30 minutes.

Sauté the onion in 1/2 cup butter in a skillet until tender. Add the mushrooms and pepper and cook until the mushrooms are tender. Stir into the rice mixture with the pine nuts.

Blend the flour with the milk in a small bowl. Add to the rice mixture and mix well. Cook until thickened, stirring constantly.

Spoon the rice mixture into a 2-quart baking dish, discarding the cheesecloth bag. Bake at 325 degrees for 30 minutes. Toss the bread crumbs with the melted butter and sprinkle over the top. Bake for 30 minutes longer.

Toasting Nuts

Toasting nuts enhances their aroma and flavor. Place nuts, either whole or chopped, in one layer on a baking sheet and toast in the oven at 350 degrees for 3 to 5 minutes or until golden brown. Shake the baking sheet once or twice during baking so that the nuts brown evenly.

Desserts

Frozen Lemon and Fresh Berry Parfaits
(Photo, pages 214–215)

My grandmother baked cookies, but she didn't believe in eating them fresh from the oven. She stored them in her cookie jar for a day or two before she would let me have any. "Wait till they come in order," Granny would say. The crisp cookies softened in their ceramic cell — their snug humidor — acquiring more flavor, ripening both in texture and in my imagination.

Bobbie Ann Mason
Clear Springs

DELECTABLE LEMON MOUSSE

Serves 8

4 egg whites (1/2 cup)	Salt to taste
4 egg yolks	1/2 teaspoon grated orange zest
1/2 cup sugar	1/3 cup finely grated lemon zest
3/4 cup fresh lemon juice	1/4 cup orange liqueur
1/4 cup water	1/2 cup sugar
2 envelopes unflavored gelatin	2 cups whipping cream
1/2 cup sugar	1/4 cup confectioners' sugar

Let the egg whites come to room temperature and stand for 1 hour. Tie a 2-inch waxed-paper collar around a 1-quart soufflé dish.

Beat the egg yolks at high speed in a mixing bowl for 3 minutes or until thick. Beat in 1/2 cup sugar 2 tablespoons at a time, beating constantly until very thick. Add the lemon juice and water gradually and mix well.

Combine the gelatin with 1/2 cup sugar and salt in a double boiler. Stir in the egg yolk mixture. Cook over, not in, boiling water for 15 to 20 minutes or until the gelatin dissolves, stirring constantly. Stir in the orange zest, lemon zest and liqueur. Cool slightly, stirring occasionally.

Spoon into a glass bowl and place in a large bowl of ice cubes. Let stand for 15 minutes, stirring occasionally, then stir constantly until the mixture mounds when dropped from the spoon.

Beat the egg whites at high speed in a mixing bowl until soft peaks form. Add 1/2 cup sugar 2 tablespoons at a time, mixing well after each addition and beating until stiff peaks form. Fold gently into the lemon mixture just until mixed.

Beat 1 1/2 cups of the whipping cream with the confectioners' sugar in a mixing bowl until soft peaks form. Fold gently into the lemon mixture. Spoon into the prepared soufflé dish. Chill, covered, for 3 hours.

Remove the collar from the dish. Whip the remaining 1/2 cup whipping cream in a mixing bowl until soft peaks form. Pipe onto the mousse using a pastry bag. Garnish with lemon slice halves.

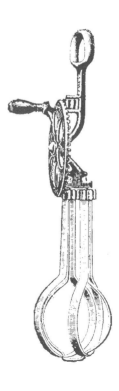

FROZEN LEMON AND FRESH BERRY PARFAITS

Created by Chef Kathy Cary, Lilly's

Serves 6

6 egg yolks
1³/4 cups sugar
1/2 cup fresh lemon juice
Grated zest of 2 lemons
1/2 cup (1 stick) butter, melted
2¹/2 cups whipping cream
1/3 cup sugar
3 ounces semisweet chocolate
7 tablespoons whipping cream
1 pint blueberries
1 pint raspberries
Lemon nut cookies, crumbled

Beat the egg yolks with 1³/4 cups sugar in a mixing bowl until thick and light yellow. Add the lemon juice and lemon zest. Spoon into a double boiler. Place over hot water and whisk in the butter. Cook until thickened, stirring constantly. Spoon into a stainless steel bowl and place a sheet of waxed paper directly on the surface. Chill in the refrigerator.

Beat 2¹/2 cups whipping cream in a mixing bowl, adding 1/3 cup sugar gradually and beating constantly until soft peaks form. Reserve 1/4 of the whipped cream. Fold the remaining whipped cream into the chilled lemon mixture. Freeze for 6 hours.

Melt the chocolate with 7 tablespoons whipping cream in a double boiler, stirring to blend well.

Spoon the melted chocolate mixture into 6 parfait glasses. Add half the blueberries, half the raspberries and top with the reserved whipped cream. Add the remaining berries and spoon the frozen lemon mixture on top. Sprinkle with cookie crumbs.

"Cooking is both an art and a passion, obviously. You have to be passionate about your cooking in order to elevate it to a fine art!"

CHEF KATHY CARY
LILLY'S

BAKED ALASKA IN ORANGE CUPS

An easy yet sophisticated ending to a dinner party.

Serves 8

8 navel oranges
4 cups (about) vanilla ice cream
8 teaspoons orange liqueur
3 egg whites
1/4 teaspoon salt
1/2 teaspoon vanilla extract
6 tablespoons sugar

Cut a very thin slice from the bottom of each orange to provide an even base. Cut a larger slice from the tops and scoop out the pulp, reserving the pulp for another purpose.

Blend the ice cream with the orange liqueur in a bowl. Spoon into the orange cups. Freeze for 2 hours or until firm.

Beat the egg whites until frothy. Add the salt and vanilla. Add the sugar gradually, beating constantly until stiff and glossy peaks form.

Spread or pipe the meringue over the orange cups, sealing to the edge. Place on a broiler pan and broil for 2 minutes or just until the meringue is light brown. Serve immediately.

PEARS IN WHITE ZINFANDEL

Aleksander House Bed & Breakfast, Louisville, Kentucky

Serves 8

8 pears
2 cups Fetzer White Zinfandel
2 tablespoons lemon juice
1 cup sugar
Grated zest of 1 lemon
2 teaspoons ground cinnamon
Nutmeg to taste
1 teaspoon vanilla extract

Peel the pears and core from the bottoms. Combine the wine, lemon juice, sugar, lemon zest, cinnamon, nutmeg and vanilla in a large deep saucepan and mix well. Bring to a boil. Place the pears stem end up in the saucepan and spoon the liquid over the tops. Simmer for 10 to 20 minutes or until the pears are tender.

Remove the pears to individual serving dishes, reserving the cooking liquid. Strain the reserved liquid back into the saucepan. Boil until reduced by half. Pour over the pears and let stand until cool. Garnish with fresh mint leaves and serve with Crème Fraîche (at right).

Crème Fraîche

Crème fraîche is a slightly tangy thickened cream with a nutty flavor and a rich, smooth texture. It can be purchased from a gourmet market or easily made at home. Combine 1 cup whipping cream and 2 tablespoons buttermilk in a glass container. Cover and let stand at room temperature (about 70 degrees F.) for 8 to 24 hours, or until very thick. Stir, cover, and store in the refrigerator for up to 10 days. Crème fraîche is wonderful spooned over fresh fruit, warm cobblers, or puddings.

SAUTÉED STRAWBERRIES IN RED WINE

Serves 6

4 cups strawberries, cut lengthwise into quarters
1 tablespoon sugar
1/4 teaspoon lemon juice
1 cup Bonterra Cabernet Sauvignon
7 tablespoons sugar
1/4 teaspoon pepper
1 (2-inch) vanilla bean
1 tablespoon cornstarch
1/4 cup Bonterra Cabernet Sauvignon
2 tablespoons unsalted butter
Pepper to taste
Vanilla ice cream

Combine the strawberries with 1 tablespoon sugar and lemon juice in a bowl and mix well. Let stand at room temperature.

Combine 1 cup wine, 7 tablespoons sugar and 1/4 teaspoon pepper in a heavy medium saucepan. Split the vanilla bean lengthwise and scrape the seeds into the saucepan. Add the bean. Cook over medium heat until the sugar dissolves, stirring constantly.

Blend the cornstarch with 1/4 cup wine in a small bowl. Stir into the hot wine mixture and cook for 2 minutes or until thickened, whisking constantly. Remove from the heat and discard the vanilla bean.

Sauté the strawberries in the butter in a large skillet over high heat for 1 minute. Add the wine sauce and pepper to taste. Bring to a boil and remove from the heat.

Spoon into 6 dessert glasses. Top with ice cream. Garnish with fresh mint sprigs.

Sauce may be prepared 1 day in advance. Cool, cover, and store in refrigerator.

RASPBERRY CRÈME BRÛLÉE

Serves 8

1 pint fresh raspberries
3 cups half-and-half
1/4 cup sugar
3 eggs
2 egg yolks
1 teaspoon vanilla extract
2 to 3 tablespoons brown sugar

Rinse and drain the raspberries and sprinkle into eight 1/2-cup ramekins. Heat the half-and-half just to the boiling point in a heavy saucepan over medium-low heat.

Whisk the sugar, eggs and egg yolks in a large bowl until light and frothy. Whisk in the hot half-and-half gradually. Strain back into the saucepan and cook over low heat just until the mixture coats the back of a wooden spoon, stirring constantly. Stir in the vanilla.

Spoon into the prepared ramekins and place in a baking dish. Pour enough hot water into the larger dish to reach 2/3 of the way up the sides of the ramekins. Bake at 300 degrees for 35 to 40 minutes or until a tester inserted in the center comes out clean.

Remove from the water bath and cool slightly. Chill, covered, for 2 hours. Sprinkle with the brown sugar and place on a baking sheet. Broil just until the tops are caramelized and golden brown. Serve immediately.

ALMOND AMARETTO COFFEE

Serve the next time your neighbor stops by for a visit.

1/2 cup hot freshly brewed coffee
6 teaspoons amaretto
1 teaspoon brown sugar
Whipped cream
1 teaspoon slivered almonds, toasted

For each serving, mix the coffee, amaretto and brown sugar in a mug. Top with a dollop of whipped cream and sprinkle with the almonds.

Neapolitan Cheesecake

Serves 12 to 14

1 cup chocolate cookie crumbs
3 tablespoons butter or margarine, melted
1 teaspoon sugar
24 ounces cream cheese, softened
3/4 cup sugar
3 eggs
1 teaspoon vanilla extract
1/3 cup mashed strawberries
1 teaspoon sugar
2 (1-ounce) squares semisweet chocolate, melted
2 (1-ounce) squares white chocolate, melted
3 (1-ounce) squares semisweet chocolate
1 teaspoon shortening
2 tablespoons butter or margarine
1/2 (1-ounce) square white chocolate
5 teaspoons shortening

Mix the cookie crumbs with 3 tablespoons melted butter and 1 teaspoon sugar in a bowl. Press over the bottom of an ungreased 9-inch springform pan. Bake at 350 degrees for 8 minutes. Cool to room temperature.

Beat the cream cheese with 3/4 cup sugar in a mixing bowl until smooth. Beat in the eggs 1 at a time. Add the vanilla and mix well. Divide into 3 equal portions.

Mix the strawberries with 1 teaspoon sugar in a bowl. Stir into 1 portion of the cream cheese mixture; stir the melted semisweet chocolate into 1 portion; stir the melted white chocolate into the remaining portion. Layer the semisweet chocolate mixture, the white chocolate mixture and the strawberry mixture in the prepared springform pan.

Bake at 425 degrees for 10 minutes. Reduce the oven temperature to 300 degrees and bake for 40 to 50 minutes longer or until set. Run a knife immediately around the edge of the pan. Cool on a wire rack. Place on a serving plate and remove the side of the pan.

Melt 3 squares semisweet chocolate with 1 teaspoon shortening and 2 tablespoons butter in a double boiler. Spoon over the cheesecake; mixture may drip down the side slightly. Melt 1/2 square white chocolate with 5 teaspoons shortening in a double boiler. Drizzle in lines or other design over the top. Store in the refrigerator.

Hints for Perfect Cheesecake

• *When adding eggs, keep the mixer on low. Beating the cheesecake mixture at too high a speed causes too much air to get into the batter and produces an inferior cheesecake.*

• *Invest in a good oven thermometer and use it to check the accuracy of your oven temperature.*

• *Place the cheesecake in the refrigerator immediately after it has finished baking. This will prevent the development of cracks and chasms.*

• *Bake a cheesecake two days before serving and allow it to mellow in the refrigerator.*

(continued at right)

PUMPKIN CHEESECAKE WITH WALNUT TOPPING

Serves 12

1¹/₂ cups zwieback cracker crumbs
¹/₄ cup sugar
6 tablespoons butter, melted
¹/₈ teaspoon cinnamon
24 ounces cream cheese, softened
³/₄ cup sugar
³/₄ cup packed light brown sugar
5 eggs
1 (16-ounce) can pumpkin
¹/₄ cup heavy cream
Nutmeg to taste
1³/₄ teaspoons cinnamon
1 cup coarsely chopped walnuts
6 tablespoons butter, softened
1 cup packed light brown sugar

Mix the zwieback cracker crumbs, ¹/₄ cup sugar, 6 tablespoons butter and ¹/₈ teaspoon cinnamon in a medium bowl. Press over the bottom and up the side of a lightly buttered 9-inch springform pan. Chill in the refrigerator.

Beat the cream cheese at medium speed in a mixing bowl until smooth. Add ³/₄ cup sugar and ³/₄ cup brown sugar gradually, beating until smooth. Add the eggs 1 at a time, beating until light. Beat in the pumpkin, heavy cream, nutmeg and 1³/₄ teaspoons cinnamon at low speed.

Spoon into the prepared springform pan. Bake at 325 degrees for 1 hour and 35 minutes.

Mix the walnuts, 6 tablespoons butter and 1 cup brown sugar in a bowl. Sprinkle over the cheesecake. Bake for 10 minutes longer. Cool on a wire rack. Chill in the refrigerator for several hours. Place on a serving plate and remove the side of the pan.

- *While storing in the refrigerator, do not cover a cheesecake with foil or plastic wrap because condensation will cause moisture to collect on top of the cheesecake. If the cheesecake is still in the springform pan, cover it with a piece of cardboard. If it is out of the pan, store the cheesecake in a cardboard cake box.*

- *Remove a cheesecake from the refrigerator several hours before serving. A cheesecake's sensuous texture is enhanced if it is not served too cold.*

DEEP-DISH APPLE COBBLER

Created by Chef Kathy Cary, Lilly's

Serves 4 to 6

Woodford Reserve Bourbon Ice Cream

1 cup sugar	3 egg yolks
2¹/2 tablespoons flour	1¹/2 tablespoons vanilla extract
¹/4 teaspoon salt	6 tablespoons Woodford Reserve
3 cups milk	Bourbon
3 eggs	1¹/2 cups cream

Cobbler

6 cups sliced Granny Smith or Jonathan apples, about 5 apples	1¹/2 teaspoons cinnamon
Juice of 1 lemon	1 cup (2 sticks) butter, softened
¹/2 cup sun-dried cherries	1 cup packed brown sugar
¹/2 cup water	1¹/2 cups flour
	Bourbon Hard Sauce (at right)

For the ice cream, whisk the sugar, flour, salt and milk in a heavy 4-quart saucepan. Bring to a boil over medium heat and cook until slightly thickened, stirring frequently.

Beat the eggs and egg yolks in a medium mixing bowl. Beat a small amount of the hot mixture into the eggs; beat the eggs into the hot mixture. Cook until thickened enough to coat a spoon, stirring occasionally. Remove from the heat and stir in the vanilla and bourbon. Cool completely. Add the cream and pour into an ice cream freezer container. Freeze using the manufacturer's instructions.

For the cobbler, spread the apples in an 8 × 8-inch baking pan and drizzle with the lemon juice. Add the cherries and pour the water into the pan; sprinkle with the cinnamon.

Mix the butter, brown sugar and flour in a bowl. Crumble over the apple mixture. Bake at 350 degrees for 50 minutes.

To serve, spoon the cobbler into serving dishes. Top with the ice cream and Bourbon Hard Sauce.

BOURBON HARD SAUCE

¹/4 cup (¹/2 stick) butter, softened
1 cup confectioners' sugar
3 tablespoons Woodford Reserve Bourbon

Process the butter and confectioners' sugar in a food processor. Add the bourbon gradually, processing until smooth. Chill in the refrigerator.

BAKED PEACH COBBLER

Serves 6 to 8

2 cups sliced fresh peaches
1/4 cup (1/2 stick) butter, softened
3/4 cup sugar
1 cup flour
1 teaspoon baking powder
1/2 teaspoon salt
1/2 cup milk
1 cup sugar
1 tablespoon cornstarch
1/4 teaspoon cinnamon
1/4 teaspoon salt
1 cup boiling water

Spread the peaches in an 8 × 8-inch baking pan. Cream the butter and 3/4 cup sugar in a mixing bowl. Mix the flour, baking powder and 1/2 teaspoon salt together. Add to the creamed mixture alternately with the milk, mixing well after each addition. Spread over the peaches.

Mix 1 cup sugar, cornstarch, cinnamon and 1/4 teaspoon salt in a bowl and sift the mixture over the batter. Pour the boiling water over the top; do not mix.

Bake at 325 degrees for 50 minutes. Serve warm with ice cream.

For variety, substitute 1 cup of raspberries or blackberries for 1 cup of the peaches.

Pretty as a Peach

Fresh peaches are available in most regions of the United States from May to October. When selecting fresh peaches, look for an intensely fragrant fruit that gives slightly when squeezed and is free of bruises. Underripe peaches can be ripened in a paper bag with small holes cut in several places. Set the bag out at room temperature for several days. Adding an apple to the bag will hasten this process because apples give off ethylene gas, which speeds ripening. Before peeling peaches, blanch them in boiling water for about 30 seconds, then plunge into ice water. The thick, fuzzy skin can then be easily peeled away.

MANGO AND RASPBERRY HAZELNUT CRISP

Serves 4

2/3 **cup finely ground hazelnuts**
3/4 **cup flour**
1/3 **cup sugar**
1/8 **teaspoon salt**
6 tablespoons unsalted butter, softened
3 mangoes, peeled
2 tablespoons fresh lemon juice
3 tablespoons sugar
1 tablespoon flour
1/2 **pint raspberries**
1 teaspoon cinnamon
4 teaspoons sugar
Chantilly Cream (at right)

Whisk the hazelnuts, 3/4 cup flour, 1/3 cup sugar and salt in a medium bowl. Cut in the butter until the mixture is crumbly. Press the mixture together to form pea-size to 1/2-inch crumbs.

Cut the mangoes into 3/4-inch cubes. Combine with the lemon juice, 3 tablespoons sugar and 1 tablespoon flour in a medium bowl; mix well. Add the raspberries and mix gently. Spoon into 4 individual baking dishes. Sprinkle with the crumb mixture, allowing the fruit to show through.

Bake at 350 degrees for 25 to 30 minutes. Sprinkle with a mixture of the cinnamon and 4 teaspoons sugar. Bake for 10 minutes longer or until the top is golden brown and the fruit is thickened and bubbly. Let cool on a wire rack until slightly warm. Serve with Chantilly Cream.

CHANTILLY CREAM

1 cup whipping cream
1 teaspoon vanilla extract, almond extract or orange liqueur
1/4 **cup sugar**

Combine the whipping cream and vanilla in a mixing bowl. Beat at medium speed for 1 minute. Add the sugar and beat for 3 minutes or until soft peaks form. Serve with Mango and Raspberry Hazelnut Crisp (at left) or other desserts.

PEAR AND TART CHERRY CRISP

Serves 6 to 8

Crisp

8 medium pears, peeled
  (about 2³/4 pounds)
²/3 cup dried tart cherries, dried
  blueberries or dried cranberries
  (about 3³/4 ounces)
2 tablespoons fresh lemon juice
2 teaspoons finely grated
  lemon zest
6 tablespoons butter, softened
²/3 cup flour

²/3 cup rolled oats or
  quick-cooking oats
²/3 cup packed light brown sugar
¹/2 cup coarsely chopped pecans
  (about 2¹/4 ounces)
1 teaspoon ground cinnamon
1 teaspoon ground ginger
¹/2 teaspoon ground allspice
¹/8 teaspoon grated nutmeg

Lemon Honey Cream

1 cup heavy cream
2 teaspoons fresh lemon juice

2 tablespoons honey

For the crisp, slice the pears ¹/4 inch thick. Combine with the cherries, lemon juice and lemon zest in a large bowl and toss to mix well. Spoon into a 9 × 13-inch baking dish.

Cut the butter into the flour in a large bowl until the mixture resembles coarse meal. Add the oats, brown sugar, pecans, cinnamon, ginger, allspice and nutmeg and mix until the mixture begins to stick together. Sprinkle evenly over the fruit and press down lightly.

Bake at 375 degrees for 40 minutes or until the pears are tender and the topping is golden brown.

For the cream, mix the heavy cream and lemon juice in a bowl until the mixture thickens slightly. Stir in the honey. Serve with the warm crisp. Garnish with additional grated lemon zest.

To keep pear slices from turning brown, combine them with ice water mixed with lemon juice and let stand until ready to use. Drain well before assembling the crisp.

SILVER BELLS PUNCH

Makes 24 (6-ounce) servings

1 (46-ounce) can
  unsweetened pineapple
  juice, chilled
2 cups piña colada drink
  mix, chilled
1 (12-ounce) can frozen
  orange juice concentrate,
  thawed
1 (1-liter) bottle club soda,
  chilled
1 (1-liter) bottle lemon-lime
  soda, chilled
1 (10-ounce) package frozen
  raspberries in syrup,
  slightly thawed

Combine the pineapple juice, drink mix, orange juice concentrate, club soda and lemon-lime soda in a punch bowl and mix well. Stir in the raspberries just before serving. Ladle into punch cups.

THE OAKROOM'S BREAD PUDDING

This recipe for The Oakroom's Bread Pudding with Woodford Reserve Bourbon Crème Anglaise was created by Chef Jim Gerhardt, The Seelbach Hilton. This tantalizing time-honored southern dessert will surely bring rave reviews.

Serves 16

Pudding
6 each day-old muffins, Danish pastries and croissants,
  or the equivalent amount
7 eggs
2 cups milk
2 cups heavy cream
2 cups sugar

Woodford Reserve Bourbon Crème Anglaise
3 to 4 cups heavy cream
1 1/2 cups sugar
1/2 to 3/4 cup Woodford Reserve Bourbon
2 tablespoons cornstarch
2 tablespoons water

For the pudding, crumble the breads into a buttered 9 × 13-inch baking dish and mix. Whisk the eggs, milk and heavy cream in a bowl. Whisk in the sugar. Pour over the bread and mix well.

Bake at 350 degrees for 20 to 30 minutes or until the center is still moist and the top is golden brown. Test the center of the pudding to determine if the liquid is set.

For the crème, combine the heavy cream, sugar and bourbon in a saucepan and bring to a boil. Blend the cornstarch and water in a cup until smooth. Stir into the cream mixture and simmer until thickened, whisking constantly. Serve warm over the pudding. Garnish with a sprinkle of cinnamon.

JACK DANIEL'S CHOCOLATE ICE CREAM

Makes 1 1/2 quarts

2 cups heavy cream
2 cups half-and-half
2/3 cup sugar
1/3 cup unsweetened Dutch
   baking cocoa

2 1/2 ounces semisweet chocolate,
   coarsely chopped
1/4 teaspoon vanilla extract
6 eggs, beaten
1/3 cup Jack Daniel's

Bring the heavy cream and half-and-half to a simmer in a large heavy saucepan. Add the sugar and baking cocoa and cook until the sugar dissolves, stirring constantly. Remove from the heat and stir in the chopped chocolate and vanilla.

Stir 1/2 cup of the hot chocolate mixture into the eggs; stir the eggs into the hot chocolate mixture. Cook over medium-low heat for 10 to 15 minutes or until the mixture thickens enough to coat the back of the spoon and leaves a path when a finger is drawn across the spoon, stirring constantly.

Strain into a bowl set into a large bowl filled with ice. Let stand until cool, stirring frequently. Stir in the whiskey. Spoon into an ice cream freezer container and freeze using the manufacturer's instructions. Place in the freezer for several hours to blend flavors.

FABULOUS FUDGE SAUCE

Makes 2 cups

1/2 cup (1 stick) butter
1 cup sugar
1 teaspoon instant coffee granules
2 tablespoons rum
1/3 cup baking cocoa

1/8 teaspoon cinnamon
1/8 teaspoon salt
1 cup heavy cream
2 teaspoons vanilla extract

Melt the butter in a saucepan and stir in the sugar, coffee granules, rum, baking cocoa, cinnamon and salt. Add the heavy cream. Bring to a boil and reduce the heat. Simmer for 5 minutes, stirring frequently. Remove from the heat and stir in the vanilla. Serve warm or cool.

BANANA LAYER CAKE

Serves 12

2¹/₄ cups cake flour
³/₄ teaspoon baking soda
¹/₂ teaspoon baking powder
¹/₂ teaspoon salt
¹/₈ teaspoon cinnamon
1 cup mashed ripe bananas
¹/₄ cup buttermilk
1 teaspoon vanilla extract

¹/₂ cup (1 stick) unsalted butter, softened
1¹/₃ cups sugar
2 eggs
Cream Cheese Frosting (at right)
2 large bananas, sliced
¹/₂ cup chopped walnuts (optional)

Combine the cake flour, baking soda, baking powder, salt and cinnamon in a bowl and mix well. Combine the mashed bananas, buttermilk and vanilla in a bowl and mix well. Beat the butter and sugar in a mixing bowl until blended. Beat in the eggs 1 at a time. Add the dry ingredients alternately with the banana mixture, beginning and ending with the dry ingredients and beating just until blended after each addition. Spoon the batter equally into 3 lightly buttered and floured 8-inch cake pans.

Bake at 350 degrees for 20 minutes or just until the layers begin to brown and a wooden pick inserted in the center comes out with a few crumbs attached. Cool in the pans on a wire rack for 10 minutes. Run a sharp knife around the outer edges of the layers to loosen. Invert onto the wire rack to cool completely.

Place 1 of the cake layers on a cake plate. Spread with ¹/2 cup of the frosting. Arrange with half the banana slices and ¹/3 of the walnuts to within ¹/4 inch of the edge. Spread ¹/4 cup of the frosting over the top of another cake layer. Place the cake layer frosting side down over the prepared layers. Spread with ¹/2 cup of the frosting. Top with the remaining banana slices and ¹/2 of the remaining walnuts. Spread the remaining cake layer with ¹/4 cup of the frosting. Place the cake layer frosting side down over the prepared layers. Spread the remaining frosting over the side and top of the cake. Sprinkle with the remaining walnuts.

You may prepare up to 1 day in advance and store, covered, in the refrigerator. Let stand at room temperature for 1 hour before serving.

CREAM CHEESE FROSTING

16 ounces cream cheese, softened
1 cup (2 sticks) unsalted butter, softened
1 tablespoon vanilla extract
¹/₈ teaspoon salt
1¹/₂ cups confectioners' sugar

Beat the cream cheese and butter in a mixing bowl until light and fluffy, scraping the bowl occasionally. Beat in the vanilla and salt. Add the confectioners' sugar gradually, beating constantly until blended. Chill, covered, for 15 minutes or until of spreading consistency.

*Photo on facing page,
Longfield Farm,
Goshen, Kentucky*

BLUEBERRY LEMON CAKE

Serves 12

Cake

1 (2-layer) package lemon cake mix
1/2 cup orange juice
1/2 cup water
1/3 cup vegetable oil
3 eggs
1/8 teaspoon finely shredded
   lemon zest

1 1/2 cups fresh or drained frozen
   blueberries
1 tablespoon finely shredded
   orange zest
1 tablespoon finely shredded
   lemon zest

Citrus Cream Cheese Frosting

1/4 cup (1/2 stick) butter, softened
3 ounces cream cheese, softened
3 cups confectioners' sugar, sifted
2 tablespoons orange juice

1/8 teaspoon vanilla extract
1 cup whipping cream, whipped
2 tablespoons grated orange zest
1 tablespoon grated lemon zest

For the cake, combine the cake mix, orange juice, water, oil, eggs and
1/8 teaspoon lemon zest in a mixing bowl and beat at low speed for
30 seconds. Beat at medium speed for 2 minutes. Fold in the blueberries,
orange zest and 1 tablespoon lemon zest. Spoon into 2 greased and lightly
floured 8- or 9-inch round cake pans.

Bake at 350 degrees for 35 to 40 minutes or until a wooden pick inserted
near the center comes out clean. Cool in the pans on wire racks for
10 minutes. Remove to the wire racks to cool completely.

For the frosting, cream the butter and cream cheese in a medium mixing
bowl until fluffy. Add the confectioners' sugar, orange juice and vanilla and
beat until smooth. Add the whipped cream, orange zest and lemon zest and
beat at low speed to mix well.

Spread the frosting between the layers and over the top and side of the
cake. Garnish with orange zest curls.

BLUEBERRY ICE CREAM

Makes 1 quart

2²/₃ cups blueberries
²/₃ cup sugar
2²/₃ tablespoons water
1 (2-inch) strip lemon zest
Zest of 1 navel orange, removed in strips
1¹/₃ cups heavy cream
²/₃ cup half-and-half
1¹/₃ tablespoons orange liqueur
2 tablespoons fresh lemon juice
¹/₃ teaspoon vanilla extract
Salt to taste

Combine the blueberries, sugar, water, lemon zest and orange zest in a large saucepan and bring to a boil. Cook, covered, for 5 minutes, stirring occasionally. Simmer, uncovered, for 5 minutes longer. Discard the lemon and orange zests.

Purée the mixture in batches in a food processor. Combine with the heavy cream, half-and-half, liqueur, lemon juice, vanilla and salt in a bowl and mix well. Press through a fine sieve into a large bowl. Chill, covered, for 1 hour.

Pour into an ice cream freezer container and freeze using the manufacturer's instructions. Store in an airtight container in the freezer for up to 5 days.

SOUTHERN COMFORT CAKE

Serves 16

Cake
1 cup chopped pecans
1 (2-layer) package butter-recipe cake mix
1 package vanilla instant pudding mix
4 eggs
1/2 cup cold water
1/2 cup Southern Comfort

Southern Comfort Glaze
1 cup (2 sticks) butter
2 cups sugar
1/2 cup cold water
1 cup Southern Comfort

For the cake, sprinkle the pecans in a greased and floured 10-inch bundt pan. Combine the cake mix, pudding mix, eggs, cold water and liqueur in a mixing bowl and mix until smooth. Spoon into the prepared pan.

Bake at 325 degrees for 1 hour. Cool in the pan on a wire rack.

For the glaze, combine the butter, sugar and cold water in a saucepan. Bring to a boil and boil for 5 minutes, stirring to dissolve the sugar completely. Remove from the heat and stir in the liqueur.

Prick the cake and pour the glaze over the top. Let stand for 8 hours or longer before removing to a serving platter.

MISS PEPPER'S CHRISTMAS CAKE

Serves 16

 **2 pounds candied fruit, such as cherries, apricots, pineapple or
pears, chopped**
1 pound dates, chopped
1 pound flaked coconut
1 pound nuts, such as pecans, walnuts, hazelnuts or Brazil nuts, broken
2 (14-ounce) cans sweetened condensed milk

Butter a 10-inch bundt or tube pan and line with waxed paper, leaving
1 inch extending over the top of the pan; butter the paper. Have a glass of
mulled wine.

Combine the candied fruit, dates, coconut and nuts in a large bowl and mix
with your hands or a wooden spoon. Add the sweetened condensed milk
and mix well.

Pack the mixture firmly into the prepared pan, pressing firmly; smooth the
top with a wooden spoon. Bake at 250 degrees for 3 hours. Cool the cake
in the pan.

Invert onto a Lenox serving plate and serve in small slices with eggnog,
coffee or tea during the holidays.

*For a little extra zip, wrap the cake in a cotton kitchen towel soaked in
Jack Daniel's Tennessee Whiskey and let it stand for 8 hours. To keep this
delicious cake moist, store it wrapped in the whiskey towel until the last
morsel is devoured.*

*Christmas in
Kentucky*

*In Kentucky there are
certain tell-tale signs that
the holidays are coming.
The weather may be bleak,
but kitchens across the
Commonwealth are filled
with the warmth of scenes
such as this:*

*"We began cracking nuts for
our fruitcakes and mixing
batters and blending in the
jam for Christmas jam cakes
and measuring out dried
fruits for our plum puddings.
I told my mother how Aunt
had filled the Lighthouse
with much the same odors,
in the bleak weeks before
Christmas. Yes, there was a
nip in the air in Kentucky,
and we saw Canada geese
come down the flyway of
the river."*

SENA JETER NASLUND
"KENTUCKY SEASONS"
AHAB'S WIFE

Amaretto Buttercream Chocolate Cake

Serves 12

Cake

2¹/₄ cups sifted flour

2 teaspoons baking soda

¹/₂ teaspoon salt

¹/₂ cup (1 stick) butter or
    margarine, softened

2¹/₄ cups packed light brown sugar

3 eggs

1¹/₂ teaspoons vanilla extract

3 (1-ounce) squares unsweetened
    chocolate, melted, cooled

1 cup sour cream

1 cup boiling water

Amaretto Buttercream

3 tablespoons butter, softened

1¹/₂ cups sifted confectioners' sugar

5 to 6 tablespoons amaretto

¹/₂ teaspoon vanilla extract

Assembly

Chocolate Ganache (at right)

For the cake, sift the flour, baking soda and salt together. Combine the butter, brown sugar and eggs in a large mixing bowl and beat at high speed until light and fluffy. Beat in the vanilla and chocolate. Add the dry ingredients alternately with the sour cream, mixing well with a spoon after each addition. Stir in the boiling water; the batter will be thin.

Spoon the batter into 2 greased and lightly floured 9-inch cake pans. Bake at 350 degrees for 35 minutes or until the centers spring back when lightly pressed. Cool in the pans on wire racks for 10 minutes. Remove to the wire racks to cool completely.

For the buttercream, combine the butter, confectioners' sugar, amaretto and vanilla in a mixing bowl and beat until very smooth.

To assemble, spread the buttercream between the layers. Place in the refrigerator or freezer for 15 minutes. Place the cake on a rack over a baking sheet. Pour the ganache over the cake, allowing it to drip down the side and spread with a spatula. Spoon excess ganache into a plastic bag and cut off a small corner. Pipe over the cake. Garnish with chocolate curls and strawberries dipped in the ganache.

Chocolate Ganache

¹/₄ cup heavy cream

4 ounces semisweet
    chocolate, chopped, or
    chocolate chips

2 tablespoons butter,
    softened

Pour the heavy cream into a microwave-safe bowl and microwave on Medium for 2 minutes. Add the chocolate and whisk until blended; microwave for 1 minute longer if necessary to melt completely. Whisk in the butter. Let stand for 30 minutes or until thickened.

SWIRLED PECAN POUND CAKE

Serves 16

1/2 cup (1 stick) butter or margarine, softened
1/2 cup shortening
3 cups sugar
5 eggs
3 cups flour
1/2 teaspoon baking powder
1/4 teaspoon salt
1 cup milk
1 teaspoon vanilla extract
1 (1-ounce) square unsweetened chocolate
1 tablespoon shortening
1/8 teaspoon vanilla extract
Cinnamon to taste
1/2 cup chopped pecans

Beat the butter and 1/2 cup shortening at medium speed in a mixing bowl for 2 minutes or until light. Add the sugar gradually, beating constantly at medium speed for 5 to 7 minutes or until fluffy. Add the eggs 1 at a time, beating just until mixed after each addition.

Combine the flour, baking powder and salt in a bowl and mix well. Add to the creamed mixture alternately with the milk, mixing at low speed after each addition and beginning and ending with the dry ingredients. Stir in 1 teaspoon vanilla.

Melt the chocolate with 1 tablespoon shortening in a small heavy saucepan, stirring to blend well. Stir in 1/8 teaspoon vanilla. Remove 2 cups of the cake batter to a small bowl. Stir in the chocolate mixture.

Add the cinnamon to the remaining cake batter and spoon 1/3 of the batter into a greased and floured 10-inch tube pan. Layer the chocolate mixture and the remaining plain cake batter in the prepared pan. Swirl with a knife to marbleize. Top with the pecans.

Bake at 350 degrees for 1 hour and 10 minutes or until a wooden pick inserted near the center comes out clean. Cool in the pan on a wire rack for 10 to 15 minutes. Remove to the wire rack to cool completely.

IRISH COFFEE EGGNOG PUNCH

2 quarts eggnog
1/3 cup packed brown sugar
3 tablespoons instant coffee granules
1/2 teaspoon cinnamon
1/2 teaspoon nutmeg
1 cup Bushmills Irish Whiskey
1 quart coffee ice cream

Combine the eggnog, brown sugar, coffee granules, cinnamon and nutmeg in a mixing bowl. Beat at low speed until smooth. Stir in the whiskey. Chill, covered, for 1 to 2 hours. Pour into a punch bowl. Top with scoops of the ice cream. Ladle into punch cups.

For **Homemade Eggnog,** combine 2 beaten eggs, 1 (14-ounce) can sweetened condensed milk and 2 teaspoons vanilla extract in a mixing bowl and mix well. Add 4 cups milk gradually, beating constantly. Cover and chill. Whip 2 cups whipping cream and fold into the chilled mixture.

ROSE GERANIUM CAKE

Serves 16

1 cup (2 sticks) butter, softened	1 cup sour cream
2¹/₂ cups sugar	2 teaspoons vanilla extract
6 eggs, beaten	2 tablespoons Rose Water (below)
3 cups flour	5 or 6 rose geranium leaves,
¹/₂ teaspoon baking soda	chopped
¹/₄ teaspoon mace	1 cup confectioners' sugar
¹/₂ teaspoon salt	2 tablespoons Rose Water (below)

Cream the butter and sugar in a mixing bowl until light and fluffy. Beat in the eggs. Mix the flour, baking soda, mace and salt together. Add to the creamed mixture alternately with the sour cream, mixing well after each addition. Stir in the vanilla and 2 tablespoons Rose Water. Fold in the rose geranium leaves.

Spoon into a greased and floured 10-inch tube pan. Bake at 350 degrees for 60 to 70 minutes or until a tester comes out clean; do not overbake. Cool in the pan on a wire rack for 30 minutes. Remove to a wire rack to cool completely.

Blend the confectioners' sugar and 2 tablespoons Rose Water in a small bowl. Spread over the top of the cake. Garnish with fresh rosebuds.

ROSE WATER

Makes 4 cups

4 cups water	2 cups organically-grown rose petals

Bring the water to a full boil in a saucepan. Pour over the rose petals in a heatproof bowl. Let stand until cool. Strain, reserving the liquid. Store in an airtight container in the refrigerator.

Rose in Gelée

To create a beautiful garnish for any dish, invert a rose into the bottom of a plastic bowl slightly larger then the flower. Tape across the bowl crosswise to hold the rose securely in place. Mix ²/₃ cup sugar and 2 envelopes unflavored gelatin in a heatproof bowl. Add 2 cups boiling water, stirring until dissolved. Add 1 cup ice cold water gradually, stirring constantly until mixture is clear. Let cool. Pour down the sides of the plastic bowl, being careful to not dislodge the flower. Refrigerate for 8 to 10 hours. Once gelée is set, slightly moisten plastic bowl and invert rose gelée into center of a serving platter.

You may use a variety of different medium-size flowers in place of the rose, or even a small bunch of violets or sprig of holly with berries. To bring even more color to your garnish, add a few drops of food coloring to the gelatin.

ELEGANT PUMPKIN ROLL

This pumpkin roll is a striking alternative to classic pumpkin pie.

Serves 12

3/4 cup cake flour
1 1/2 teaspoons cinnamon
1 1/4 teaspoons ground ginger
3/4 teaspoon ground allspice
1/8 teaspoon nutmeg
6 egg yolks
1/3 cup sugar
1/3 cup packed brown sugar
2/3 cup canned pumpkin
6 large egg whites

1/8 teaspoon salt
Confectioners' sugar for rolling and
  sprinkling
1/4 cup toffee chips or chopped
  toffee candy
Toffee Rum Filling (at right)
1 1/2 cups commercial caramel
  sauce
1/2 cup toffee chips or chopped
  toffee candy

Sift the flour, cinnamon, ginger, allspice and nutmeg into a small bowl. Combine the egg yolks, sugar and brown sugar in a mixing bowl and beat for 3 minutes or until very thick. Beat in the pumpkin at low speed. Mix in the sifted dry ingredients.

Beat the egg whites with the salt in a mixing bowl until stiff but not dry. Fold into the batter 1/3 at a time. Spoon into a 10 × 15-inch baking pan sprayed with nonstick cooking spray.

Bake at 375 degrees for 15 minutes or until a tester inserted into the center comes out clean. Run a knife around the edges to loosen and invert onto a smooth kitchen towel generously sprinkled with confectioners' sugar. Fold the towel over 1 long side of the cake and roll in the towel from the long side. Place seam side down and let stand for 1 hour or until cool.

Unroll the cake and sprinkle with 1/4 cup toffee chips. Spread with the Toffee Rum Filling and roll again from the long side to enclose the filling. Cover the roll with foil and chill in the refrigerator. Trim the ends of the roll on a slight diagonal.

Dust the cake with additional confectioners' sugar. Warm the caramel sauce in a small saucepan and spoon some over the cake; sprinkle with 1/2 cup toffee chips. Slice and serve with the remaining caramel sauce.

TOFFEE RUM FILLING

1 teaspoon unflavored
  gelatin
2 tablespoons rum
1/4 teaspoon vanilla extract
1 cup whipping cream, chilled
3 tablespoons confectioners'
  sugar
10 tablespoons toffee chips

Sprinkle the gelatin over the rum in a small heavy saucepan and let stand for 10 minutes or until softened. Cook over low heat just until the gelatin dissolves completely, stirring constantly. Stir in the vanilla. Beat the whipping cream with the confectioners' sugar in a large bowl until soft peaks form. Beat in the gelatin mixture. Fold in the toffee chips.

PLUM TORTE

Serves 8

 ¹/₂ **cup (1 stick) unsalted butter, softened**
³/₄ cup sugar
1 cup unbleached flour, sifted
1 teaspoon baking powder
¹/₈ teaspoon cinnamon
¹/₈ teaspoon salt (optional)
2 eggs
24 Italian purple plum halves
Sugar to taste
Lemon juice to taste
1 teaspoon cinnamon, or to taste

Cream the butter and ³/₄ cup sugar in a mixing bowl until light and fluffy. Add the flour, baking powder, ¹/₈ teaspoon cinnamon, salt and eggs; beat until smooth. Spoon into an 8- to 10-inch springform pan.

Arrange the plums cut side down on top of the batter. Sprinkle with additional sugar and drizzle with lemon juice. Sprinkle with 1 teaspoon cinnamon.

Bake at 350 degrees for 1 hour. Cool slightly, remove the side of the pan and serve warm with whipped cream if desired. Store in the refrigerator or freezer.

WOODFORD RESERVE CHOCOLATE TORTE

Serves 12

Torte
16 ounces semisweet chocolate
1¹/₄ cups (2¹/₂ sticks) unsalted butter
¹/₄ cup Woodford Reserve Bourbon
2 tablespoons instant coffee granules
5 egg yolks, at room temperature
5 egg whites, at room temperature

Chocolate Ganache
10 ounces bittersweet chocolate
¹/₂ cup heavy cream
2 tablespoons dark corn syrup

For the torte, melt the chocolate with the butter in a double boiler over hot water, stirring to blend well. Cool to room temperature.

Combine the bourbon and coffee granules in a small bowl and mix well. Beat the egg yolks in a mixing bowl until thickened. Add the bourbon-coffee mixture and egg yolks to chocolate mixture and mix well.

Beat the egg whites until stiff peaks form. Fold into the chocolate mixture. Spoon into a greased 9-inch springform pan.

Bake at 375 degrees for 12 minutes; the torte will appear underbaked. Cool on a wire rack.

For the ganache, chop the chocolate in a food processor. Scald the heavy cream in a small saucepan. Add the chocolate and mix well. Stir in the corn syrup.

Place the torte on a serving plate. Pour the ganache over the top. Chill in the refrigerator.

Chocolate Curls

Garnish chocolate recipes with these elegant curls:

- *Melt semisweet chocolate squares or chips on the stove top or in the microwave.*

- *Use a spatula to spread melted chocolate into a very thin layer on a baking sheet. Chill until firm but still pliable, about 10 minutes.*

- *To curl chocolate, slide the tip of a metal spatula under the edge of the chocolate. Push the spatula along the baking sheet, under the chocolate, until the chocolate curls as it is pushed. Make the curls as long or as short as you want.*

- *Use a wooden pick to pick up each curl and carefully transfer to a waxed paper-lined baking sheet. Chill until firm, about 15 minutes.*

OLD FORESTER BOURBON BALLS

Bourbon balls are a Kentucky gift-giving tradition. Add these to your holiday cookie plate or Derby gift basket.

Makes 12 dozen

 5 cups vanilla wafer crumbs
2 cups confectioners' sugar
1/4 cup baking cocoa
2 cups chopped nuts
6 tablespoons light corn syrup
1 cup Old Forester
Confectioners' sugar for coating

Combine the cookie crumbs, 2 cups confectioners' sugar, baking cocoa and nuts in a bowl and mix with a large spoon. Add the corn syrup and bourbon and mix well.

Shape into small balls and roll in additional confectioners' sugar, coating well. Store in the refrigerator or freezer.

APRICOT SHORTBREAD SQUARES

Makes 16 to 25

1/2 cup (1 stick) butter, softened
1/2 cup packed brown sugar
1 cup flour
1/2 cup apricot preserves
1/8 teaspoon vanilla extract
1 teaspoon grated lemon zest
1/3 cup toasted chopped pecans

Combine the butter, brown sugar and flour in a mixing bowl and mix until smooth. Press into an 8- or 9-inch-square baking pan. Bake at 350 degrees for 12 minutes or until golden brown.

Combine the apricot preserves and vanilla in a bowl and mix well. Spread over the shortbread. Sprinkle with the lemon zest and pecans. Bake for 20 minutes longer. Cool on a wire rack. Cut into small squares to serve.

CHOCOLATE CHESS BARS

Makes 16

1 cup flour
1/4 cup confectioners' sugar
1/2 cup (1 stick) butter, melted
1 1/2 cups sugar
3 1/2 tablespoons baking cocoa

1/8 teaspoon salt
2 eggs, beaten
1/4 cup (1/2 stick) butter, melted
1 (5-ounce) can evaporated milk
1 teaspoon vanilla extract

Combine the flour, confectioners' sugar and 1/2 cup butter in a bowl and mix well. Press over the bottom of a greased 8 × 8-inch baking pan. Bake at 350 degrees for 20 minutes.

Combine the sugar, baking cocoa and salt in a bowl. Add the eggs, 1/4 cup butter, evaporated milk and vanilla and mix well. Spread over the warm baked layer. Bake for 40 to 50 minutes longer or until set. Cool on a wire rack. Cut into bars to serve.

SIMPLY SESAME COOKIES

These cookies will make it to the top of your most-requested list.

Makes 4 dozen

2 cups (4 sticks) butter, softened
1/8 teaspoon vanilla extract
1 1/2 cups sugar
3 cups flour

1 cup sesame seeds
2 cups shredded coconut
1/2 cup finely chopped almonds

Cream the butter and vanilla in a mixing bowl until light. Add the sugar gradually, beating until fluffy. Add the flour gradually, beating constantly until smooth. Stir in the sesame seeds, coconut and almonds.

Shape into logs 3 to 5 inches long and 2 inches in diameter. Wrap in waxed paper and chill in the refrigerator for 3 hours or longer.

Cut into 1/4-inch slices and arrange 1 inch apart on ungreased cookie sheets. Bake at 300 degrees for 25 to 30 minutes or until light brown.

Professional Results

Use black baking pans when baking. A dull, dark, or black surface absorbs more of the radiant energy coming from the oven walls than a bright, shiny, or white surface.

TRIPLE-CHOCOLATE MALTED COOKIES

Makes 2 dozen or more

1 cup butter-flavor shortening
1¼ cups packed brown sugar
½ cup malted milk powder
2 tablespoons chocolate syrup
1 tablespoon vanilla extract
1 egg
2 cups flour
1 teaspoon baking soda
½ teaspoon salt
1½ cups semisweet chocolate chunks
1 cup milk chocolate chips

Combine the shortening, brown sugar, malted milk powder, chocolate syrup and vanilla in a mixing bowl and beat for 2 minutes. Beat in the egg.

Mix the flour, baking soda and salt together. Add to the chocolate mixture gradually, mixing well after each addition. Stir in the chocolate chunks and chocolate chips.

Shape into 2-inch balls and arrange 3 inches apart on ungreased cookie sheets. Bake at 375 degrees for 12 minutes or until golden brown. Cool on the cookie sheets for 2 minutes. Remove to a wire rack to cool completely.

Homemade Vanilla Extract

Combine 3 whole vanilla beans with ½ teaspoon light honey and 7 ounces Finlandia Vodka in a bottle. Cover and let stand for 4 to 8 weeks before using. Remove the vanilla beans to store for longer than 8 weeks.

CRANBERRY CARAMEL SQUARES

Makes 2 dozen

1 cup fresh cranberries
1/2 teaspoon fresh lemon juice
2 tablespoons sugar
2 cups flour
1/2 teaspoon baking soda
2 cups rolled oats
1/2 cup sugar
1/2 cup packed brown sugar
1/4 cup finely chopped toasted pecans
1 cup (2 sticks) butter or margarine, melted
10 ounces dates, chopped
3/4 cup chopped pecans
1 (12-ounce) jar caramel sauce
1/3 cup flour

Combine the cranberries with the lemon juice and 2 tablespoons sugar in a small bowl and mix well.

Mix 2 cups flour, baking soda, oats, 1/2 cup sugar, brown sugar and 1/4 cup pecans in a bowl. Stir in the butter and mix until crumbly. Reserve 1 cup of the mixture and press the remaining mixture over the bottom of a lightly greased 9 × 13-inch baking pan.

Bake at 350 degrees for 15 minutes. Sprinkle with the dates, 3/4 cup pecans and cranberries.

Mix the caramel sauce with 1/3 cup flour in a small bowl. Spoon over the cranberries and sprinkle with the reserved flour mixture. Bake for 20 minutes longer or until light brown. Cool on a wire rack and cut into squares.

CRANBERRY KIR NOËL

3 cups fresh cranberries
3 cups water
2 cups sugar
1 teaspoon whole allspice
2 cinnamon sticks
4 whole cloves
Korbel Brut Champagne, chilled

Combine the cranberries, water, sugar, allspice, cinnamon sticks and cloves in a saucepan and mix well. Bring to a boil; reduce heat. Simmer for 5 to 10 minutes or until the cranberries begin to pop, stirring occasionally. Cool to room temperature. Strain the syrup into a container with a cover, discarding the solids. Cover and chill in the refrigerator. For each Cranberry Kir Noël, place 1 1/2 tablespoons of the cranberry syrup in a Champagne flute. Add enough Champagne to fill the flute. Garnish with additional whole cranberries. Store leftover syrup, covered, in the refrigerator.

CURRANT JELLY COOKIES

Makes 16

^{1}/$_2$ cup (1 stick) butter or margarine, softened
^{1}/$_2$ cup sugar
1 egg yolk
^{1}/$_2$ cup ground almonds
^{1}/$_2$ teaspoon grated lemon zest
^{3}/$_4$ cup flour
^{1}/$_4$ teaspoon cinnamon
^{1}/$_8$ teaspoon nutmeg
^{1}/$_4$ teaspoon salt
1 egg white, lightly beaten
2 tablespoons sliced almonds
^{1}/$_3$ cup currant jelly

Cream the butter and sugar in a mixing bowl until light and fluffy. Beat in the egg yolk. Stir in the ground almonds and lemon zest.

Mix the flour, cinnamon, nutmeg and salt together. Add to the creamed mixture and mix well. Divide into 2 equal portions.

Pat each portion over the bottom of a generously greased 8 × 8-inch baking pan. Brush one layer with the beaten egg white and sprinkle with sliced almonds.

Bake at 350 degrees for 18 to 20 minutes or until golden brown. Cool in the pans for 3 minutes. Invert the baked layers onto waxed paper.

Spread the jelly over the bottom of the plain layer. Place the other layer almond side up on the jelly. Cut into bars or squares with a sharp knife while warm.

GONE-IN-A-DAY COOKIES

Makes 6 to 7 dozen

1 cup (2 sticks) margarine, softened
1 cup sugar
1 cup packed brown sugar
1 egg
1 to 2 teaspoons vanilla extract
1 cup rolled oats
1 cup crushed cornflakes
1 cup chopped pecans or walnuts
1 cup shredded coconut
1/8 teaspoon cinnamon
1 cup vegetable oil
3 1/2 to 4 cups sifted flour
1 teaspoon baking soda
1 teaspoon salt

Cream the margarine, sugar and brown sugar in a mixing bowl until light and fluffy. Beat in the egg and vanilla. Add the oats, cornflakes, pecans, coconut, cinnamon and oil and mix well.

Sift the flour, baking soda and salt together. Add to the oats mixture and mix well. Chill in the refrigerator.

Shape into 1-inch balls. Place on ungreased cookie sheets and press with a fork dipped in water to flatten. Bake at 325 degrees for 12 to 15 minutes or just until golden brown; do not overbake. Cool on the cookie sheets for several minutes. Remove to a wire rack to cool completely.

Which Oats to Use?

After a process of being cleaned, toasted, hulled, and cleaned again, whole oats become oat groats. Depending on further processing, oat groats can be classified in three categories:

- Rolled oats (also called old-fashioned) are steamed and flattened with large rollers. They take about 15 minutes to cook.

- Quick-cooking rolled oats are groats that have been cut into pieces before being steamed and flattened. They cook in about 5 minutes. Old-fashioned oats and quick-cooking oats can usually be interchanged in recipes.

- Instant oats cannot be interchanged because they are precooked and dried before the rolling process. The precooking softens the oats, and any baked goods made with them can turn into a gooey mess.

PRALINE CHEESECAKE BARS

Created by Chef Kathy Cary, Lilly's

Makes 20

2 cups graham cracker crumbs
6 tablespoons sugar
7 ounces (1³/4 sticks) butter, melted
1 tablespoon cinnamon
36 ounces cream cheese, softened
2 cups sugar
4 eggs
9 ounces pecan pieces
¹/2 tablespoon vanilla extract
2 cups packed brown sugar
1 cup (2 sticks) butter

Mix the graham cracker crumbs, 6 tablespoons sugar, melted butter and cinnamon in a bowl. Press over the bottom of a 9 × 13-inch baking pan. Bake at 350 degrees for 20 minutes.

Process the cream cheese and 2 cups sugar in a food processor until smooth. Add the eggs and process until mixed. Add the pecans and vanilla and pulse until mixed. Pour over the baked layer. Bake at 350 degrees for 25 minutes or until set in the center.

Combine the brown sugar and 1 cup butter in a saucepan and cook until the butter melts and the brown sugar dissolves, stirring to mix well. Pour over the cream cheese layer. Broil until bubbly.

Cool on a wire rack. Cut into bars to serve.

PRALINE COOKIES

These delightful cookies combine pecans and brown sugar to achieve the flavor of that delicious southern confection known as a praline.

Makes 3¹/₂ dozen

Cookies
1²/₃ cups sifted flour
1¹/₂ teaspoons baking powder
¹/₂ teaspoon salt
¹/₂ cup (1 stick) butter, softened
1¹/₂ cups packed brown sugar
1 egg
1 teaspoon vanilla extract
1 cup pecan halves, broken into pieces

Praline Frosting
1 cup packed brown sugar
¹/₂ cup cream
1 cup confectioners' sugar

For the cookies, sift the flour, baking powder and salt together. Beat the butter in a mixing bowl until light. Add the brown sugar gradually, beating until fluffy. Beat in the egg and vanilla. Add the dry ingredients gradually, mixing well after each addition.

Drop by rounded teaspoonfuls onto cookie sheets. Bake at 350 degrees for 10 to 12 minutes or until golden brown. Cool on the cookie sheets on wire racks for 2 minutes. Top with the pecan pieces. Remove cookies to wire racks to cool completely.

For the frosting, combine the brown sugar and cream in a small saucepan and bring to a boil, stirring constantly. Boil for 2 minutes and remove from the heat. Stir in the confectioners' sugar; thin with a few additional drops of cream if necessary for spreading consistency. Spread over the cookies. Do not substitute margarine for butter in this recipe.

"IRISH CREME" LIQUEUR

Makes 8 (6-ounce) servings

1 (14-ounce) can sweetened condensed milk
2 cups half-and-half
2 cups Early Times
¹/₂ teaspoon instant coffee granules
2 ounces coffee liqueur

Combine the sweetened condensed milk, half-and-half, whisky, coffee granules and liqueur in a pitcher and mix well. Refrigerate until chilled. Pour over ice to serve.

Sugar and Spice Ginger Cookies

Makes 8 dozen

1 cup shortening
¹/₂ cup (1 stick) margarine, softened
2 cups sugar
2 eggs
¹/₂ cup molasses
4 cups flour
4 teaspoons baking soda
2 teaspoons cinnamon
1¹/₄ teaspoons ginger
1¹/₂ teaspoons ground cloves
¹/₈ teaspoon allspice
¹/₂ teaspoon salt
Confectioners' sugar

Combine the shortening, margarine and sugar in a food processor and process until light and fluffy. Add the eggs and molasses and process until smooth.

Sift the flour, baking soda, cinnamon, ginger, cloves, allspice and salt together. Add to the food processor and process until well mixed. Shape into balls and place on cookie sheets; press to flatten.

Place on the upper oven rack and bake at 350 degrees for 5 minutes. Move to the lower oven rack and bake for 5 minutes longer; do not overbake. Sift confectioners' sugar over the cookies and remove to wire racks to cool. Freeze in airtight plastic bags if desired.

CRANBERRY PIE

Serves 8

 1 pound fresh cranberries
(about 4 cups)
1¹⁄₂ cups sugar
2 tablespoons flour
¹⁄₂ teaspoon cinnamon
¹⁄₄ teaspoon salt
³⁄₄ cup chopped walnuts

1 small orange, peeled, sectioned,
chopped
¹⁄₄ teaspoon grated orange zest
¹⁄₂ cup raisins
1 recipe (2-crust) pie pastry
2 tablespoons butter
Sugar for sprinkling

Combine the cranberries, 1¹⁄₂ cups sugar, flour, cinnamon and salt in a large bowl. Stir in the walnuts, orange, orange zest and raisins. Spoon into a pastry-lined 9-inch pie plate. Dot with the butter.

Top with the remaining pastry; seal and flute the edge and cut vents. Brush with water and sprinkle with sugar.

Cover the edge with foil and place on a baking sheet. Bake at 375 degrees for 25 minutes. Remove the foil and bake for 30 to 35 minutes longer or until the cranberries are tender and the crust is golden brown. Serve warm or cool with ice cream if desired.

EARLY TIMES TRIPLE TURF PIE

Serves 6 to 8

¹⁄₂ cup (1 stick) butter, melted,
cooled
¹⁄₂ cup flour
2 eggs, lightly beaten
1 cup sugar

Early Times to taste
1 teaspoon vanilla extract
1 cup chocolate chips
1 cup chopped pecans
Pastry Shell (at right)

Combine the butter, flour, eggs, sugar, whisky and vanilla in a bowl and mix well. Stir in the chocolate chips and pecans. Spoon into the unbaked Pastry Shell. Bake at 350 degrees for 30 minutes. Garnish with sprigs of fresh mint. Serve with whipped cream or ice cream.

PASTRY SHELL

Makes 1 pastry shell

1¹⁄₄ cups flour
¹⁄₄ cup sugar
Cinnamon to taste
¹⁄₂ cup (1 stick) butter, chilled
1¹⁄₂ tablespoons beaten egg
¹⁄₂ teaspoon vanilla extract

Combine the flour, sugar, cinnamon and butter in a food processor container and process until crumbly. Add the egg and vanilla in a stream, processing constantly until the mixture forms a ball. Wrap in plastic wrap and chill in the refrigerator for 1 hour. Roll to fit a 9-inch pie plate on a lightly floured surface and fit into the pie plate.

For a baked shell, prick all over with a fork and bake at 350 degrees for 10 minutes.

SOUTHERN APPLE TART

Serves 8 to 10

Tart Pastry
1/3 cup butter, softened
1/3 cup sugar
1/8 teaspoon cinnamon
1/4 teaspoon vanilla extract
1/8 teaspoon salt
1 cup sifted flour

Filling
4 cups sliced peeled apples
8 ounces cream cheese, softened
1/4 cup sugar
1 egg
1/4 teaspoon lemon juice
2 teaspoons grated lemon zest
1/4 teaspoon almond extract
1/8 teaspoon salt
1/4 cup sugar
1/2 teaspoon cinnamon
1/4 cup sliced almonds

For the pastry, cream the butter, sugar, cinnamon, vanilla and salt in a medium mixing bowl until light and fluffy. Add the flour and mix until crumbly. Pat over the bottom of a 9-inch springform pan.

For the filling, spread the apples in a shallow baking dish and cover with foil. Bake at 400 degrees for 15 minutes. Reduce the oven temperature to 350 degrees.

Beat the cream cheese and 1/4 cup sugar in a medium mixing bowl until smooth. Add the egg, lemon juice, lemon zest, almond extract and salt and beat until smooth. Spoon into the prepared springform pan. Arrange the apples in a circular pattern over the top.

Mix 1/4 cup sugar and cinnamon in a small bowl. Sprinkle over the apples and arrange the almonds over the top. Bake at 350 degrees for 40 to 60 minutes or until the filling is set and the crust is light brown.

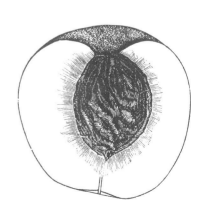

FRESH LIME AND MACADAMIA TART

A palate-pleasing tart.

Serves 6 to 8

Tart Pastry

1¹/₂ cups unbleached flour
¹/₂ cup (1 stick) unsalted butter,
**   chilled, chopped**
1 tablespoon sugar

¹/₂ teaspoon grated lime zest
¹/₈ teaspoon salt
1 egg yolk
1 to 2 tablespoons ice water

Filling

2 large limes
¹/₂ cup ground unsalted
**   macadamias**
¹/₂ cup sugar

2 eggs
6 tablespoons unsalted butter,
**   melted**

For the pastry, combine the flour, butter, sugar, lime zest and salt in a food processor container and process until the mixture resembles coarse meal. Add the egg yolk and process to mix. Add enough ice water to form a ball, processing constantly. Shape into a ball, dust with flour and wrap with plastic wrap. Chill for 1 hour or longer.

Roll the dough into a 12-inch circle on a lightly floured surface. Place in a 9-inch tart pan. Trim and flute the edge and prick the bottom with a fork. Line with baking parchment and weight with dried beans or pie weights. Bake at 400 degrees for 15 minutes. Remove the weights and parchment and cool on a wire rack.

For the filling, remove the zest from the limes with a vegetable peeler; reserve the limes and chop the zest fine. Combine the zest with the ground macadamias, sugar and eggs in a food processor. Process for 30 seconds. Squeeze in the juice from the limes and add the butter. Process for 10 seconds or until well mixed.

Pour into the tart shell. Bake for 30 minutes or until the filling is set and light brown. Cool to room temperature. Cut into wedges and garnish the servings with whipped cream and whole macadamias or thinly sliced lime wedges.

Quick Tarts

For a quick-and-easy dessert, fill purchased tart shells with the following:

- *A scoop of ice cream topped with fresh fruit*

- *A favorite pudding topped with whipped cream*

- *Sliced fresh fruit brushed with melted seedless jam*

Wine Guide

White Varietal Wine

VARIETAL	STYLE	COMMON AROMAS & FLAVORS	MENU EXAMPLES
CHARDONNAY (Shar-doe-NAY)	*Lighter* Light yellow, lighter body, emphasis on fresh fruit, crisp	Green apple, lemon, orange	Corn chowder, Grilled chicken, and Shrimp salad
	Barrel-fermented Medium yellow, medium-full body, oak influence	Apple-spice, pineapple-tropical fruit, citrus, buttery	Roast chicken, Seafood and shellfish, Veal piccata
	Reserve/Barrel-fermented Medium-dark yellow, full-bodied, rich with oak emphasis	Pineapple-tropical fruit, vanilla, nutty, toasty, spicy	Crab cakes, Fettuccine Alfredo, Sautéed/grilled prawns or scallops with rich sauces
PINOT GRIGIO/PINOT GRIS (PEE-no GREE-gee-oh/ PEE-no GREE)	Pale yellow, light oak in some styles	Lemon, melon, floral	Slightly spicy appetizers, Fresh seafood, Vegetarian dishes
VIOGNIER (VEE-oh-NYAY)	*Dry* Medium yellow, medium-full body, varied styles—stainless steel or barrel-fermented	Floral, peach, apricot, honeysuckle	Slightly spicy appetizers, Grilled Halibut, Smoked foods
GEWÜRZTRAMINER (Ga-VERTZ-trah-ME-neer)	*Off-dry* Light-medium yellow, light-medium body, hint of sweetness	Apricot, peach, Oriental spice, tropical fruit, honey	Prosciutto and melon, Oriental and Latin dishes, fresh fruit
	Dry Light-medium yellow, medium-full body, bone dry, hint of bitterness	Green apple, pear, floral	Sausages, Pâté, Chicken or seafood with light cream sauce
JOHANNISBERG RIESLING (Joe-HAHN-nis-berg REEZ-ling)	*Off-dry* Light-medium yellow, medium body, hint of sweetness	Apricot, peach, pear, honey, floral	Baked ham, Oriental and Latin dishes
	Dry Light yellow, light-medium body, dry, crisp	Green apple, pear, mineral	Smoked salmon or trout, Fresh oysters, Oriental and Latin dishes
SAUVIGNON BLANC FUMÉ BLANC (SOW-veen-yonh BLONK) (Foo-may Blonk)	*Grassy/herbal* Light-medium yellow, medium body, crisp	Lemon, grapefruit, smokey, grassy, dill, green olive	Salads, Fillet of sole, Vegetarian dishes, Steamed clams
	Barrel-aged Medium-yellow, medium-full body, oak influence	Fig, melon, orange, lemon, vanilla, herbal	Veal piccata, Roast chicken, Grilled shrimp

Photo on facing page,
Tobacco barn and field
Carroll County, Kentucky

Reprinted with permission from Fetzer Vineyards.

Wine Guide

RED AND BLUSH VARIETAL WINE

VARIETAL	STYLE	COMMON AROMAS & FLAVORS	MENU EXAMPLES
CABERNET SAUVIGNON (Cab-bear-NAY SO-veen-YONH)	*Medium* Crimson-medium red, medium body, smooth, fruity, soft	Cherry, berry, spice	Grilled meats, Beef or lamb stew, Pasta with olives and tomato sauce
	Barrel-aged/Reserve Medium-dark red, medium-full body, oak influence, more complex	Cherry, currant, chocolate, cedar, mint, vanilla	Grilled meats, Roast rack of lamb with Dijon mustard, Roast pork, Aged cheeses
MERITAGE (MEHR-i-taj)	Medium-dark red, medium-full body, tannic when young	Currants, berries, cedar, cocoa, vanilla	Fillet of beef, Roast pork, Game, Hearty cheeses
MERLOT (Mare-LOW)	Medium-dark red, medium body, soft, round mouthfeel	Berry, cherry, orange zest, tea, vanilla	Veal ragout, Roast duck, Grilled tenderloin of pork
SANGIOVESE (San-joh-VAY-zeh)	Ruby-garnet, medium body, dry	Blackberry, cherry, licorice, earthy	Tomato-based pastas, Roast meats, Duck
NEBBIOLO (Neb-be-YOH-LO)	Medium-dark red, full body, rich, intense	Blackberry, spice, earthy, tar	Veal, Pork, Duck in red wine sauce, Aged cheeses
SYRAH/PETITE SIRAH (Sih-RAH/ Puh-TEET Sih-RAH)	Dark red-purple, full body, tannic	Blueberry, currant, plum, licorice, pepper	Grilled lamb, Game dishes, Hearty cheeses
PINOT NOIR (PEE-no NWAH)	Ruby-medium red, light-medium body, soft, fruity	Cherry, spice, cedar, coffee, earthy, mushrooms	Chicken in red wine sauce, Grilled salmon or tuna, Grilled squab or quail
ZINFANDEL (ZIN-fan-dell)	Medium-dark red, medium-full body, lively	Blackberry, raspberry, jammy, spice, pepper	Pasta with garlic-tomato sauce, Roast chicken, Grilled meats and ribs, Hearty cheeses
WHITE ZINFANDEL (White ZIN-fan-dell)	Pink-coral, light body, hint of sweetness, lively	Strawberry, orange zest	Asian or Latin dishes, Grilled chicken, Pasta salad
PORT (PORT)	Dark red, full-bodied, intense, rich	Ripe berries, chocolate, vanilla	Chocolate desserts, Coffee desserts, Hearty cheeses

REPRINTED WITH PERMISSION FROM FETZER VINEYARDS.

Wine Guide

REGIONAL ITALIAN BLENDS — WHITE

VARIETAL	STYLE	COMMON AROMAS & FLAVORS	MENU EXAMPLES
SOAVE (*SWAH-vey*)	Pale yellow, dry, light-bodied	Apple, pear, honeydew melon, almond	Cold appetizers, Chicken or seafood salads, Pastas
ORVIETO (*Or-vee-YEE-toe*)	Light straw, medium-bodied, fruity, dry	Fresh apple, citrus, pear	Pastas, Chicken or seafood with cream sauce, Herbed cheeses
FRASCATI (*Fras-KAHT-ee*)	Bright, translucent, clean, crisp	Floral, slight perfume	Salads, Pastas, Mild seafood dishes, Poultry

REGIONAL ITALIAN BLENDS — RED

VARIETAL	STYLE	COMMON AROMAS & FLAVORS	MENU EXAMPLES
VALPOLICELLA (*VAL-poli-TCHELLAH*)	Ruby red, dry, medium-bodied	Delicate spice, ripe cherry, almonds, raisins	Roast beef, Beef stew, Pasta with red sauce
CHIANTI (*KEE-ahn-tee*)	Ruby-garnet red, dry, medium-full bodied	Plum, ripe raspberry, cherries, spice	Grilled red meats, Veal and tomato-based dishes, Duck
BARDOLINO (*BAR-doh-LEENO*)	Bright ruby-red, dry, slightly spritzy	Spicy cherry, raspberry	Smoked fish, Salads, Barbecued ribs, Pizza

CHAMPAGNE & SPARKLING WINE STYLES

VARIETAL	STYLE	COMMON AROMAS & FLAVORS	MENU EXAMPLES
BRUT (*Brute*)	Light-medium yellow, crisp, lively	Yeasty, citrus, apple	Fresh oysters, Seafood with light sauces, Smoked salmon
BLANC DE NOIR (*Blonk duh Nwah*)	Cherry-pink color, medium-full body, rich	Toasty, nutty, cherry	Seafood or poultry with richer sauces, Grilled meats
CHARDONNAY CHAMPAGNE (*Shar-doe-NAY Sham-PANE*)	Medium yellow, medium-full bodied, rich	Apples, ripe pears, melon, creamy	Appetizers, Seafood, Veal and poultry dishes
ASTI SPUMANTE (*AS-tee Spoo-MAHN-tee*)	Full bodied, refreshing	Peaches, apricots	Appetizers, Apple tarts, Lemon pie

REPRINTED WITH PERMISSION FROM FETZER VINEYARDS.

Acknowledgements

Splendor in the Bluegrass would never have been possible without the insight, commitment and common vision of countless individuals. Our heart-felt thanks and appreciation go to all those listed here. It is our sincerest hope that we have not overlooked anyone. We are indebted to you for your time, talent, energy and resources.

A very special thanks to . . .

Brown-Forman Corporation
   Exclusive Corporate Sponsor
Owsley Brown Frazier Family Foundation
Lois Mateus, Brown-Forman Corporation
Early Times Old Style Kentucky Whisky
Woodford Reserve Kentucky Straight
   Bourbon Whiskey
Labrot & Graham Distillery
Brown-Forman Wines International
Bourbon Street Cafe at
   Brown-Forman Corporation
Fetzer Vineyards
John Ash, Brown-Forman Wines
Architype
Bittners
Louisville Stoneware Company
F.B. Purnell Sausage Company
Julius Friedman
Doug Van Houten
Ott Communications, Inc.
Favorite Recipes® Press
Dan Dry & Associates
Tricon Global Restaurants and KFC
Churchill Downs®
Joe Brotzge, Colonial Design
Bruce Richardson, Elmwood Inn Fine Teas
Vince Staten, Vince Staten's
   Old Time Barbecue
Dean Newal Hunter, Jr., Sullivan College
   National Center for Hospitality Studies
Aleksander House Bed & Breakfast
   Innkeeper Nancy Hinchliff
Inn at the Park Bed & Breakfast
   Innkeeper Sandra Mullins
Inn at Woodhaven Bed & Breakfast
   Innkeeper Marsha Burton
Pinecrest Cottage Bed & Breakfast
   Innkeeper Nancy Morris
Nancy and J.D. Cooper
James C. Eaves, Jr.
   Greenebaum Doll & McDonald, PLLC
Philip C. Eschels
   Greenebaum Doll & McDonald, PLLC
Omni Graphics
Celebrations, Inc.
Kentucky Writers' Coalition, Inc.

Professional Credits

Architype
   Rhonda Goodall, Project Manager
   Julius Friedman, Project Designer
   Doug Van Houten, Graphic Designer

Ott Communications, Inc.
   Joyce Goldsmith, Senior Photographer
   Sheri Mivelaz, Vice President/
      Group Director
   Sandra Perry, Assistant Stylist
   Marilyn Rollins, Director of
      Food Marketing

Dan Dry & Associates
   Dan Dry, Owner and Photographer

Favorite Recipes® Press
   Bob Johnson, Regional Sales Manager
   Mary Cummings, Managing Editor
   Mark Sloan, Production Manager
   Elizabeth Miller, Project Manager

Featured Chef Contributors

Chef Kathy Cary, Lilly's
Chef John Castro, Winston's at
   Sullivan College
Chef Agostino Gabriele, Vincenzo's
Chef Jim Gerhardt, The Oakroom at
   The Seelbach Hilton
Lynn Winter, Lynn's Paradise Cafe
Chef Jim McKinney, Club Grotto
Chef Anoosh Shariat, Shariat's

Special Contributors

John Ash, *From the Earth to the Table*, used
   by permission, publisher: Dutton/Signet
   Books (Tamarind Tea with Scented
   Geraniums and Grilled Veal Chops with
   Cabernet-Wild Mushroom Sauce)
John Ash (Strawberry Sparkler)
Chef Sara Gibbs, Bourbon Street Cafe
   (Cranberry Kir Noël, Roasted Tomato Clam
   Chowder, Mediterranean Meatball Soup,
   Southern Comfort Pork Tenderloin, Early
   Times Mustard Chicken, Southern Sweet
   and Spicy Pork Chops and Bay Scallop
   Risotto with Herbs)
Bourbon Street Cafe (Finlandia Cosmopolitan
   Martini, Korbel Mimosa, The Woodford
   Reserve Mint Julep, Southern Spicy
   Chicken with Comfort, Louisiana Grilled
   Salmon, Southern Comfort Muffins, Jack
   Daniel's Chocolate Ice Cream, Old Forester
   Bourbon Balls, Southern Comfort Cake
   and Woodford Reserve Chocolate Torte)
Capriole Goat Cheese, Capriole, Inc.
   Greenville, Indiana
Courier-Journal & Louisville Times Co.
   Copyright © 1999, reprinted with
   permission (Raspberry Lemonade and
   Watermelon Lemonade)
Doll's Market (Katherine Doll's
   Cheese Torte)
Ed's Breads, Ed Penziner (Herb
   Cheddar Rolls)
Elmwood Inn, Fine Teas & Gourmet Foods
   (Hazelnut Scones and Rose
   Geranium Cake)
*Jack Daniel's Home Town Celebration Cookbook
   Volume II*, Copyright © 1990, published
   by Rutledge Hill Press, reprinted with
   permission (Miss Pepper's Christmas Cake)
The Cheddar Box Café (Derby
   Pasta Salad)
The Seelbach Hilton
   (The Seelbach Cocktail)
Vince Staten, author of *Real Barbecue* and
   Jack Daniel's Old Time Barbecue Cookbook and
   owner of Vince Staten's Old Time Barbecue

Featured Writers and Publishers

Side Bar, page 46
Max Allen, Jr., The Seelbach Hilton
  Bartender Emeritus

Side Bars, pages 112, 204, and 231
Martha Barnette
Excerpts from *Ladyfingers and Nun's Tummies*
Copyright © 1997 by Martha Barnette
Reprinted by permission of Times Books, a
  Division of Random House, Inc., New York
All Rights Reserved

Chapter Opener, page 104
Wendell Berry
"Prayer after Eating," from *Collected Poems
  1957-1982*
Copyright © 1964, 1968, 1969, 1970, 1973,
  1977, 1980, 1982, 1984 by Wendell Berry
Reprinted by permission of Perseus Books
  Group, New York
All Rights Reserved

Side Bar, page 174
Marie Bradby
Excerpt from *Momma, Where Are You From?*,
  illustrated by Chris K. Soentpiet
Copyright © 2000 by Marie Bradby
Reprinted by permission of the publisher,
  Orchard Books, New York
All Rights Reserved

Side Bar, page 18 and Chapter Opener,
  page 24
Thomas D. Clark
From *The Kentucky*
Copyright © 1942 by Thomas D. Clark
Reprinted by permission of Henry Holt
  & Co., LLC, New York
All Rights Reserved

Side Bar, page 109
Derek Cooper
Reprinted by permission of Derek Cooper

Chapter Opener, page 152
From *The Geography of the Imagination* by
  Guy Davenport
Reprinted by permission of David R. Godine,
  Publisher, Inc.
Copyright © 1997 by Guy Davenport

Chapter Opener, page 152
Guy Davenport
Excerpt from *The Geography of the Imagination*
Copyright © 1997/A Common Reader Edition
  published by The Akadine Press, Inc.
  by arrangement with the author

Reprinted by permission of The Akadine
  Press, Inc., Pleasantville, New York
All Rights Reserved

Chapter Opener, page 8
John Egerton
Excerpt from *Southern Food: At Home, on the
  Road, in History*
Copyright © 1987 by John Egerton
Reprinted by permission of Alfred A. Knopf, a
  Division of Random House, Inc., New York
All Rights Reserved

Side Bars, pages 121 and 175
Excerpt from *Express Lane Cookbook* by
  Sarah Fritschner
Copyright © 1995 by Sarah Fritschner
Reprinted by permission of Houghton Mifflin
  Company, New York
All Rights Reserved

Side Bars, pages 71, 176, and 208
Excerpt from *Vegetarian Express Lane Cookbook*
  by Sarah Fritschner
Copyright © 1996 by Sarah Fritschner
Reprinted by permission of Houghton Mifflin
  Company, New York
All Rights Reserved

Chapter Opener, page 172 and Side Bars,
  pages 57 and 77
Camille Glenn
Excerpt from *The Heritage of Southern Cooking*
Copyright © 1986 by Camille Glenn
Used by permission of Workman Publishing
  Co., New York
All Rights Reserved

Side Bar, page 34
Lincoln Henderson, Master Distiller
  Brown-Forman Corporation

Chapter Opener, page 80
Ronni Lundy
Reprinted by permission of copyright holder
  Ronni Lundy

Chapter Openers, pages 196 and 216
Bobbie Ann Mason
Excerpt from *Clear Springs*
Copyright © 1999 by Bobbie Ann Mason
Reprinted by permission of Random House,
  Inc., New York
All Rights Reserved

Side Bar, page 237
Sena Jeter Naslund
Excerpt from "Kentucky Seasons," *Ahab's Wife*

Copyright © 1999 by Sena Jeter Naslund
Reprinted by permission of William Morrow
  & Co., New York
All Rights Reserved

Chapter Opener, page 54
Charles Patteson with Craig Emerson
Excerpt from *Charles Patteson's
  Kentucky Cooking*
Copyright © 1988 by Charles Patteson
Reprinted by permission of copyright holders,
  Charles Patteson, Craig Emerson and
  Jane Ross Associates, Inc.
Harper & Row, Publishers, New York
All Rights Reserved

Side Bar, page 11
Genie K. Potter, author, *Kentucky Women*

Side Bar, pages 160–161
Jane Lee Rankin
Excerpt from *Cookin' Up a Storm — The Life and
  Recipes of Annie Johnson*
Copyright © 1998 by Jane Lee Rankin
Reprinted by permission of Grace Publishers,
  South Fallsburg, New York
All Rights Reserved

Chapter Opener, page 128
Frederick L. Smock and Editor
  L. Elisabeth Beattie
Excerpt from "One Writer's Beginning,"
  Savory Memories
Copyright © 1998 by Frederick Smock
Reprinted by permission of copyright holder,
  Frederick Smock
The University Press of Kentucky,
  Lexington, Kentucky
All Rights Reserved

Side Bar, page 93
Lucinda Dixon Sullivan
Excerpt from *It Was the Goodness of the Place:
  A Novel*
Reprinted by permission of copyright holder,
  Lucinda Dixon Sullivan

Side Bar, page 146
Richard Taylor and Editor
  L. Elisabeth Beattie
Excerpt from "Guineas and Griddle Cakes,"
  Savory Memories
Copyright © 1998 by Richard Taylor
Reprinted by permission of copyright holder,
  Richard Taylor
The University Press of Kentucky,
  Lexington, Kentucky
All Rights Reserved

Splendor in the Bluegrass Committee

Chair
Jennifer A. Kohler

Editor
Maria Kaufmann

Advisors
Nancy Cooper
Susan D. Phillips
Leslie F. Westberry

Design and Production Chair
Jamie B. Estes

Recipe Collection Co-Chairs
Karen McKelvey Andersen
Ramona Hornbuckle Carter

Recipe Testing Co-Chairs
Lisa W. Nash
Dana M. Tilley

Chapter Chairs
Karen L. Crain and Cindy Purnell
    Entertainment
Meredith K. Parks
    Appetizers & Beverages
Abby Russell Jackson
    Soups & Salads
Mary C. Sullivan
    Breads & Breakfast
Anne Crecelius
    Meats
Kay Richard
    Poultry
Judy Hoge
    Seafood
Faith S. Atwell
    Vegetables & Side Dishes
Carol D. Whalen
    Pasta & Grains
Lisa Runkle
    Desserts

Marketing Co-Chairs
Karen M. Le Blond
Laura Petry

Special Events Co-Chairs
Sarah Hulette Dilger
Abby Russell Jackson

Corporate Liaisons
Helen Overfield
Cindy Purnell

Subcommittees

Design and Production
Maria Kaufmann
Jennifer A. Kohler
Karen M. Le Blond
Leslie F. Westberry

Editorial Team
Valerie Kremer
Maria R. Schapker
Stephanie Smith

Editorial Contributors
Anne Crecelius
Valerie Kremer
Kay Richard

Recipe Collection
Lara Custer
Anne Crecelius
Angela Queenan Porter
Cindy Purnell

Recipe Testing
Lisa Tate Austin
Donna G. Dutton
Mary Elizabeth Embry
Belle Maloy Fosbury
Kimberly Logan
Anne Milton McMillin
Carolyn Perkins

Marketing
Amy Ashton
Paula L. Campbell
Kelly Gant
Kimberly Logan
Mary D. Stuckert
Laura L. Suggs

Special Events
Karen McKelvey Andersen
Amy H. Baughman
Ramona Hornbuckle Carter
Anne Crecelius
Kelly Gant
Maria Kaufmann
Angela Queenan Porter
Laura Avance Pruniski
Cindy Purnell
Kathryn Roberts
Maria R. Schapker
Mary D. Stuckert
Cheryl Forino Wahl

Recipe Screeners and Testers

Colleen M. Amoss
Karen McKelvey Andersen
Amy Ashton
Faith S. Atwell
Laurie Atwell
Lisa Tate Austin ❦
Teresa M. Baker
Dana Lee Barnes
Madison R. Bennett
Lisa Bentley
Marcia M. Biery
Elizabeth Boland
Elizabeth Lee Bond
Margaret Hulette Borders
Elizabeth Brodt ❧
Nancye Callahan ❧
Paula L. Campbell
Ramona Hornbuckle Carter
Andrea M. Cheek
Dana Lucas Collins
Nancy Cooper
Jennifer Toombs Corum
Anne Crecelius ❧
Jenifer T. Daunhauer
Sarah Hulette Dilger
Leigh Ann Duque
Donna G. Dutton ❦
Mary Elizabeth Embry ❦
Kate Erdmann
Mary Eschels
Jamie B. Estes
A. Halle Evert
Ann Fleming
Belle Maloy Fosbury ❦ ❧
Kelly Gant
Stephanie Geddes
Judy Golliher
Angela M. Gulley
Elizabeth Hanauer
Angela Henry
Macon S. Hillebrand

Judy Hoge
Rosemarie Baylon Hollenbach
Lynn Howard
Courtney R. Howell
Abby Russell Jackson
Fofo Johnson ❧
Frani K. Jones
Carol Kaufmann
Maria Kaufmann
Pam Klinner
Jennifer A. Kohler ❧
Cynthia Kohorst
Susan Kosse
Valerie Kremer
Karen M. Le Blond
Kimberly Logan ❦
Patty Logan
Libby Maddox
Courtney L. McCall
Dodie L. McKenzie
Anne Milton McMillin ❦
Millicent Meehan
Sarah Metry
Lourdes Miller
Jennifer B. Mitchell
Tammy K. Moorman
Lisa Morsman
Lynne Mueller ❧
Eileen Muench
Lisa W. Nash ❧
Aimee Norman
Elaine O'Donel
Meredith K. Parks ❧
Liz Shepherd Patrick
Carolyn Perkins
Laura Petry
Susan D. Phillips ❧
Cindy Purnell ❧
Kathy Purnell
Mary Pope Quinn
Becky Kuster Ragland

Dishin' It Out Contributors

Kay Richard
Kristin Riddick
Kim Rietze
Juli Roberts
Eleanor R. Robinson
Margaret Morsman Ruggles
Lisa Runkle
Maria R. Schapker
Ann Walker Schechter
Monica Schroeder
Sharron Shariat ✍
Stephanie Smith
Amy Jo Sorrell
Cathy Franck Spalding
Elizabeth B. Straub
Mary D. Stuckert
Mary C. Sullivan
Angela H. Tafel
Elizabeth Taylor
Lisa Thomas
Jennifer Blair Thompson
Kitty Tichenor ✍
Jane S. Tierney
Dana M. Tilley ✍
Tracee Troutt
Heather A. Turner
Carol Tway ✍
Cheryl Forino Wahl
Melissa N. Webb
Leslie F. Westberry
Carol D. Whalen
Michelle Black White
Meredith L. Williams
Nicole Willingham
Beth Wilmes
Kim Wilson
Erin Yates

♟ Team Captain
✍ Screener

Executive Chef
($300 and up)
Mr. and Mrs. Owsley Brown, II
Mary Eschels
Jennifer A. Kohler
Karen M. Le Blond
Dodie and Jeff McKenzie
Millicent A. Meehan
Helen and John Overfield
Jennifer Blair Thompson
Michele L. Trible

Sommelier
($200 to $299)
Anita Barbee
Holly H. Gathright
Deanna K.W. Pelfrey
Nancy O. Stablein

Sous Chef
($100 to $199)
Claire Arnold
Eunice F. Blocker
Jennifer and Jonathan Blum
Joni Knight Burke
Christine L. Champlin
Nancy Cooper
Juliet Cooper Gray
Lynn Howard
Lounette Humphrey
Abby Russell Jackson
Deede Baquié Jones
Susan Yeager Judge
Pam Klinner
Anne Miller
Meredith and Michael Parks
Susan D. Phillips
Mrs. John S. Rankin
Kay and Dick Richard
Margaret Morsman Ruggles
Sue A. Russell
Lourdes Schoen
Vicki Hundley Smith
Mrs. Peter Spalding, Jr.
Elizabeth B. Straub
Susan E. Viers
Louise R. Wall

Pastry Chef
($50 to $99)
A-C Brake Co., Inc.
Annemarie Aldrich
Reah Robinson Allen
Dan and Karen Andersen
Shannon Armstrong
Amy Ashton
Teresa M. Baker
Amy H. Baughman
Mrs. Colley W. Bell III
Suzanne Helm Blake
Mrs. Bruce J. Block
Cynthia L. Coffee
Mrs. G. Richard Day
Melanie Miller Deck
Laurie Diebold
Sarah Hulette Dilger
Leigh Ann Duque
Donna G. Dutton
Jamie B. Estes
Jenny Crawford Fendig
Roberta M. Fischer
Lizzy Fitzgerald
Ann Rankin Fleming
Marea B. Gardner
Meredith A. Gault
Teri Glick
Mrs. William H. Grant
Mr. and Mrs. Mark K. Gray
Lee A. Hancock
Kelly S. Henry
Frances Starks Heyburn
Judy Hoge
Ava Kaelin-Whitmore
Patty Kantlehner
Maria Kaufmann
Melony J. Lane
Kate Lindsay
Sallie Mossman Manassah
Sherry R. Moak
Lynne Mueller
Linda Fry Mulloy
Lisa W. Nash
Kelly Sorrell Nett
Penny Peavler
Sherry P. Porter
Nancy Ragan
Caroline D. Robinson
Mr. and Mrs. Jerry L. Rogers
Maria R. Schapker
Ann Walker Schechter
Marylin Collis Sexton
Mary Shands
Liz Shepherd
Anne C. Sloan

Mollie Smith
Sharon Sparrow
Diane Stege
Anne T. Stewart
Loren Stinnett
Catherine H. Stopher
Jane K. Stough
Laura Strickland
Laura L. Suggs
Tiffany Sulzer
Mrs. Robert E. Sutherland
Sally C. Taylor
Susan Thurman
Dana M. Tilley
Jonna Ann Timmering
Mrs. Rudy F. Vogt
Delia C. Walker
Mrs. Will (Cissee) Ward, Jr.
Leslie F. Westberry
Carol and John Whalen
Cheri Collis White
Michelle Black White
Katie E. Williams
Sherry Wilmes

Recipe Contributors

1823 Historic Rose Hill Inn
  Innkeeper Sharon Amberg
Bunny Abbott
Cynthia Mink Adelberg
Theresa Albers
Annemarie Aldrich
Aleksander House Bed &
  Breakfast, Innkeeper
  Nancy Hinchliff
Max Allen, Jr., Bartender
  Emeritus, The Seelbach Hilton
Alpine Lodge Bed & Breakfast
  Innkeepers Dr. & Mrs. David
  Livingston
Colleen M. Amoss
Sandy Andersen
Karen McKelvey Andersen
Arbor Rose Bed & Breakfast
  Innkeeper Judy Melzer
Debbie Arnold
Amy Ashton
Catherine Astorino
Lisa Tate Austin
Amy Axel
Joan Axel
Lynne B. Baker
Darla Baldridge
Anita Barbee
Dana Lee Barnes
Mildred Barnes
Bauer Haus Bed & Breakfast
  Innkeeper Marian Bauer
Amy H. Baughman
Wanda Bell
Berea's Shady Lane
  Bed & Breakfast
  Innkeeper Clarine M. Webber
Ellana Bessen
Marcia M. Biery
Beth Blythe
Elizabeth Lee Bond
Sharon Boyd
Margaret Braden
Carla A. Brawner
Cecy Brewer
Linda Brissette
Elizabeth Brodt
Amy Brooks
Kim Brown
Pamela A. Brown
Brown-Forman Corporation
  Employees
Margaret Burcham
Burlington's Willis Graves
  Bed & Breakfast, Innkeeper
  Nancy Swartzel

Ramona Hornbuckle Carter
Sue Carter
Betty J. Cary
Cindy Cayot
Cincinnati's Weller Haus
  Bed & Breakfast, Innkeepers
  Mary M. & Vernon Weller
Jef Conner
Nancy Cooper
Jennifer Toombs Corum
Kristine Crawford
Anne Crecelius
Cumberland House Bed &
  Breakfast, Innkeeper
  Jo Ann May
Mary Craig Czerwonka
Bob Dahlem
Catherine S. Dahlem
Judy Dahlem
Jenifer T. Daunhauer
Joan Daunhauer
Melanie Miller Deck
Regina Derloshon
Laurie Diebold
Sarah Hulette Dilger
Leslie Dobbins
The Doctor's Inn Bed &
  Breakfast, Innkeepers
  Dr. Bill & Biji Baker
Mary Beth Doheny
Merry W. Dougherty
Stephen Drake
Ann Dreisbach
Chris Dreisbach
Shirley Rankin Dumesnil
Donna G. Dutton
Laura H. Edwards
Leah Eggers
Dana Elbert
Mary Elizabeth Embry
Mary Eschels
Jamie B. Estes
Buff Fallot
Katherine J. Felfeli
Jenny Crawford Fendig
Nancy Fifield
Rosalind Finlow
First Farm Inn Bed & Breakfast
  Innkeeper Jen Warner
Ann Fleming
Dee Dee Ford
Belle Maloy Fosbury
Deborah E. S. Fosbury
Connie Fowler
Owsley B. Frazier
Tamara Lee Fulkerson

Teresa Fulton
Gambill Mansion Bed &
  Breakfast, Innkeeper
  Ella V. Seals
Meredith A. Gault
Stephanie Geddes
Ghent House Bed & Breakfast
  Innkeeper Diane Young
Joy Glover
Judy Golliher
Terri Thompson Gouldman
Susan A. Gracik
Heather Birt Graff
Charlie Grass
Sylvia Grass
Karen Graves
Will Graves
Greensburg Academy
  Bed & Breakfast, Innkeepers
  George & Dottie Gagnon
Angela Greenwell
Esther Greenwell
Meredith S. Grider
Carisa Groomes
Angela M. Gulley
Leslie Hagan
Robin Bradley Hansel
Susan Harris
Sara Haynes
Anne Scholtz Heim
Denise M. Helline
The Helton House
  Bed & Breakfast
  Innkeeper Grace E. Conley
Kelly S. Henry
Mary Scott Herrington
Kathy Hickerson
Adeline A. Hoagland
Jennifer Curry Hoertz
Judy Hoge
Donna Holstine
Jimmy M. Hornbuckle, Jr.
Sankie S. Hornbuckle
Deb Hoskins
Lynn Howard
Courtney R. Howell
Nancy J. Huddleston
Sarah Huddleston
Inn at Morgan
  Innkeeper Victoria L. Cozadd
Inn at the Park Bed &
  Breakfast, Innkeeper
  Sandra Mullins
Inn at Woodhaven Bed &
  Breakfast, Innkeeper
  Marsha Burton

Kimberly M. Jackson
Alma Jacobs
Sherry Jelsma
Frani K. Jones
Haley Jones
Tessa Jones
Cassie Joyce
Evelyn Kaelin
Ava Kaelin-Whitmore
Patty Kantlehner
Barbara Kaplan
Jennifer Karem
Maria Kaufmann
Kavanaugh House
  Bed & Breakfast
  Innkeeper Kay Clark
Elizabeth Keenan
Karen L. Keith
Dana Kisor
Amy S. Koerner
Gloria Kohler
Jennifer A. Kohler
Mary Jane Kot
Nancy Kratz
Corey Cole Kuhn
Sarah A. LaBeau
Michele Lamb
Royce Lamb
Margaret Lanier
Christi Lanier-Robinson
Meredith Leathers
Karen M. Le Blond
Bernice A. Lee
Sandra Lee
Steve Lee
Dan Leese
Katy Leese
Trish Loehnert
Judy Logan
Kimberly Logan
Vivian Logan
Deborah Mariotti
Lisette Markham
Lois Mateus
Lynn McCarty
Linda S. McClure
Martha McCoy
Nancy Whitsett McDill
Gaye McGill
Carolyn McKelvey
Anne Milton McMillin
Mary P. McMillin
Jenny Hall Medley
Millicent Meehan
Marilyn Meeks
Jeanette Melis

264

Sarah Metry
Teresa A. Metzger
Jinks Miles
Lourdes Miller
Betty Jane Mills
Jennifer B. Mitchell
John Mitchell
Morning Glory Bed & Breakfast
 Innkeeper Sally M. Goodloe
Laura Morris
Jeanne C. Morsman
Lisa Morsman
Lynne Mueller
Eileen Muench
Dottie Mullane
Debra Murphy
Myrtledene Bed & Breakfast
 Innkeeper James Spragens
Sandee Nasello
Lisa W. Nash
Sissy Nash
Mary Lee Nelson
Jayne Nendorf
Aimee Norman
Margaret D. Norris
Sandra T. O'Brien
Mary Lee O'Bryan
Rhonda Odom
Carol Ohanian
Allison Overfield
Helen Overfield
Jenny Overfield
John Overfield
Shelly Overfield
Kathy Oyler
Joyce Parks
Meredith K. Parks
Michael Parks
Bryant Peavler
Patty Peavler
Penny Peavler
Laura Petry
Ben Phillips
Susan D. Phillips
Pineapple Inn Bed & Breakfast
 Innkeeper Muriel R. Konietzko
Pinecrest Cottage Bed & Breakfast
 Innkeeper Nancy Morris
Kristen Poindexter
Laura Avance Pruniski
Ann Purnell
Cindy Purnell
Kathy Purnell
Nancy Ragan
Randolph House Bed & Breakfast
 Innkeeper Georgia B. Heizer

Martie Driskill Rankin
Elizabeth Ray
Eileen Meyer Renco
Marchant S. Reutlinger
Sharron Reynolds
Hollie J. Rich
Kay Richard
Allison Richardson
The RidgeRunner Bed &
 Breakfast, Innkeeper
 Susan Richards
Ridley House Bed & Breakfast
 Innkeeper Rita G. Ridley
Kim Rietze
Grace K. Riley
C. Rinehart
River's Edge Country Inn
 Innkeeper Donna Caldwell
The Rocking Horse Manor
 Innkeeper Diana Jachimiak
Rosedale Bed & Breakfast
 Innkeeper Katie Haag
Sarah Rowe
Margaret Morsman Ruggles
Lisa Runkle
Josephine Y. Runnels
Chef Nancy Russman
Kathy Saldana
Patti Salzenberg
Elizabeth Shwab Sanders
Barbara Sandford
Maria R. Schapker
Ann Walker Schechter
Lourdes Schoen
Monica Schroeder
Molly Schuette
Mary C. Segeleon
Kim Seibert
Marilyn Collis Sexton
Shaker Tavern Bed & Breakfast
 Innkeeper Jo Ann Moody
Alison Shiprek
Diana Dean Sideman
Della Smith
Jill Lewis Smith
Vicki Hundley Smith
Sheila Sollberger
Amy Jo Sorrell
Cathy Franck Spalding
Rick Spillard
Nancy Stevens
Loren Stinnett
LeAnn Stokes
Jane K. Stough
Louis R. Straub, II
Amy L. Streeter

Mary D. Stuckert
Laura L. Suggs
Mary C. Sullivan
Joan Puddephatt Swenson
Angela H. Tafel
Elizabeth Taylor
Mary C. Taylor
Matthew Thistleton
Becky Thompson
Dana M. Tilley
Don Tilley
Rita Tilley
Heather B. Tompkins
Holly Tompkins
Katherine Hayes Trentham
Susan Barlow Tucker
Heather A. Turner
Carol Tway
Joanna Veirs
Cheryl Forino Wahl
Delia C. Walker
Kimberly L. Walker
Gingy Wallace
Susan M. Warner
Linda Watson
Clarine M. Webber
Helen I. Weber
Leslie F. Westberry
Carol D. Whalen
Whispering Winds Inn
 Innkeeper Calvin S. Fisk
Charles White
Cheri Collis White
Michelle Black White
Sandra Wicker
Meredith L. Williams
Nicole Willingham
Beth Wilmes
Kim Wilson
Thomas B. Wilson
Erin Yates
Paul Zurkuhlen

Index

Quick or Easy

The above symbol used with the recipes denotes which recipes are either quick or easy to prepare.

To obtain additional copies of *Splendor in the Bluegrass* for $29.95 each,
plus tax and shipping, please contact the Junior League of Louisville, Inc. at:

P.O. Box 6066

Louisville, Kentucky 40206-0066

(502) 584-7271

Fax (502) 584-3562

E-mail: jll@ntr.net

www.juniorleaguelouisville.org